Punishment

First published in 1989, *Punishment* examines the practice of punishment, not simply as a typical sanction employed by the state but as a pervasive feature of social organisation in both past and contemporary societies. With depth and rigour, they consider penal practice in a variety of historical and cultural contexts, such as the family, kinship and tribal groupings, small communities, educational institutions, the workplace and the commercial environment, criminal organisations, and the wider international community, as well as that of the state. In this way they widen the scope of the debate about the use of punishment as an instrument of human organisation, presenting different perspectives on the phenomenon of punishment and questioning the boundaries between different disciplines – juridical, philosophical, sociological, psychological and historical – within which the subject has been considered in the past. This book will be of interest to students and teachers of history, sociology, criminology, law, philosophy and psychology.

Punishment

Rhetoric, Rule, and Practice

Christopher Harding and Richard W. Ireland

Routledge
Taylor & Francis Group

First published in 1989
by Routledge

This edition first published in 2022 by Routledge
4 Park Square, Milton Park, Abingdon, Oxon, OX14 4RN
and by Routledge
605 Third Avenue, New York, NY 10017

Routledge is an imprint of the Taylor & Francis Group, an informa business

Publisher's Note
The publisher has gone to great lengths to ensure the quality of this reprint but points out that some imperfections in the original copies may be apparent.

Disclaimer
The publisher has made every effort to trace copyright holders and welcomes correspondence from those they have been unable to contact.

A Library of Congress record exists under ISBN: 0415023408

ISBN: 978-1-032-34525-3 (hbk)
ISBN: 978-1-003-32266-5 (ebk)
ISBN: 978-1-032-34533-8 (pbk)

Book DOI 10.4324/9781003322665

PUNISHMENT

Rhetoric, rule, and practice

CHRISTOPHER HARDING

and

RICHARD W. IRELAND

Routledge

London and New York

First published in 1989 by Routledge
11 New Fetter Lane, London EC4P 4EE
29 West 35th Street, New York, NY 10001

© 1989 Christopher Harding and Richard W. Ireland

Photoset by Rowland Phototypesetting Ltd
Bury St Edmunds, Suffolk
Printed in Great Britain by St Edmundsbury Press Ltd
Bury St Edmunds, Suffolk

British Library Cataloguing in Publication Data

Harding, Christopher
Punishment, rhetoric, rule, and practice.
1. Punishment. Sociological perspectives
I. Title   II. Ireland, Richard W.
303.3'6

ISBN 0-415-02340-8

Library of Congress Cataloging in Publication Data

Harding, Christopher, 1951–
Punishment – rhetoric, rule, and practice / Christopher Harding and
Richard W. Ireland.
p.   cm.
Bibliography: p.
Includes index.
1. Punishment.   I. Ireland, Richard W., 1955–   II. Title.
HV8675.H37 1989
364.6 – dc19   88-26335

Chris Harding died on New Year's Eve 2021, unaware of Routledge's decision to reprint our book. He would have been delighted to learn of it. We planned and wrote the book together and it is not easy to add even this brief note without his presence. Chris was throughout his career a generous collaborator with a range of colleagues, but it was something with which, in general, I was less comfortable. It fell on him to keep the project on track, and to put up with my sometimes precarious descents into anxiety and despair. We wrote it, then, not simply as colleagues with shared interests, but as friends. That friendship survived intact until Chris's death. The reprinting of this volume celebrates this relationship as well as the material within the text.

So what of the text? Our publisher thinks it is worth reprinting, which is very gratifying. But is it? We were aware of the temporal as well as the geographical contingency of even the most 'theoretical' discussion from the outset: "[W]e shall not restrict the scope of our study and argument to the contemporary and the topical. To begin with, the idea of the contemporary is based to some extent on fleeting phenomena: what is relevant at this moment may not appear so much so in ten or twenty years' time" (p.16). Rather longer than that has now elapsed since those words were written, and the question of whether we succeeded in transcending the concerns of the 1980s is one which will depend on the judgment of the reader. Certainly we would have used other examples in places if we were writing today and at times different language. Our own investigations of the topic of punishment continued long after the manuscript was sent off, and so, of course did those of many other scholars. The fields of philosophy, history, anthropology, sociology, criminology and psychology were all touched upon in our study and those disciplines, unlike the text of our book, have not stood still. There is, no doubt, much research and writing in those and other areas, which we would have had to include if this text were written *de novo*. But is *Punishment: Rhetoric, Rule and Practice* still worth reading despite its relative antiquity? The reader will, of course, expect my affirmative answer to that question, but I must say that it is not simply personal and shared pride which drives it, but the same critical reflective judgment which led to its publication in the first place.

We wrote the book in response to what we felt to be the narrowness of the treatment of punishment in the existing literature, particularly in the corpus of work which did not question (or perhaps, in some cases, inadequately questioned) the acceptance of the position of judicial punishment of the criminal as a phenomenon, or at least a paradigm, insulated from its appearance in other areas of social life. The text, then, set out to re-position that practice within a wider and more interconnected landscape; to see it, in our terminology, as a 'technique' rather than an 'institution.' We thought that what we were doing was a first, but not the last, step in challenging traditional discussions: "[W]e have moved towards a multicentred view of the subject, which is an admittedly ambitious position to adopt, and this book is by way of a first report on such a project: an identification of issues, problems, and themes, and a prospectus for further studies" (p.2). In that statement of intent, the book may perhaps be regarded as a break from tradition, and historically interesting on that account.

The question of contemporary relevance is not however answered by such a claim. If the book had resulted in a paradigm shift, in the efflorescence of writing from the same inclusive 'multicentred' perspective, then it could rest, unread but nodded to, in the footnotes of more developed analyses, and itself gathering dust on library shelves. I may have missed that shift, that efflorescence, those footnotes, and I am quite sure many good things have been written about punishment since 1989, but I don't think this text is redundant. It would be so only if discussion of the topic, particularly in Law Schools, did not seek to circumscribe its scope by concentration on judicial sanctions alone; if jurisprudential investigation of the practice raised its head from the well-worn recital of 'retributive' as against 'consequentialist' theory; if writers ceased to try to resolve social practices into stipulative definitions; if a consciousness of their own geographical, cultural and temporal approach disturbed them as much as I think it disturbed us.

It is not for me to say whether the book deserves to be read by a new generation of scholars. Clearly, I think that it does: the reprinting of a piece of work which has nothing useful to say can't even satisfy an author's vanity, for the knowledge of its redundancy taints the satisfaction caused by its existence. I think we made some good and important points in this book, points which certainly remain worthy of consideration. But, as ever, the truth of that assertion depends not on my assertion, but on the judgment of the reader.

I think that Chris would have agreed with this analysis. I don't think it is customary to dedicate a book to one of its authors. My attempt to do that here would have made him smile.

Richard Ireland
March 2022

CONTENTS

PREFACE

In a house in the village of Llanbrynmair near Machynlleth in Mid-Wales two portraits were discovered beneath some panelling. These were of a former owner of the property and his wife, both supporters of the Royalist cause in the English Civil War. Parliamentarian soldiers, having taken the house but not its occupants, had riddled these portraits with musket-shot, so executing in effigy the Royalist sympathizers. Some kind of punishment? But of whom, exactly, and precisely by whom, and for what offence? Punishment in the proper sense of the term, or in some attenuated form? A significant instance of penal practice, or simply military excess? Working from one such example, these questions may be asked and lead generally to a closer understanding of the phenomenon of punishment. It is with such questions that we are concerned in the work which follows. And there is a further point in opening our discussion with the above example of punishment *in absentia*, if indeed this would be such a case. That incident – of local interest to ourselves, of more general interest to historians, but probably not one which would immediately engage the attention of those who usually take part in discussion of punishment – may serve to emphasize the diverse range and character of penal phenomena. It is undeniable that the practice of punishment is a significant and pervasive aspect of human organization and occurs at many social levels, from the everyday regulation of the behaviour of children to the imposition of severe sanctions by the state or indeed against the state. It is this total panorama of penal activity, and not just punishment within the familiar context of state criminal law, that we propose to discuss here.

Speaking as authors, we must undoubtedly have made our first acquaintance with the subject of punishment as children when we

1

were ourselves the subject of parental discipline. Our interest in punishment as a subject (what is sometimes referred to as the 'theory' of punishment) was later fostered when we were required as students of law to confront certain topics of jurisprudence. Our first reflection on the question of punishment in an academic rather than a personal sense was therefore very much along juristic lines. Since then, the experience of teaching, discussing and writing on the subject has led us to acquire, with more or less proficiency, a number of further perspectives. Not surprisingly, as teachers of law, we gradually became more familiar with what might be termed the 'sociological' slant on the subject, but increasingly we have come to view other academic standpoints as both important and necessary: the historical, the psychological, the anthropological, for instance, to cite some of the more well-established labels. (But we must take care in applying such labels, since in this context they indicate boundaries between fields of knowledge and study that are arbitrary and open to argument, a point that is developed as a theme in our own discussion.) In short, we have moved towards a multicentred view of the subject, which is an admittedly ambitious position to adopt, and this book is by way of a first report on such a project: an identification of issues, problems, and themes, and a prospectus for further studies.

A major aim of the present work is to treat punishment as a subject in its own right, not simply as a topic within a more established field of study. Jurists have been customarily preoccupied with the definition of and justification for punishment, usually by the state; sociologists and penologists have been interested in the methods and impact of punishment as one kind of state activity; social anthropologists have treated punishment as one aspect of social organization in the societies they have examined; psychologists have sometimes turned their attention to the consequences of punishment in interpersonal relations and in the context of child-rearing; and very recently social historians have shown an interest in the evolution of state systems of punishment, or, more exceptionally, the phenomenon of punishment in other social contexts (what some writers refer to as 'civil society'). We would like to present here the thesis that our general understanding of penal practice may be enhanced by an investigation of the subject in a wide range of social contexts, what Stanley Cohen has referred to as the 'overall social space', and that many contemporary arguments concerning the use of punishment might be better informed by an appreciation of such a broad-based view. In particular, we wish to break with that tradition of scholarship which assumes such a crucial relation between the state and the employment of penal measures. Undeniably the state is a significant actor in this respect but it has, we believe, been given a role in much of the theory of punishment which is disproportionate to its place in penal practice – hence, the reference in the title of this work to both the 'rhetoric' and the 'practice' of punishment; or, more simply, what is said and what is done. We have been concerned therefore to extend the scope of the discussion further into the realm of what sociologists sometimes term 'civil society': that area of social relations existing alongside or independently of the state.

In carrying out such a project, we have also inevitably been involved in an investigation of the relation between penal theory and penal practice, in so far as these aspects of the subject may in fact be clearly distinguished. Naturally, we ourselves have to provide some theoretical structure within which to discuss the subject and in doing so we are concerned to emphasize and explore, in the middle section of the book, the crucial relation between the use of punishment and the application of norms. But within our basic theoretical scheme we have felt it important to roam freely for empirical purposes, for we wish to keep theoretical limitations on the discussion to a minimum, and in particular we hope to avoid as far as possible the resort to stipulative definitions, which on occasion has characterized the existing debate on punishment and has been used at times in that context to establish a boundary between the state and other manifestations of social organization.

But we also wish to stress the perception that, in an ultimate sense, all penal theory is connected with penal practice. The process of discussing punishment is itself often a reaction to existing penal practice and may inform the content of later practice. The theorist does not occupy a position of Olympian isolation but is part of the total picture of penal activity, affected by his or her own experience, social and personal. In this connection it is interesting to reflect on the extent to which different societies produce different levels and kinds of debate and literature on the question of punishment within those societies. But, with few exceptions, writers on punishment have generally tended to distance themselves from their subject without appearing to be conscious of their own locus. We should ourselves admit at the outset that the ambitious reach of our discussion is likely to be affected by the fact of our own location and experience within a particular time and culture. Although some of our hypotheses and conclusions may then be coloured by that fact, we would not want to be wholly defeated by a consciousness of cultural relativism and would none the less hope that the approach to the subject which we are putting forward may be considered by those who deal with the subject in other contexts and from other backgrounds.

We need to acknowledge the support we have received from a number of people in the preparation of this work. Our colleagues at the Department of Law at Aberystwyth were prepared to shoulder an extra teaching burden during part of the time that we were writing this book, and a number of colleagues at UCW Aberystwyth and friends elsewhere have shown an encouraging interest in our work and provided a sounding board for some of our ideas. In the Hugh Owen Library at Aberystwyth, Bill Hines and Meirion Derrick have once more given us much assistance. We should like to express our thanks to all of these collectively.

Christopher Harding would like to express his thanks more particularly to Jenny Harding, who has taken the brunt of periods of abstraction and sometimes irritability, and to a number of people outside Aberystwyth who have shown an encouraging interest in this work, more especially Trish Harding and Non Vaughan-Thomas. It was also useful to have some critical response to our ideas in seminars at Aberystwyth and Gregynog, including the suggestion made by Peter Alldridge of the Cardiff Law Faculty that the hapless professor who enters the scene in our second chapter should experience as his ultimate punishment the knowledge that he appears in a book of this kind!

Richard Ireland would like to thank a number of people. Firstly, Chris who, as well as enduring the many other frustrations to which the enterprise of co-authorship exposed him, also volunteered to type the entire manuscript, much of this exercise being undertaken late at night and in response to tedious dictation. Secondly, Richard would like to thank the staff at Bronglais Hospital, whose decision to put him in plaster on two separate occasions in late 1987 kept him in one place long enough to tackle some difficult jurisprudential issues; and also John Williams, whose voluntary taxi service ensured that libraries could still be visited. To the many friends whom, as the work progressed, he showered with gloom and despair with all the discrimination of a rogue crop-sprayer, and in particular to Gwyneth Owen and David Salter, he gives his apologies and thanks for tolerance. Finally, and for reasons which only they will understand, he would like to express his appreciation of all the members of his family.

Aberystwyth, Summer 1988

A NOTE ON TERMINOLOGY

It would be useful at the outset if we are able to clarify the common use of certain key terms and concepts throughout the following pages. For the sake of exposition, a certain core terminology is inevitable, but some of this will comprise commonly used terms in writing on philosophy and social science, and these terms are sometimes given a specific or ideologically charged meaning by certain writers. To avoid misunderstanding, therefore, our own intention in using such terms should be made as clear as possible. Consistent with the main thrust of our argument, we would not wish to insist upon a very hard-and-fast usage of many of these words and would prefer to employ a flexible terminology, which can take its meaning from context. It will seem odd then to encounter something resembling a glossary at the outset. However, such has been the impact of stipulative definition or ideological colouring in relation to some words and concepts that we should at least try to make it clear what meanings should *not* necessarily be read into our use of certain terms. Whilst, as will be explained, we do not wish to answer complex questions by definitional means, it is important that we are not trapped by the specialist meaning given to terms by other writers. What follows, therefore, is intended as a general aid but should not be seen as superseding in any way the arguments developed in the course of this book.

Having said that, we must straightaway admit that, for purposes of our own argument, we have used some very general terms in a specific way which may not accord with everybody's preferred usage but which we have adopted ourselves for the sake of clear and unencumbered explanation. Thus, in the later portions of the book in particular we have used the terms 'subject' and 'object' of punishment in a technical fashion. 'Subject' refers to the person, or, more arguably, animal or inanimate entity, that is being punished, or 'subjected' to the process of punishment. 'Object' has, in our usage, a rather more problematical meaning. For want of any better term coming to mind, we use it to describe that which is of value or significance to the subject of punishment and is being targeted by those carrying out punishment to give effect to the penal measure, e.g. the body, freedom, property of the subject. The term 'object' is being used here to facilitate discussion of methods of punishment.

Convenient description of the actors in the penal process is not always easy. 'Subject' will probably be accepted as a fair enough indication of the person being punished but there is no one word in the English language, it seems, that simply and commonly describes the person or entity that punishes. Modern writing tends to use general terms such as 'penal agent' or 'penal authority' but otherwise we are forced to describe more specific roles, such as that of 'executioner'. The word 'punisher' may appear in the dictionary but is not part of common or academic usage. Indeed, it is a linguistically intriguing point that neither English nor French has a word that is commonly and appropriately used to signify 'one who punishes'. We do not have the time or space at present to speculate whether this is a recognition, through the use of language, of that social and institutional complexity of the act of punishment which we discuss in Chapter 8. Suffice it to say that we have found it useful to distinguish for some purposes between two principal actors – the person who decides upon the use of punishment, whom we term the penal 'authority', and the person who carries the punishment into effect, the penal 'agent' in our terminology. 'Agent' in particular is a term of great potential ambiguity, and we need therefore to stress our preferred use of the term for purposes of this book. We may summarize our terminology thus far by saying that we shall refer to the decision of a 'penal authority' that punishment should be imposed by a 'penal agent' (or 'agency') on the 'subject' of such punishment by means of targeting some 'object' connected with the 'subject'.

The whole process of using or experiencing punishment sometimes needs a shorthand description when writing or discussing the topic. The 'penal' or 'punitive' process are inoffensive general terms for this purpose, but tend to lack argumentative force. The temptation then is to use richer terminology, and two terms in particular require mention in this connection: 'penality' and 'social control'. 'Penality' is, in dictionary terms, a somewhat archaic word that has been recently revived by some writers to indicate the overall complex of penal relations and procedures. But it has also been employed with a more definite theoretical thrust, as, for instance, by David Garland and Peter Young, when they argue that analyses of penal action should 'reject the question-begging notion of "punishment" and install in its place a less tendentious term, such as the "field of penal practices" or "penality", which would signify a complex field of institutions, practices and relations rather than a singular and essential type of social event' (*The Power to Punish: Contemporary Penality and Social Analysis*, London: Heinemann, 1983, p. 14). We can accept that 'punishment' is a question-begging term – indeed, that is a major reason for writing the present book – but we would be more uneasy about the substitution of the apparently descriptive term 'penality', since this fails to suggest the important questions that are implicit in the term 'punishment'. However, 'penality' is a useful descriptive term and we do use it as such, to signify just what Garland and Young refer to as the 'field of penal practices' (or something like the 'penal realm', for those who like to rise above the prosaic).

'Social control' is, perhaps, an even more problematical term, since it clearly refers to a major subject-matter of much sociological and criminological writing. It is axiomatic to assert that punishment is a technique of social control, in that it is, in general terms, a reaction to conduct that is disapproved. But it is easy to slip from an understanding of 'social control' in its most spare meaning to one that is coloured by political or social theory. So, for example, 'social control' may be used to indicate ideological control, for instance, by the state to repress interests hostile to those of the ruling elite. To then use the term 'punishment' in such a context is to invite a critical interpretation which, while relevant to that particular use of the technique of punishment, may not be appropriate in a discussion of punishment more generally. In short, the concept of 'social control' has a complex theoretical history since its first appearance in sociological literature at the beginning of this century, and in occasionally using the term we do not wish to become embroiled in that particular ongoing theoretical debate. We use the term in its sparest form and the 'social' can refer to any relevant grouping, the state or otherwise, that is able to employ punishment as part of its organization. Of course, neither punishment nor social control operate in an ideological vacuum; but the terms refer to general social practice, which is not

9

dependent upon any specific ideology, although it can provide a means for the expression of the latter.

A similar point may be made in relation to our use of the term 'discourse', which our readers should also understand in an ideologically neutral fashion. The term is no more than a convenient shorthand, like 'penality' referred to above, to describe the body of discussion, argument, and theorizing about the practice of punishment: punishment-talk, as distinct from punishment-in-action. But 'discourse' is useful as implying something wider than 'theory', since it may embrace an important area of non-academic debate, which may have a significant impact on the practice of punishment. This aspect of penal debate comes to the fore in particular in the area we refer to under the heading of 'popular penality' (see Chapter 2). In analytical terms, it may not be easy to distinguish between the discourse or theory of punishment on the one hand and its practice on the other. But for purposes of exposition some distinction has to be made and we shall sometimes use the term 'discourse' as a way of signifying discussion of punishment at a number of levels.

In academic and technical contexts the discussion of punishment has frequently been accorded the more scientific label of 'penology'. This is a term best reserved for a certain kind of expertise on the subject and it should be borne in mind that much of the time 'penological' endeavour is concerned with modern state systems of punishment and this is how we prefer to use the term. The development of such 'penology' is considered further in Chapter 4. Thus, for our purposes, penology is not so much a *general* 'science' of punishment (we suspect that few readers would readily describe this work as one of 'penology') as a particular outgrowth of state systems of punishment and the term would not, in its normal usage, sufficiently describe the whole body of writing, research, and thought on the subject.

Finally, we should say a little about some more specific terms that are necessarily used a good deal in certain parts of the book. 'Incarceration' in its most proper sense refers to the practice of imprisonment. However, we suspect that the adoption of the term 'carceral' by Foucault and other writers has given currency to a wider meaning of the term, to signify a more general institutional confinement. Certainly, we are happy to use it in this wider sense, especially in Chapter 10, where the term is used to encompass a range of situations of enforced confinement as part of a typology of methods of punishment. We are especially concerned to employ this wider sense of the term to reinforce the observation that penal confinement extends in practice well beyond the more usually documented area of state imprisonment. We shall sometimes refer to penal measures as 'sanctions', as indeed they are, but this does not imply that punishment and sanctions are exclusively synonymous. There are other forms of sanction in addition to punishment and we are concerned, in Chapter 7, to draw some distinctions between punishment and other sanctioning processes. Finally, we also use the term 'socialization', frequently employed in psychological and sociological literature, in a number of places. Our use of the term will refer generally to the process of transmission of culture and cultural norms. It is not intended in itself to answer questions concerning the techniques through which this process is attempted. The role of punishment in the transmission of cultural norms and its interplay with other techniques is a matter concerning which we shall have more to say in due course.

1

THEMES AND ANALYSES

In both the practice and the theory of adverse social reaction the process of punishment occupies a significant and problematical position. As a means of responding to undesired and proscribed behaviour, punishment stands out as a highly meaningful and potent social practice, so that its distinctive features have become a favourite subject of philosophical argument and its practical application – in some spheres at least – an important concern of sociological enquiry. Viewed in its widest context (as is not often done), it can be seen as one amongst a number of techniques that may be used by a social grouping to deal with conduct that is disapproved of within that group. Disapproval alone, techniques of socialization, processes of education and supervision: these are all sensible and commonly used methods of confronting the socially wayward. Punishment, although it may be interwoven with these other methods, occupies a distinct functional and symbolic position, which heightens its profile in general social consciousness. It is our object here to explore the distinctive character of penal practice, to clarify the use of punishment in place of other possible methods as a response to undesired conduct in many instances, and to indicate some of the more important moral and practical problems associated with the punitive response.

In carrying out this task, we consider that it is necessary to adopt the widest possible perspective on penal activity and in particular to take our analysis beyond the conventionally favoured paradigm of punishment as a state activity. We are therefore interested in the practice of punishment in the context of a wide range of social groups; not only the modern nation-state and legal order; but also 'stateless societies'; kinship and family groupings; local communities; spiritual,

13

educational, professional and labour organizations; 'subcultural' or 'underworld' groupings; clubs; and the international community – to name only the more familiar of such different social contexts. This may appear to some as an exercise in eclecticism as much as useful analysis, and it has to be admitted that such a wide-ranging investigation requires careful handling to maintain a manageable and helpful perspective on the subject. In particular, it may be objected that our proposed analysis comprises so many situations that are socially far-removed from each other that little of use can be gleaned from such an investigation: penalties within, for instance, a family and within a state legal system are so different in their aims and social context as to deny the unity of the theoretical structure within which we are intending to present the subject. The short answer to such an objection resides in our insistence upon viewing punishment as a social method or technique, rather than as an institution (which is how it is sometimes spoken of). It is a characteristic type of social response, with distinctive features and often distinctive purposes, and as such is available to any social group with a minimum degree of cohesion. The long answer will be presented in the unravelling of our discussion, during which we hope to demonstrate some of the advantages of adopting this wider context for analysis and to clarify, via this approach, the reasons why punishment may be used instead of other available social responses in certain kinds of situation.

It will be seen that much of this discussion revolves around some basic and seemingly straightforward questions about the use of punishment. Enough has been said already perhaps to make it clear that a central question that we seek to address is that of 'Why use punishment?', and the resolution of that enquiry, we suggest, lies in a consideration of the purposes held in mind when punishment is used, rather than other social techniques. But we shall also turn our attention to questions of agency, subject, and method: 'Who punishes whom, by what means?' These additional questions, which occur haphazardly in much of the existing discussion of the subject, deserve a central location within the discourse on punishment since they elucidate much that is important and problematical about the practice. At the very least, we would argue, this realignment of the groundplan of discussion can illuminate a number of questions. And these questions are better handled, we feel, by extending the lines of enquiry into the whole penal complex, by roving throughout the penal realm rather than basing ourselves in what many have regarded as the capital site of that activity.

It will also be clear by now that our enquiry relies upon a wide range of sources. In the Middle Ages it was possible for a man to sit and write a text entitled *De Universo*, reflecting the fact that knowledge of the world then was not only limited but also general.[1] The world of knowledge is a different one at present and in it the specialist is supreme; academics know much more about much less; historians foreclose discussion with a succinct 'outside my period'; anthropologists distrust any theory of universals and study instead individual social systems. The broad statement now exists primarily in the mouth of the bar bore and the taxi driver. Against such a background, a book which attempts to incorporate material from the specialist disciplines of philosophy, history, anthropology, psychology, penology, and others, especially when written by persons whose own academic background lies in law, needs some explanation and possibly, an apology. Apologies always proving difficult, we shall offer explanation first.

COMPARISONS AND THEORY

A central aim of our enquiry is to discover more effectively the essential elements of penal activity. We have been concerned to discover more about its enduring appeal to a wide range of societies over a considerable period of time and in relation to a broad spread of social situations. In order to carry through this exercise, we have departed from the main stream of debate on the subject in some important respects and the result of this has been to produce a discussion that is obviously much more broadly based, though, we hope, not more loosely structured.

Firstly, it has to be admitted that much of the existing discussion, which provides our point of departure, has taken place in the context of western culture and in its literary form has been generated to a large extent in the modern period (that is, from the eighteenth century onwards),[2] although, of course, much of this literature is derived ultimately from earlier discourse. Since we ourselves are in some respects responding to this 'western' tradition of discussion, we are also in some senses located within it, a continuation of, addition to, or development from that tradition, however it may be viewed. But, although our discourse is positioned, as we are physically, in a western context, we are concerned that the substance of our discussion should extend beyond the boundaries of what may be thought of as 'western civilization' and take into account practices and views of punishment as they occur in other cultures. This is consistent with our perception of punishment as a pervasive feature of human organization and the misgiving that any discussion of the subject with exclusive or even particular reference to how it is used and viewed in 'western' society many result in a partial understanding of some of the essential features of the practice. Our choice of examples and our analysis is therefore global in scope, although we are aware that, in a more personal sense, our discussion will undoubtedly run the risk of being culturally specific. But we cannot so easily shed our own experience, training, and expectations.

Secondly, we shall not restrict the scope of our study and argument to the contemporary and the topical. To begin with, the idea of the contemporary is based to some extent on fleeting phenomena: what is relevant at this moment may not appear so much so in ten or twenty years' time. Nor should it be necessary to stress the importance and utility of a historical perspective in casting light on the present. One of the most significant areas of study of penal practice to emerge in recent years has been the social history of state punishment, together with an investigation of some other social and punitive collectivities, such as the family; much of this, as we shall discuss later, is carried out, at least partly, with the object of assessing critically contemporary penality. Moreover, as should become evident, there are sometimes some illuminating parallels to be drawn between apparently diverse instances of penal practice occurring at very different times. Those who design deterrent strategies, for instance, may gain some useful insights from the study of earlier models.

Finally, our discussion will try to achieve a broader base in another important way, already mentioned. Much of the discussion of punishment (again, we are referring to the 'western' debate on the subject) has been concerned with punishment as an exercise of state power, carried out within the framework of a state legal system or, more precisely, system of criminal law. While it is a commonplace observation that punishment operates in other social contexts, such as the family or the workplace or within educational, religious, or military institutions, for example, there has been a noticeable tendency on the part of many writers on the subject, whether they be philosophers, jurists, or sociologists, to relegate such instances of penality to a less significant or secondary place in the order of discussion, if they are considered worthy of mention at all. In short, with the exception of a small number of writers, there has been a strong tendency to present a paradigm of punishment in the form of a state institution (and again it is significant that state, in this context, is primarily understood in a western sense). There is one important area of discussion and research where this has not been the case – that of social anthropology – and that may be partly explicable by reference to the focus of much of the work in that field on less-developed societies which have lacked the conventional paraphernalia of statehood.[3] Whatever the reasons, social anthropology, through its interest in punishment (among other phenomena) in the context of a number of different social groupings, has provided a major source for our present study and has been a highly suggestive force in the evolution of our analysis.

It is at this point that we should acknowledge some of the pitfalls that may be inherent in our proposed method. Firstly, there is the possibility that our account will become merely a collection of details, concerning various practices occurring at different times and within different social groupings, which we decide to categorize as 'punishment'. Hopefully, our analysis of the distinctive features of penal response will provide theoretical unity to what may otherwise appear as a list. But the other danger is that, when we seek to impose an order or theoretical structure on such instances, we may commit the greater sin of producing abstract principle or theory out of widely differing social practices, which may be easily misunderstood outside their more specific social context. This last pitfall is one routinely ignored by some practitioners of jurisprudence, whose supposedly general ideas about the nature of, for example, law is coloured by preconceptions derived from their own experience of a particular type of legal system.[4] But since such work is often read within the same cultural tradition, it is rarely challenged on that ground. In our case, however, the obviously comparative nature of our own enterprise should make us acutely aware of the danger of removing a practice from its origianl context and forcing it into a theoretical framework that does not accommodate such problems of comparative analysis. And our own dilemma is inevitably compounded by our lack of experience of some of the disciplines that we are obliged to draw upon. It is at this point that apology may be in order. But if we do stray into either naivety or error, then we would at least hope that others will correct or develop our ideas so as to lead to a fruitful outcome.

INSTITUTION OR METHOD?

The subject of punishment has a secure place in academic discourse. In much of the discussion it is an 'institution', which needs to be 'defined' and then 'justified'. In this process, contending factions attack each other's philosophies. Kantian ghosts stalk the gallows of the civil society dissolving itself and, as the last murderer is hanged, a smile plays on their thin lips because they are witnessing what is inherently right.[5] On the other hand, Utilitarians or 'consequentialists', wearing nineteenth-century top hats or doctors' white coats,[6] are reluctantly obliged to imprison the innocent and the insane and sometimes to disembowel the parking offender 'pour encourager les autres'.

Obviously the arguments in this dialogue are more subtle than may be suggested by our cartoon presentation, and we shall consider them seriously at a later point (see, in particular, Chapter 6). But for the present we shall restrict ourselves to some comments on the manner of this approach to the subject. Undoubtedly, it is an important task to justify the state's use of unpleasant measures against persons subject to its power: this is a central concern of both political and moral philosophy. But the customary approach adopted in this kind of endeavour is framed in terms of justifying the 'institution' of punishment (or of 'criminal' punishment, if the disputants are rather more careful in their choice of words).[7] These terms of argument may conceal more than they reveal, being both too wide and too narrow. In the first place, we would argue that punishment is not an institution in any sense: it is an instrument, a tool, a technique of social control. Nor does the addition of the adjective 'criminal' in any way evade this objection, for it is in that word that the question of institutionality lies buried, in issues such as the legitimate scope of state regulation of conduct and intervention in the lives of individuals. Moreover, not all criminals are, in practice, subjected to punishment. It may be argued, in effect, that state intervention is better viewed on wider grounds than merely the way in which such action manifests itself in the use of punishment. The latter question (i.e. punishment by the state) both excludes the problem of the general legitimacy of state intervention and ignores other forms of coercion by the state, such as hospitalization and other non-punitive detention. Since our interest here is in punishment rather than state control of individuals, we are therefore keen to eschew the focus on the latter, which may undoubtedly be regarded as an 'institution'.

18

Our deviation from the traditional framework of discussion is certainly not intended to deny the need to justify punishment in its application to particular cases.[8] But it is more conducive to clarity of thought if we say that what is being defended in such cases is the way in which a particular method or tool of social control is being used, rather than the tool itself. To draw a brief analogy: in the context of mechanics, we argue about whether a tool should be used for a particular purpose, rather than whether the existence of that tool is justified. Of course, it may be objected that use of a particular tool may never be justified in any circumstances (although such an extreme view is seldom voiced). Yet, unless we investigate the purposes that underlie punishment and consider whether they may be adequately served by other techniques, such an objection is merely dogmatic. This viewpoint connects with another central element in our analysis, concerning the essential relation between punishment and norms and rules (see Chapter 5), a relation that occurs in a much more extensive fashion than many theorists have been willing to consider and in contexts very far removed from the model of the centralized state that has formed the juristic paradigm.

Moreover, the term 'institution' itself, so widely used in this context, is redolent with ambiguity. Writers who refer to the 'institution of punishment' tend not to define or explain clearly their use of this basic term. In so far as it is intended to signify no more than familiar usage, its adoption is not objectionable. But in much of this discussion the word 'institution' bears connotations of organization and establishment, suggesting that punishment can stand alone as an autonomous phenomenon rather than something which depends for its organizable features upon an institution properly so called, such as the state or the family, which may employ punishment in certain cases. When writers refer, for example, to the 'institution of criminal punishment', the institution mentioned is, strictly speaking, the framework of state organization that makes use of this particular technique of social control. In another context, the term 'institution of criminal punishment' may conjure up (reasonably enough) the vision of a Victorian prison façade. 'Institution' in this sense suggests an ordered edifice planned by an architect, which is far removed from our view of punishment as an organic growth within general social practice.

THE PROBLEM OF RATIONALIZATION

One difficulty with which discussion of the subject of punishment is fraught is the tendency towards *ex post facto* rationalization, by which we mean the practice of supplying an explanation or justification for something after the event, of a kind that does not correspond with the motives and aims that actually preceded that event. Just as we know that judges may justify sentences that seem intuitively correct by using the language of retribution, deterrence, reform, or any other penal aim, so we should question whether existing penal philosophies are, in themselves, anything other than intricate *ex post facto* rationalization of an unarticulated social practice. In other words, we need to take care to enquire whether theorists are imposing their own explanations on a social actuality that may not justify such explanation. This danger has been recognized by Torstein Eckhoff when he concedes:

> Too often it is taken for granted that punishment should be used roughly to the extent and in the way that it is actually used in one's own country at the present time; much of the discussion concerning justification has been a search for premises suited to back up this preconceived conclusion.[9]

Eckhoff's call is for a 'more critical' attitude,[10] and our approach is accordingly critical. But we shall not be critical in the sense of assessing the present usage of punishment, except in so far as we would stress that the reality of the ethical question of whether punishment is justified lies – once we have established how punishment and state are related – in an examination of how and in what circumstances the social technique is used rather than whether the 'institution' is justified. So, for example, the question of whether it is justifiable to punish one innocent person in order that ten other innocent persons shall be spared is a genuine ethical problem. But this is not a problem that can be satisfactorily answered by searching for a 'proper' justification for the 'institution of punishment'. Our approach will attempt to be critical rather in the sense of challenging the significance of much of the traditional argument in this area. It is important to remember that punishment has been and is routinely practised at times and in places where the names of Bentham, Kant, Hart, *et al.*, are wholly unknown. That may seem an obvious statement, but it gives rise to two further important points. One is the possible ethnocentricity and attendant tendency towards rationalization in much of the well-known theorizing. The other is to make clear that we do not for such reasons deny the importance of much of the contemporary ethical argument but would seek to give it a more precise location in a wider scheme of analysis. And it should also be said that the ideas which form the fulcrum of such philosophical investigation are not necessarily unfamiliar to the minds of persons of remote times and cultures, even if they are not so fully articulated in such contexts. One advantage, therefore, in adopting a broader scheme of enquiry, is that we may thereby minimize the risk of interpreting according to the preconceptions of one's own society and culture and consequent misleading rationalization.

LIMITING DEFINITIONS

Another danger that we are seeking to avoid – indeed, our eagerness to avoid it may attract considerable criticism from some quarters – is that of using stipulative definitions to close off the subject-matter for analysis. Philosophers of punishment have not always resisted this temptation, not through any sinister motive but simply because their sphere of investigation has been limited and they have accordingly adopted limited definitions. But, once these self-imposed terms of reference are challenged, the definitions produced by such theorizing appear as manifestly arbitrary. So, for example, H. L. A. Hart, in his influential writing on the subject, has been concerned to avoid what he calls use of a 'definitional stop', which simply rules out of court any discussion of matter not contained within the convenient definition.[11] He does this, more precisely, by listing a number of 'substandard' or 'secondary' cases of punishment, which include 'among many other possibilities':

(a) Punishments for breaches of legal rules imposed or administered otherwise than by officials (decentralized sanctions).
(b) Punishment for breaches of non-legal rules or orders (punishments in a family or school).
(c) Vicarious or collective punishment of some member of a social group for actions done by others without the former's authorization, encouragement, control or permission.
(d) Punishment of persons (otherwise than under (c)) who neither are in fact nor are supposed to be offenders.[12]

21

That the contents of this list may perfectly properly be described as instances of punishment is clear from the fact that Hart himself uses that term. But what Hart has done is to move the definitional stop from the definition of 'punishment' to that of the 'standard' or 'central' case of punishment. While it may be accepted that this definition provides the standard case for Hart, that is also to accept Hart's position as a legal philosopher; but there is no other reason, certainly none supplied by Hart himself, why *we* should adopt the same viewpoint, nor why, for example, a man who loses his job because he has taken home the company's stationery or a boy who has been slapped by his father for being insolent should be corrected when they say that they have been punished but reassured that their statements are true in a substandard or secondary sense.

Hart's own introduction to this question of definition itself raises the issue that he is content to marginalize by definition rather than by argument. He states:

> There is, I think, an analogy worth considering between the concept of punishment and that of property. In both cases we have to do with a social institution of which the centrally important form is a structure of *legal* rules, even if it would be dogmatic to deny the names of punishment or property to the similar though more rudimentary rule-regulated practices within groups such as a family or a school, or in customary societies whose customs may lack some of the standard or salient features of law (e.g. legislation, organized sanctions, courts).[13]

Leaving aside the question of whether the analogy is appropriate (i.e. whether punishment can be spoken of in the same way as property, as an institution), the reasons for designating one instance of punishment (the 'legal') as 'the most centrally important form' really ought to be stated. Certainly, the self-evidence of this presumed centrality is not warranted on grounds of popular contact with, or perhaps even popular perception of, punishment (though the latter is an untestable hypothesis). Many more readers of this book will have been punished at home or at school than will have encountered the penal process of the legal system.[14]

Nor do the reasons of those writers who seek to articulate their reasons for such a standpoint necessarily impress any more than Hart's silence. The editors of a work entitled *Contemporary Punishment* show that they are sufficiently aware of the problems being discussed here to observe (with what justification we shall discuss later) in relation to Flew's classic definition of punishment: 'If quarrels must be picked with such a masterly performance one might raise the question of punishment for the breach of rules outside the legal realm.'[15] But they proceed to explain their preferred focus on criminal law punishment: 'It is here that the problems of social control by coercive means take on a crucial significance. Not only are the means frequently harsh, such as loss of liberty, but they always involve [the] latent quality of moral condemnation.'[16]

This simply will not do. The first limb of the distinction differentiates criminal law punishment only on the ground of its severity, a weak enough distinction, even if true; but it is a difference that, in any case, would be disputed by the relatives of those punished for breaching the rules of criminal gangs such as the Mafia, who may have suffered a much more severe penalty than that imposed by many legal codes. Nor is the second limb of the distinction, that of moral condemnation, convincing. It is neither sufficient to include cases where a breach of the law does not provoke a moral censure but may be met with either moral indifference or even popular support, nor does it cater for other cases where rules are supported by moral censure (such as rules of morality themselves!), yet attract no legal sanction. The easy conflation of law and morality with no further investigation is simply inadequate as an argument.

The other line of enquiry into punishment, which has become significant recently once again, tends to concern itself with punishment as employed by the state – indeed, it is this relation it is most eager to explore. Although the editors of a recent 'sociological' critique, arguing for a critical reappraisal of thoughts about punishment, are well aware that the practice is to be found in social contexts other than that of state intervention, their recogntion of this fact is consigned to a footnote, so as to concentrate on their concept of 'penality', which is one related to state activity.[17] Indeed, much recent critical investigation often sees its task as being an explanation of 'the roots of the modern penal system'. To be sure, this is a valuable enterprise, yet once more we would simply assert that much of this work, while purporting to examine the implement, is in fact fascinated by the user. State-centred theorists use the model of the western industrialized capitalist state (the existence of which is not, of course, a precondition for the use of punishment) and tell us how it uses its tools. The danger in such discussion is that the language and ideology entailed in a critique of the agent (the state) becomes too closely identified with the instrument of punishment itself. Moreover, such an argument does not consider some ideas which, in our view, should be seen as fundamental. It is not, we suggest, absurd to regard as crucial in the history of state punishment, the question of when and how the state arrogated to itself the right and the power to punish, taking it away, in whole or in part, from other social groupings, such as the kindred or the local community. With few exceptions,[18] the power of the state to punish has been received as a datum and what are investigated are rather the changes in the exercise of that power (see our discussion at the beginning of Chapter 10). Such transitions in the exercise and forms of punishment are important,[19] but to accept that point need not lead us to ignore the logically anterior question of the assumption of this power by the state, which is not a matter lost in the mists of ancient history (certainly not in the case of British penal practice), but is itself a subject of important enquiry and one that we shall return to in due course.

2

PUNISHMENT, STATE, AND SOCIETY

Before embarking upon an analysis of the distinctive features of the punitive method, it may be helpful if we elaborate further our own approach to the subject. This can be done in three stages: firstly, by emphasizing and explaining in more detail our insistence upon an examination of penal practice in a range of social contexts; secondly, by demonstrating some of the useful perspectives that may be gained through this method (Chapter 3); and then by locating this approach more specifically in the theoretical spectrum of debate by saying something about the previous and existing discussion of the subject. We shall then be in a better position to enter upon the central part of our own work, namely an analysis of the principal features of punishment.

The impression derived from much of the existing discussion on the subject of punishment is similar to that provided by a zoologist who provides a detailed account of the characteristics of a lion, characteristics that may, admittedly, include awesome power and dangerous ferocity, without pointing out that the lion is part of a much wider genus, the cat family. If it is then objected: of course the lion is a type of cat; or of course punishment is found in families, schools, criminal organizations, 'stateless societies', etc., but investigation of the genus does not tell us much more about the individual types, then we must state firmly our disagreement. If the zoologist wishes to understand biological or behavioural differences between a lion and a wolf, then surely some insight may be gained from the knowledge that the two animals each belong to a different genus. In the same way, if we try to understand why, in a particular social situation, punitive rather than other methods are used to achieve social control in that situation, and wish to work out the consequences, advantages, and disadvantages of the use of one rather than another, then we may be aided in such endeavours by bearing in mind the characteristic features of the social methods in question. And this exercise may be useful even when we compare social practice in widely different contexts. If we note, for example, that banishment may appear to be a more effective form of punishment within some social groupings than within some others, our comparative analysis of the practice in these different contexts should provide us with some insight into the potential and limits of that penal measure. Indeed, we shall be drawing some such comparative observations in our final three chapters, when we shall consider generally questions relating to agency, subject, and method.

Let us begin in this chapter then by making the case for founding our analysis within a societal as opposed to a legal context of punishment and exorcizing the state-centred model of penal activity, the Hartian 'standard case'. In his review of 1970s social histories of punishment, Michael Ignatieff argued:

> If we are going to get beyond our present almost exclusive focus on the state as the constitutive element of order, we will have to begin to reconstitute the whole complex of informal rituals and processes within civil society for the adjudication of grievances, the settling of disputes and the compensation of injury . . . the crimes which [the state] visits with punishment ought to be interpreted as the tip of an iceberg.[1]

Ignatieff identifies the challenge in this way: to explore the network of penal activity which handled the 'dark figure' of crime. While we would endorse much of the theoretical blueprint being developed there by Ignatieff, we would also, importantly, wish to take it further. Clearly, we are interested in the network of penal activity that exists in a wide substratum beneath the more visible peak of state penality. But we are not only interested in this penal network in so far as it handles a dark figure of crime. We are also equally interested in the response to non-legal breaches, 'offences' within distinct normative systems, which do not necessarily overlap with breaches of a formal criminal code. In fact, we would go so far as to overturn the conventional order of discussion, which tends to view the state as the primary *locus* of penal activity, and argue that that the location of penality is much more widely dispersed throughout society as a whole. We must emphasize the wide diaspora of penal situations. The state, by virtue of its general prominence in modern political and social discourse, has become more, and more visible as, a *locus* for the application of penal measures. But punishment does not begin with the state, but in wider society. Let us take a hypothetical example to illustrate this point.

THE CASE OF THE MUCH-PUNISHED PROFESSOR

We are following here the hypothetical penal career of a university professor, a man respected in his field of work and who has a satisfying lifestyle and pleasing network of family and friends. He has also been entrusted with the management of funds, collected for a very well-regarded charitable purpose, but in a moment of temptation he diverts some of this money to his own account. This is later discovered and he is subsequently prosecuted, tried, and convicted of the relevant criminal offence under the system of law in his country. Let us consider some of the possible consequences of this situation. Leave aside for present purposes the question of their degree of probability and whether they are all likely to occur in cumulation; a possibility of each in itself is unlikely to be in doubt.

Following his conviction for the criminal offence, the professor is due to be sentenced to some punishment under the system of criminal law. For our purposes, let us say that he is sentenced to a suspended term of imprisonment and ordered to pay back the money he has wrongfully diverted from the charity fund. This is what some writers would term the 'formal' or 'legal' punishment for the offence, and for many this kind of measure would be regarded as being of central concern in any discussion of punishment.

The trial for the offence has been held in public and has attracted a fair amount of publicity. The professor is a well-known member of both his local and campus community and being both conscious of his status and naturally sensitive, is keenly aware of how this has affected other people's perception of his character. He has been personally humiliated by both his appearance in the court and the accounts of his offence and trial in the press. The professor experiences this sense of degradation independently of any specific personal reaction by others to his offence and conviction.

After his conviction, his employer, the university, informs the professor that he has been suspended from his post. He will in due course have to appear before a disciplinary body within the university, which will then decide whether or not he should be dismissed from his position. If this were to happen, he would then lose pension rights and would find the prospect of employment in another comparable position very unlikely.

The professor's family have been ostracized by some of their former friends. His children have been jeered at in school and his wife either ignored by former friends or treated to their patronizing sympathy. The cumulative effect of this has been to introduce a high level of stress into relations within the professor's family such that he seriously fears the break-up of his marriage under the personal and social strain.

The professor had also been a leading member of the local poetry society and had published a volume of poems. He is expelled from the society on account of his offence and at one of its meetings a number of its members organize a public burning of their copies of the professor's book of poems and send a formal report of this to him.

A lonely and depressed figure, the professor is walking by himself over the local common, thinking over his fall from grace. He encounters a group of youths who recognize him: they shout abuse and then spit at him, push and shove him to the ground. After this incident, he returns home and commits suicide.

Many of these penal incidents are in themselves plausible, reflecting what may be to many readers familiar and understandable social responses to unacceptable behaviour. The cumulative character of the example will no doubt appear as far-fetched. While this does not affect the individual credibility of the various punitive actions, it does provoke the important question: why would we not expect all of this to happen to the professor? The short answer, for present purposes, is likely to be that each of the social groups mentioned above who are in a position to apply a sanction to the professor would no doubt bear in mind the likelihood of other sanctions originating elsewhere and at least consider whether it would be necessary on either moral or practical grounds to pile on to him the maximum possible number of penalties. Underlying this consideration is an important point, which will require further elaboration below. Given that a single instance of behaviour may offend concurrently against the rules of a number of social groups, it may have to be decided in each group what account is to be taken of possible sanctions of another kind. Sometimes there may not be such mutual awareness of each group's penal power; but often there is, and in such cases it is a significant problem of social organization, both in moral and political terms. Decisions of this kind are frequently taken by a range of persons and authorities. How should an employer or educational authority, for instance, respond to the fact that an employee or student has been convicted of a serious criminal offence? Conversely, should a court of law, in sentencing, take into account the fact that an offender has been beaten up, has lost his professional status or the affection of his family, through the commission of his offence? There is, moreover, another important element in such decisions, which we should introduce briefly at this point and discuss further in due course. This resides in the fact that one penal authority may desist from action, not simply because there are other possible sources of punishment (it is not so much a question of respect for competing authorities) but most probably through deference to an idea of what would amount to a proportionate response. To inflict punishment more than once in respect of the same offence may violate a deeply held commitment to a conviction of proportional reaction.

But there appears to have been little academic interest in or systematic investigation of how such decisions are taken. The possibility of concurrent sanctions has typically attracted most interest at a legal level, where more than one legal system has jurisdiction over the same offence, in which situation the principle *non bis in idem*, guarding against so-called 'double jeopardy' has evolved.[2] But more generally a significant area of decision-making, involving a comparison of different forms of punishment, has received little attention and this has contributed to the narrow and partial theorizing about punishment that is found in much philosophical and sociological discussion.

But let us return for the present to the most obvious point about the example presented above: that it is misleading to think of offences or other socially undesirable behaviour being dealt with in a punitive isolation and in particular to take the view that it is only the authorities set up under a state's legal system who will react to the commission of an act that is disapproved. In our example, a number of sanctions emanating from different social groupings could be listed in addition to the 'formal' punishment applied by the state: the censure of public or community opinion; measures taken by an employer (suspension, dismissal, loss of pension rights); peer-group reactions in the form of ostracism by former friends and formal exclusion and symbolic rejection by a specific group (the poetry society); vicarious punishment of the offender's family; possible rejection of the offender by members of the family; physical violence as an expression of community censure; and arguably, at the end, self-inflicted punishment through the act of suicide. And it may be fairly asked which of these sanctions are the more significant from the point of view of the offender. It is unlikely that the professor is most concerned by the suspended prison sentence or compensation order in themselves: censure, ostracism, and loss of position surely have much greater impact on his personal situation. There is an important lesson here for those who design penalties from a deterrent or preventive perspective, and this is another important issue which deserves further discussion.

Furthermore, we should stress that we would not want our example of the professor's plight to reinforce a state-centred view of penal activity. For, although we begin the story with the imposition of state punishment, most of the penal reaction described there is separate from the sphere of state action and is unlikely to be dependent upon the latter, but may occur rather in spite of it. *A fundamental point to be made here is that our example refers to a widely spread punitive impulse throughout society as a whole, which itself feeds the state procedures and may also be manifested in the reaction of other groupings.* What the case of the professor serves to show is that state penality is neither anterior to nor has it supplanted the possibility of these other penal processes. It may be that a state prosecution triggers the other reactions, but in the sense of promoting awareness of the offending conduct. Admittedly, in some situations, a parent, schoolteacher, or employer may say in effect: 'I shall leave the law to take its course here', and allow formal penality to deal with the matter. But there is no evidence, so far as we are aware, that this is a necessary, invariable, or even predominant reaction in the total field of penal responses. To be sure, this question is not easily tested in an empirical fashion but it seems, in any case, that there has been little attempt to probe this matter. The propriety of any or all of these measures in legal or ethical terms is not here our concern. It is the fact of their possible occurrence to which we would draw attention.

However, we may conclude for immediate purposes by making clear one further point. That is, when a number of social groupings respond punitively to fraudulent conduct, they are not all thereby punishing a criminal offence. We should not view the sanctions of non-state groupings as a usurpation of the role of the state authorities. Such groups, when they react in this way, are responding to a parallel breach of their own norms of conduct, however this breach may be described in each system; in the case of the professor, it would doubtless amount to a breach of trust or an act of unfair advantage in most of the punitive contexts considered there. In other words, the penal activity in each instance arises *ab origine* and any ordering of the exercise of penal authority occurs at a later point, through the recognition that punishment in another context may be more appropriate and for it to take place a number of times would result, overall, in a disproportionate reaction.

From this point, it may now be useful to explore further the common perception that the state has a primary role in penal activity, and then to expand upon our location of the source of penal action in society generally.

THE DISCOURSE AND THE PRACTICE OF PUNISHMENT

In order to clarify the high profile which the state has achieved in relation to penal activity, it may be useful to distinguish between punishment in its actual social manifestation – when and how it takes place in concrete instances – and punishment as a subject of discourse. When we look at the practice of punishment it may still be safely asserted that more punishment is handed down by families, institutions of work, and education, and within the interpersonal sphere than is dealt out by the state. Indeed, many members of society will never experience 'formal' punishment by the state although they will inevitably experience punishment in other aspects of their lives. Nor may punishment by the state automatically take precedence because of some qualitative difference: the majority of state punishments are likely to have a predictable or even routine character, which allows them to be tolerated as easily, if not more easily, than a number of non-legal sanctions. In a British study by Willcock and Stokes, it was found, for example, that fear of family reaction loomed larger for a group of potential delinquents than the possible impact of measures that may be taken by the state.[3] In relation to the occurrence of punishment, therefore, the state does not appear to deserve the pride of place allocated to it in much of the literature on the subject.

But what characterizes much of the modern writing on the subject is its concern generally with the exercise of state power. The state is seen as the site of politics, the prime mover of the social, the economic, and the cultural. At the same time, in much of the discussion of punishment, the state is taken for granted as an omnipresent, monolithic constant in penal relations. The result is that, for many writers, the subject of punishment has become enmeshed in theorizing about the state and has also developed into a potent representation of a form of power that excites a general level of concern. This intellectual process has been described by Peter Young in the following terms:

> The state is encapsulated in contemporary sociological explanations of penality by two inter-related movements. One movement presents a conceptual homology between the idea of theorising and the idea of the state, and the other movement cements this by virtue of the political propensities of radical work. Consequently, the state appears as a natural, convenient and powerful explanatory tool. However, what is problematic about this encapsulation is that it takes place more or less entirely within the realm of abstracted theory. Conclusions are reached a priori of any investigations of the specific nature of penality.[4]

This relocation of the subject of punishment from the actual to the theoretical plane is a feature of philosophical as well as sociological accounts and, similarly, in the former the state is often adopted as an explanatory tool. So, for instance, J. D. Mabbott asserts: 'This connection, on which I insist, between punishment and crime, not between punishment and moral or social wrong, alone accounts for some of our beliefs about punishment.'[5] What is being argued by both sociologists and philosophers in such cases is not simply that punishment by the state is the most significant instance of punishment, but that it is punishment in an epistemologically exclusive sense: if it is not defined in this restrictive manner, we will not understand its essential character and operation. Surely, however, these writers are concerned not so much with punishment as an autonomous social activity, but with analysis of the state and of its related legal system. In the same way that some sociological analyses are not interested in social organization distinct from the state, there is a type of philosophical investigation which confines itself to a box, in this instance the box of the state's legal system. Mabbott argues that his approach enables us to understand better our reaction to such phenomena as retroactive legislation and bad law, implying that these are problems peculiarly relevant to the formal legal realm.[6] But retroactive rule-making and the moral content of rules are subjects for discussion in any normative system, whatever the relevant social grouping.

To argue otherwise is to resort to a form of juridical apartheid, which has a basis in theory and can be substantiated only by a partial observation of social organization.

In the traditional areas of debate about punishment, there has often been a keen resistance to any attempt to challenge the state-centred analysis of punishment. Take, for example, the curt dismissal by Mabbott of Flew's argument for a wider definition of punishment:

> Punishment is not to be limited to the State. Any rule-making authority or its agents can rightly be said to punish. Penance and excommunication, expulsion from club or union, the chastisement of children by parents or teachers, the 'penalties' in games, are to be included as examples of the standard use of 'punishment'. I am not so sure about this, but I do not think anything serious depends on it.[7]

Whether or not anything serious does depend upon a wider view of punishment is, of course, the subject-matter of much of this present work; for the present, Mabbott's one-line dismissal exemplifies well the unwillingness to move outside the paradigm of state systems of punishment. But even amongst writers who do wish to undertake a wider analysis, there appears to be some difficulty in taking the plunge. One of the few philosophers seriously to question the state-centred view of the subject, H. J. McCloskey, opens his discussion forcefully:

> much contemporary writing on punishment commits the Platonic fallacy of assuming that there is a single, core, paradigm use of 'punishment' which is to be found by elucidating the concept of legal punishment. Against this I wish to argue that there is not a single core, basic use of punishment, that there are a number of distinct but related concepts of punishment, that legal punishment is no more basic or central to the concept of punishment than are other forms of punishment, and that a consideration of the nature of punishment in its other contexts throws light on the concepts of punishment, deserving of punishment, deserved punishment, justifiable punishment.[8]

He then goes on to consider a number of different instances of punishment, such as 'divine' punishment, and punishment within the

33

context of the family, education, games, and voluntary associations. However, McCloskey then distinguishes 'parasitic' forms of punishment, for example, punishment within gangs, interpersonal punishment of friends and colleagues, and the punishment of pet animals, which presumably constitute penality of a lower order.[9] While his further distinction of 'poetic' uses of the term punishment ('a punishing work schedule', 'a boxer punishing his opponent') are sensible because there the use of the term is, we believe, for reasons to be explained later, metaphorical, it is difficult to see why the penalizing of gang members or pets should be put into marginal categories. They reflect a normative situation, although perhaps within a social grouping that may be considered in some respects by some people irregular. But such doubts arise from value-judgements concerning the propriety of the existence of the system of rules, not from its normative character.

In the same way, some sociological discussion that identifies the need for a wider basis for analysis of punishment also fails to carry this perception very far into practice. Garland and Young, for instance, point out the need in penal theorizing to 'signify a complex field of institutions, practices and relations rather than a singular and essential type of social event' so as to counteract 'the reductionist tendency implicit in sociological and philosophical analysis, which would deny in advance the diversity and complexity of the object'.[10] Such an approach should then open the discussion to include an analysis of punishment in its various social contexts. But the same authors, as we have already pointed out, state in a footnote that their discussion throughout 'is limited to the sanctions imposed by the institutions of "criminal justice" and their ancillary agencies. This focus should not be taken to deny the existence, or political importance, of other, non-legal, forms of sanctioning such as occur in, for example, domestic, educational or employment relations.'[11] This self-denying ordinance is significant enough, but its location in a footnote is even more telling. Writing individually, Young is concerned to question the central position of the state in explanations of penal relations.[12] Yet his own analysis of penal change in the late nineteenth century, while usefully and rightly emphasizing a distinction between different groups of officials and others usually lumped together as representing the state, is still an exercise performed within the parameters of the legal system and its penal apparatus.

What is required, therefore, is not only a theoretical postulation signalling a change of direction, but also evidence of serious commitment to such an enterprise through specific analyses of concrete situations and practices. But any new directions in this discussion have to overcome, in the words of Michael Mann, 'the enormous covert influence of the nation-state of the late nineteenth and early twentieth centuries on the human sciences',[13] which has resulted in the domination of both sociology and history by the model of the nation-state. Mann goes on to argue that there is within much of this work a contestable theoretical assumption: 'Because people are social animals, they have a need to create a society, a bounded and patterned social totality. But this is false. Human beings need to enter into social power relations, but they do not need social totalities. They are social, but not societal, animals.' No doubt this view may itself be contested; but the point to be made here is that the kind of historical analysis of power relations employed in Mann's work emphasizes the role of various social networks and groupings: kinship groups, mercantile, military, and religious organizations, as much as the wider, more amorphous units of discussion that are more familiar in sociological analysis. Similarly, it is within such a broad network of social groupings that we would seek the source of penal relations.

RESIDUAL AND TERMINAL FORMS OF PUNISHMENT

In his later work, *The History of Sexuality* (vol. 1), Michel Foucault explains his analysis of power relations in the following terms:

> By power, I do not mean 'Power' as a group of institutions and mechanisms that ensure the subservience of the citizens of a given state. . . . The analysis, made in terms of power, must not assume that the sovereignty of the state, the form of the law, or the overall unity of a domination are given at the outset; rather, these are only the terminal forms power takes. It seems to me that power must be understood in the first instance as the multiplicity of force relations immanent in the sphere in which they operate and which constitute their own organisation.[14]

In the same way, we would argue that penal relations (which Foucault would doubtless view as a manifestation of power relations) are immanent in society generally and that specific measures of punishment as employed by the state or any other social organization are the terminal forms arising from penal relations. The source of penality lies diffuse throughout human society and is drawn upon by different social groupings as they emerge and develop their own normative framework. In this way punishment by the state is no different *as a method of social control* from punishment within any other social group; the difference, in so far as it exists, is to be found in the measures applied, the associated procedures and organizational paraphernalia, and, of course, the ambit of the society in question. The penal totality therefore comprises a number of different social groups, each with its distinct normative system and capacity to resort to penal methods.

The discursive tradition that has stood in the way of this approach to the subject has been described by the anthropologist Leopold Pospisil in the following terms:

> Traditionally, law has been conceived as the property of society as a whole. As a logical consequence, a given society was thought to have only one legal system that controlled the behavior of all its members. Without any investigation of the social controls that operate on the subsociety levels, subgroups (such as associations and residential and kinship groups) have been *a priori* excluded from the possibility of regulating their members' behavior by systems of rules applied in specific decisions by leaders of these groups – systems that in their essential characteristics very closely parallel the all-embracing law of the society. This attitude was undoubtedly caused by the tremendous influence the well-elaborated and unified law of the Roman Empire exerted upon the outlook of the European lawyer. Had classical Greece exercised such influence over the legal minds of our civilization, our traditional concept of law might have been much more flexible and, cross-culturally speaking, 'realistic'.[15]

This is not the place to consider further Pospisil's explanation for the theoretical predominance of state-centred views of social organization; nor would we be wholly happy with the implications of his term 'subsociety levels'. But his statement indicates well enough the theoretical obstacles to the line of enquiry that we propose: an unwillingness to accept the independent vitality of non-legal (i.e. not state-centred) normative systems.

Yet some theorists have pointed in the direction that we favour and provided the necessary components of a convincing theoretical structure, which others could have then used.[16] Ehrlich, developing the earlier approach of Von Gierke, argued that individuals acted as members of subgroups within society rather than as independent actors in society as a whole and that law could be regarded as an ordering of behaviour in any group of interacting people, no matter what the size or complexity of that group.[17] Max Weber was prepared to identify within such social groupings an authority, analogous to legal authorities of the state system, that could employ physical or psychological means of coercion.[18] This complex of social groupings with its consequent multiplicity of sanctions has been recognized by anthropologists. As Epstein has indicated:

> Each group and subgroup within a society tends to develop its own distinctive pattern of usages and the means of maintaining them without necessary recourse to the municipal law. Sanctions therefore come to operate within every conceivable set of group relationships: they include not only the organized sanctions of the law but also the gossip of neighbours or the customs regulating norms of production that are spontaneously generated among workers on the factory floor.[19]

The possibility of conflict between the norms of the different social groups is recognized by Hoebel, whose observation is again worth quoting:

> In any society there are a number of subgroups which taken together form the social whole. Every one of these subgroups will have its own code of standards and norms for its own members. Some of these standards may have a genuinely imperative quality for the membership of the subgroup. They will, then, on the level of that subgroup have a quality which is significantly similar to the 'legal'. Many social problems arise from the fact that the individual is at one and the same time a member of a number of subgroups and of the social whole and his legal relations on the separate levels of the several orders may be in sharp conflict.[20]

Once this view of social organization is accepted, the remaining principal problem is to identify with confidence the existence of such normative–punitive orders within society as a whole, so as to distinguish punishment within such contexts from acts of mere reprisal. That important problem we shall address more fully in Chapter 5. Suffice it to say for the present that our approach is based upon a view of punishment essentially as an element of the disapproval expressed

37

within a social group in respect of a breach of the norms of that group.

NON-STATE PENALITY

Should we be asked to demonstrate clearly the autonomous and significant use of punishment outside the context of state activity, there are two spheres of action in particular which may be referred to, both of which comprise a distinct organization and an enduring significance. The first of these contexts is that of supernatural and eschatological penality, where punishment resides in a system of belief related to a normative order. The second context is that of what may be described as 'popular penality', in which punitive reactions spring from a broadly accepted community ordering distinct from that represented by state authority.

Much of the discussion of punishment assumes the initiation and application of sanctions by a human agency. However, normative systems may also rely upon measures that are believed to emanate from non-human or non-physical entities: 'divine' and 'supernatural' forms of punishment. Such penality may be differentiated, according to whether it takes effect during the lifetime of the subject of the punishment and whether it is implemented by human or non-human agencies, or whether it is seen as an inevitable experience in a projected after-life or other experience after death (i.e. eschatological penality). So, for example, in the first type of case, a natural calamity, such as the Great Flood, may be confidently interpreted as divine retribution; on the other hand, Hell-fire or less explicit images of punishment in the after-life may be seen as an inevitable consequence of certain wrongdoing. Such penalties do not have to be divine in the conventional sense of emanating from an authority of God-head; another form of supernatural sanctioning authority commonly encountered in some societies takes the form of ancestral spirits who act as guardians of behaviour. So, among the Lugbara of Uganda, the ancestors of the living members of the tribe are the guardians of customary morality, continuously reviewing the actions of their descendants and punishing misdeeds (such as fratricide, incest, or disrespect towards an elder of the tribe) by the imposition of illness or misfortune.[21] The Lugbara do not have any centralized political organization but are organized instead around a cluster of locally based kinship groups, each governed for important purposes by an

38

elder, whose authority is reinforced by his role as custodian of the shrines of the ancestors. The elder will, in practice, invoke ancestral punishment in appropriate cases and instances of illness or other misfortune will be claimed as a manifestation of this penal authority; in cases where such affliction appears undeserved, it may be interpreted as the result of antisocial witchcraft. This is one example of a supernatural authority employed by a secular agency within a group, obviating the need for any substantial penal paraphernalia on the part of that agency itself.

It may be objected that since these sanctions operate in the realm of belief as distinct from physical experience, they are essentially of a different order from other forms of penality. But it may not always be easy to draw such a neat line of division, as some reflection on the idea of deterrence will show. The force of the eschatological sanction, which is based upon some reckoning in the stage of after-life, is bound to be to a large extent deterrent. In so far as a person attempts to curb his innate moral weakness through fear of some penalty after death his behaviour is conditioned by the deterrent impact of his belief. While such a belief is sincerely held it may provide an effective control over personal behaviour irrespective of the fact that the 'reality' of the sanction is not provable in terms of the experience of those persons outside the belief systems. In other words, to dismiss such beliefs as being based on superstition or an irrational fear does not bring into question the effectiveness of the sanction since the belief is real and a significant determinant of behaviour. And ultimately all systems of deterrence depend upon a belief in the probability of some sanction being applied. There may be no doubt that a certain type of penalty under a system of criminal law is available for use, but unless potential offenders strongly believe that it is likely to be applied to them, it is unlikely to have any deterrent impact. In practice, a 'real' system of criminal law may have much less deterrent effect than the 'unprovable' sanctions emanating from divine authority, spirits of ancestors, or any other mystical or spiritual source. Moreover, the more elusive the experience of the sanction, the greater may be its effect. A hardened criminal may conceivably be little concerned by the effect of any earthly penalties, yet be unnerved by the intangible and unlimited quality of Hell-fire or its equivalent.

Admittedly, the vulnerability of eschatological or other supernatural systems of penalty lies in the maintenance of the underlying system of belief. Once that begins to falter, the whole system is likely to become less convincing than one which is based upon physically demonstrable penalties. Yet, even in a situation where such systems of belief are open to serious challenge, their tenacity and appeal should not be underestimated. Eschatological religious systems are a source of comfort and provide a sense of order as well as fear of an ultimate reckoning. And, while the operation of such sanctions cannot be proved in terms of the physical world, the fact that neither may they be disproved confers a relative strength in the face of evidence of the fallibility of material penalty. Finally, even somebody who has 'rational' doubts about the operation of a system of divine punishment in the form of material unpleasantness experienced by wrongdoers, may none the less be 'irrationally' seduced by a comforting sense of justice and natural order, which may be derived from the coincidence of wrongdoing and natural calamity or bad luck. Personal feelings of guilt may also produce a sense of supernatural penalty, when a misfortune occurs after an act of wrongdoing and feelings of guilt 'irrationally' link the two (a favourite situation in literature is an unfaithful spouse's interpretation of misfortune as a penalty for adultery). However plausibly these situations may be explained as coincidence, the force of 'irrational' interpretations of such events as penal remains impressive, and the potential of such belief should not be lightly dismissed.

As regards what we have described as 'popular penalty', it is evident that community disapproval, often of morally as distinct from legally offensive conduct, may manifest itself in penal action that is separate from, and indeed may be in opposition to, any that might be taken by state authorities. In rural Bangladesh, for example, there are reported instances of the operation of the *salish*, or village court, imposing punishment for offences of adultery.[22] Such trials are carried out by village elders and the court may impose penalties, such as fines or public flogging. One view is to see the *salish* as a survival from an earlier penal order, linked to the delay and cost in securing justice through the state legal system, since the complainants and defendants involved in such proceedings invariably come from the poorer classes. However, this may be to underestimate the autonomy of such procedures, and it may be misleading to view such localized popular penalty simply in terms of the deficiencies of the formal legal system. The Bangladeshi *salish* calls to mind the whole range of formalized local community reactions that were significant in the social life of many parts of Europe until the nineteenth century: the rituals of punitive ridicule, such as the French *charivari*, the German *Katzenmusik*, and the British 'rough music', 'skimmingtons' and 'riding the stang', to list just a few names for such practices.[23] These were essentially responses to breaches of communal morality and principles of local political economy: remarriages (especially between spouses of widely disparate age), adultery, deviant sexual behaviour, husband-scolding, and wife-beating. In such cases it is clearly the community broadly conceived, not the more specific organizations of family or state, that supplies the penal reaction, although in some cases this may also have a local colouring. Moreover, in so far as such *charivaris* and the like were directed against the actions of local public authority, they invert what may be seen as the conventional direction of penal action, in that a representative of the state is being punished by the community.[24] The successors to that form of community penality may be present-day media cartoons and caricatures, which may use satire and ridicule to punish perceived breaches of popular morality.[25]

Nor should this area of penal activity be relegated to what may be viewed as a primitive realm of rural life and folklore. A more recent and notorious instance of popular punishment is provided by the spontaneous action against collaborators in Europe in the aftermath of the Second World War, in the period before formal proceedings were properly organized. In a number of countries which had been under Nazi occupation or Fascist rule, popular courts were quickly set up and ordered a number of executions and lesser punishments, such as shaving the heads of female collaborators.[26] What is remarkable about this wave of popular justice was its similarity of method over a wide and disparate area, with little evidence of central direction.

The objections that may be levelled at these manifestations of popular penality arise from their often summary character, and the attendant risk of absence of due process and inconsistent treatment. It should be said, however, that the examples that have been listed above – the *salish* in Bangladesh, rough music and *charivaris*, and the punishment of collaborators – do not necessarily demonstrate a lack of concern for procedural or evidential propriety.[27] In the final analysis, there may be two important points to be made about the phenomenon we have described as popular punishment. Firstly, it appears to serve as a primary penal response in situations where there is no more centrally organized sanctioning system available or willing

41

to deal with the matter. Not surprisingly, therefore, it is especially evident in rural and remote societies and situations of political disarray, and generally in relation to offences against community sensibilities, which are not directly protected by a legal system. Secondly, when the formal responses of the legal system are more likely to take place, popular reactions may assume a supplementary role, sometimes compensating for what may be seen by the punishing populace as a lenient official penalty. The treatment of certain kinds of offender (especially those convicted of sexual offences) by fellow prisoners provides a clear contemporary instance of this aspect of popular punishment.[28] Generally, though, popular responses, because often diffuse in occurrence and relatively lacking in central organization, may be all too easily dismissed from the overall penal picture, whereas in actuality they may provide an important indication of the force and extent of a communal penality, even in circumstances in which it has been relegated to a residual role.

Finally, let us conclude with a note of deliberate disorientation, in order to emphasize the variety of groupings which may make use of penal methods. We have suggested above the inversion of the conventional picture that occurs in the case of community punishment of officials. A perhaps even more striking inversion of the traditional view could be presented in the idea of schoolchildren punishing a teacher. Marsh, Rosser, and Harré investigated the phenomenon of classroom trouble by viewing the situation, not only from the teacher's standpoint but also from that of the pupils, who have an autonomous sense of order, within which teachers may commit offences against and receive punishment from the pupils.[29] The authors conclude:

> offences are of two types, demeaning and non-demeaning. Demeaning offences fall into two broad categories, those which are treated by [the pupils] as part of the generally resented background of personal devaluation, and those which call for specific retribution according to rule. Offences in the second category fall into two classes, exhibition of weakness where strength is expected and manifestations of loss of dignity. The former are sometimes responded to violently, the latter by a withdrawl into a reciprocal posture, exhibiting a dignity proportional to that lost by the teacher. Non-demeaning offences are dealt with according to a simple *lex talionis*.[30]

42

This may appear to be a different realm of experience altogether compared to the more familiar state legal order. Yet, for all its inversion of the traditional adult standpoint of social control, it is still a system of order, comprising norms, sanctions, and elements of reciprocity and proportionality.

3

CONFLICTS AND TENSIONS WITHIN THE PENAL NETWORK

Since we have sought to relocate the discussion of punishment within a broad context of different social groupings (sometimes interrelated, sometimes not), it will become evident that our account will also bring to the fore problems, not otherwise so much emphasized, arising from the co-existence of these penal situations. Yet in social, moral, and political terms, these may be significant problems. In the same way that an observer of the juridical world may refer to the 'conflict of laws' (or more accurately, in some instances, of jurisdictions), as observers of the penal world we may usefully talk in terms of conflicts and tensions as between different penal orders. These may be discussed under four main headings:

1 the problem of concurrent penality, where the same conduct may be subject to more than one normative and punitive order, which in turn may give rise to problems of both a moral and a practical nature;

2 the displacement of one punitive order by another, or the intrusion of one into another, particularly as regards the role of the modern state;

3 the relative impact of different punitive orders, as an aspect of social control;

4 the problem of reconciling the different cultural and moral outlooks that underlie specific spheres of penal activity – of coming to terms with 'unacceptable' manifestations of penal action.

CONCURRENT PENALITY

We have already shown how punishment may be applied by a number of different 'authorities' in relation to a single instance of offending conduct concurrently disapproved within a number of social groups. On reflection, this is such a widespread social phenomenon that it hardly requires further illustration. Most readers would be familiar with the examples of the schoolchild who, having been disciplined at school, is further chastized on reaching home by his or her parent; of the sex offender who, having been given a prison sentence, is then beaten up in prison by other inmates; of the professional who, having been convicted of a criminal offence, is then disciplined by the appropriate professional body or loses his or her employment; and of the offender who loses the respect, love, or friendship that has previously been enjoyed as well as suffering a more formally organized sanction. We need not extend the illustrative list to make the point. Recognition of these concurrent processes of penality should also serve to underline further the dangers in concentrating too much on the state's system of criminal law in discussions of punishment. For problems of a moral, political, and practical nature arise here which should seriously engage our attention.

Let us consider then the moral dilemma presented by the so-called situation of 'double jeopardy', the risk that an offender may be punished more than once in respect of the same act. There is clearly an underlying moral doubt as to the acceptability of such multiple punishment, and this is summed up in the traditional Latin maxim *Non bis in idem*, as used in continental legal systems, or *Nemo debet bis puniri pro uno delicto*, to give the variant sometimes used in common law jurisdictions.[1] Western legal theory, basing itself on Greek and Roman law principles, has generally sought to avoid the prosecution and punishment of a person more than once in respect of the same offence.[2] But it is within the internal operation of systems of criminal law that most attention has been paid to this problem, resulting in the development of such doctrines as *Autrefois Acquit* and *Res Judicata*.[3] Similarly, there has been concern at an international level about the possibility of prosecution more than once in relation to a matter which could amount to an offence in more than one jurisdiction.[4] An earlier instance of this aspect of the problem centred on the dispute between the English King Henry II and Archbishop Thomas à Becket concerning the possibility of clerks who had been convicted in ecclesiastical courts facing further punishment in the Royal courts.[5] In so far as the problem has been cast in legal terms, it has received a good deal of attention. Some of the attendant legal issues are still not easily resolved: for example, the identification of a single offence for purposes of avoiding multiple punishment in different jurisdictions,[6] or the extent to which a prosecuting authority is entitled to accumulate charges on overlapping offences in relation to a single criminal transaction.[7] But the problems are recognized and efforts are made towards their resolution.

The problem of multiple punishment as between different types of normative system (e.g. legal system and professional disciplinary action, school, and family) has received more uneven attention and is less easy to resolve, no doubt because here we are often moving beyond the boundaries of what is recognized as legal action so that the problem is moral rather than legal in character. The difficulty here of determining whether only one offence has been committed may be even greater. For different penal authorities may all punish for breach of their own normative systems, a complicating factor being that the rules of one social group may include reference to those of another group. So, for instance, it may be that the norms of a family will include a requirement that its members do not break the rules of, say, a school, or the criminal law. In such cases, the moral objection to 'multiple' punishment may then, strictly speaking, not be that the principle *non bis in idem* is infringed, for there is in reality no '*idem*'. The objection will be rather as to whether the multiplicity of penal reactions is unjust on other grounds, as compromising, for example, a principle of proportionality.

Problems of this order are encountered on an everyday basis and are confronted by courts and lawyers amongst others, but they are patchily documented. In criminal court proceedings such issues commonly arise via pleas in mitigation of sentence; in deciding on a sentence, the court is urged to bear in mind that the offender already stands to lose his job, future respect, or material well-being, family support, or whatever.[8] In that area, at least, the subject is, in fact, already subject to legal consideration, but in the form of a little-recorded, essentially discretionary body of decision-making.[9] No doubt also, prosecutors frequently take into account other possible sources of penalty in deciding whether or not to mount a formal prosecution, but again this is a largely invisible area of decision-making. Should these kinds of decision be subject to more scrutiny or based on more clearly established principles? Given the practical importance of such decisions, these would seem to be relevant jurisprudential questions.

We may push our enquiry even further, away from the familiar areas of legal decision-making. Should the teacher or parent punish when they are aware of the possibility of the other doing so? How far should they go towards clarifying to each other their own practice and intentions: what kind of moral obligation do they have in this regard? At the interpersonal level, how should the family or friends of an offender react to his punishment at the hands of another authority and distinguish between 'he has been punished enough' and 'he deserves all that he gets'?

Perhaps sufficient has been said to outline the nature of the problem indicated here. At an everyday level, in both legal and non-legal contexts, decisions have to be taken which involve the relative weighing of the effect of penalties emanating from different sources. Whether such decisions are taken by courts of law or by private individuals, they are of great importance in illustrating the consequences of social organization; certainly in some situations the reaction of another individual may be of as much, or even greater, significance for the subject of punishment as that of a formally constituted authority.[10] Yet we cannot hope to achieve an understanding of how these decisions are made or of the relation between different and competing systems of penality if our attention is focused primarily on what is happening within the state's legal system. Although the latter may be an important context for such action, and perhaps one of increasing importance in many societies, it cannot claim by any means the main share of our attention.

THE RISE AND FALL OF PUNITIVE ORDERS

Reference to the possibility of a number of co-existing and perhaps competing 'penal systems' in relation to the same behaviour, inevitably gives rise to an enquiry into the comparative effectiveness and appeal of these different types of penality. This is an inevitable product of the search for greater efficiency, economy, and (hopefully) justice in human organization. Multiple punishment may be both wasteful and inhumane. A typical reaction to our hypothetical story of the professor in Chapter 2 would be that such accumulation of punishment would be unnecessary and unfair (although to say so begs a number of questions), and that the whole scenario lacked plausibility since that would not have been society's reaction in practice. In reality, it might be said, the professor would not have suffered so badly in the penal realm. In so far as this is a true reflection of what does tend to happen in social actuality, then it evidences a drive towards establishing one or more appropriate penal agencies for particular situations. We are therefore confronting another important issue in social organization: the identification of the appropriate locus for penal intervention, so as to accommodate a sense of justice, effectiveness, and proportionality. This is a further problem alongside that discussed in the preceding section: rather than simply choosing between the operation of different systems of penalties, the issue becomes whether one should be replaced or controlled by another.

Once again, the question of the role of the state arises, although we should take care not to allow it to occupy too much of the stage. For undoubtedly, an important feature of the development of the state in the modern period has been its increasingly incursive approach to matters that have previously been regulated for the most part by individuals, smaller communities, or other institutions. This is another phenomenon which, upon further reflection, will appear quite familiar to many readers and a few examples will suffice to make the point. In the area of 'criminal' offending in Britain, for example, it is clear that over the last two hundred years state authorities have increasingly taken over responsibility for dealing with conduct that may amount to criminal offences. Whereas previously a certain amount of law-breaking was dealt with by local communities, the establishment of a centralized police force, and a greater willingness on the part of members of the public to report matters to the police resulted in an increasing involvement on the part of the state in dealing with conduct that comes within the prohibition of the criminal law.[11] When this development is combined with the tendency to expand the scope of the criminal law to include the now familiar range of 'regulatory' infractions, it can be appreciated how enforcement of the criminal code has become a major state enterprise. To be sure, there remain certain types of conduct not covered by criminal law,[12] and also institutional contexts where there is a strong impulse to stave off the possible involvement of state agencies, for example, as regards pilfering within a firm, or acts of vandalism on a university campus; in such situations the overriding principle may be expressed as 'we can deal with this ourselves; we do not need to call the police'. But this attitude tends to arise for the most part in institutional situations where there is a strong sense of community.

Another instructive case is provided by the regulation of family life. Whereas, at one extreme, Roman society allowed the head of the family (*Paterfamilias*) wide powers of regulation and control over his family unit, with minimal interference by the legal system, the trend in contemporary western society is to provide for increasing state surveillance of how parents regulate what are in any case usually much smaller family units.[13] In English law, for example, powers of chastisement are still allowed to parents over their children, but it is clearly accepted that legal limits are imposed on the exercise of such penal authority and parents' treatment of their children is 'policed' by social-work agencies.[14] The earlier concept of an 'obstinate, wilful' child who is the appropriate subject for chastisement by a parent or schoolmaster has now been largely replaced by that of a child in need of 'care and control',[15] the latter to be provided by a state agency, the parental authority having been proven to be inadequate.

A final illustration may be taken from an institution that is already in most senses a state agency, although one with a certain degree of autonomy. Since 1877, the British prison system has been organized as a centrally directed state agency, in recent years as a department of the Home Office, itself a government department. However, traditionally discipline within the prison system has been a matter for the Prison Department itself to administer, and for a long time there was a reluctance to interfere in any way in the application of penalties imposed for breaches of discipline. An analogy was drawn in particular with the imposition of disciplinary sanctions within the armed forces,[16] another area where a vaguely defined 'policy' was seen to require the use of a 'local' penal system. More recently, however, political pressure to recognize prisoners' 'rights',[17] and a tentative judicial activism have resulted in an encroachment by the state legal system in this hitherto sealed-off area of penality, in the form of some judicial review of the procedures that lead to the imposition of disciplinary punishment.[18] Generally, therefore, at least in western society, it is possible to detect an 'opening-up' of closed, more specialized systems of punishment and their resulting incorporation within, or at least supervision by, the general legal system of the state. In itself, this is a tendency that deserves much closer attention and research; but for the present, it is at least possible to propose a tentative, although in some respects puzzling, hypothesis that for some purposes at least the state is perceived as the ideal penal authority. Examined more closely, there is a complicating factor here: probably in this respect a distinction may need to be drawn between the state as a penal agency and the state as a supervisory agency of penal practice.[19] The tendency just referred to entails not so much the development of the state's penal functions as its role in supervising delegated penality. In one sense it may be meaningful to talk about a shift from 'private' and 'local' to 'public' and 'general' systems of punishment, but the latter should be understood as a form of umbrella: a collection of penal systems, alongside the central state system of criminal law, but ultimately deriving authority from and under some supervision by the state. Typical examples would be the disciplinary systems of the prisons and the armed forces, and penal elements within education and welfare systems provided by the state.

This process of transfer of penal authority is perhaps one of the major themes of contemporary penality, although it is infrequently identified as such. Certainly it deserves some reflection, because in itself it suggests much about twentieth-century views on punishment. The question 'Who punishes?' should be seen as one of the primary lines of enquiry within the discussion of the subject. Why is it the case, for example, that in many western countries the punishment of children by parents or (often as a substitute) schoolteachers is viewed with increasing unease and subject to increasing 'legal' (i.e. external) control? A simple answer, of course, is not possible, but doubtless any explanation will need to draw upon, among other things, our general perception of child development and psychology, conversely our faith (or lack of it) in certain adult authorities, our belief in the need for 'expert' responses to juvenile behaviour, and more generally prevailing contemporary notions of justice and suspicion of arbitrary reactions. Pursuing such lines of enquiry, and incidentally exploring the impact of leading theoreticians (for instance, in this context, Freudian theories of psychological development), we may approach some understanding of these perceived shifts in penal activity.[20] But it promises to be a long and difficult task.

The point to be emphasized is that the location of penal authority is unlikely to be static in most societies, especially as (or if) their organization becomes more complex and interdependent. No doubt there is always going to be some place for localized systems of punishment, if only because many infractions are so small in themselves that the need for an immediate, summary response on the part of the most convenient penal agency will remain self-evident. It would be a mistake, therefore, to envisage the phasing out of punishment in the family, the workplace, the clubroom, or the interpersonal sphere. These will undoubtedly remain important at the everyday level of individual experience. But at the same time, as regards in particular those infractions that are viewed as more serious threats to the fabric of society, there is increasing pressure for uniformity of definition, regulation, and punishment, as is evidenced by a number of developments in international law.[21] The ultimate goal in this tendency may be seen in the form of the idea (and, as yet, ideal) of an 'international penal tribunal', such as the War Crimes Tribunals in 1945 aspired to be.[22]

It should perhaps be added, for the sake of clarity, that the discussion in this section presupposes a substantial overlap of normative and penal purpose as between the punitive orders in question. What has been said above makes sense, for example, in the case of the state and the family in so far as both are concerned to prescribe acts of dishonesty and have at least some similar objectives in imposing punishment for such conduct. But it would clearly make little sense to talk of one group supplanting another for purposes of punishment, if the norms of the two groups either related to different matters or their purposes in using punishment were significantly different, as would no doubt be the case, for example, in relation to the former point, as between the state and a criminal gang.[23]

THE RELATIVE IMPACT OF PUNISHMENTS

The impact of punishment is, standing by itself, a question-begging concept, since so much depends on what effects or results are expected of punishment, either generally or in particular instances. For present purposes we may postpone detailed consideration of the expected or hoped-for results of using punishment and accept that they may reasonably include such elements as the effective communication of disapproval and persuasion towards future respect for the norms of the system, among other goals (see Chapter 6). The argument to be made here is simply that, whatever goal may be held in view by whoever is making use of punishment, it may be a useful exercise to consider which out of a range of penal alternatives provides the best or better prospect of achieving that goal.[24] Obviously, penologists already carry out this exercise within the repertoire of state measures in debating the comparative merits of, for example, imprisonment, community service, or fines. Less obviously, the same kind of exercise may have been performed by the 'old-fashioned' policeman dealing with a juvenile offender, in deciding between administering a 'clip round the ear' or setting in motion the formal process of prosecution

51

and punishment.[25] Much less obviously, and no doubt with much more difficulty, a similar process could be carried out by investigating the relative effects of punishments in relation to the same matter arising in different contexts. So, for example, as regards breach of the criminal law, it may be asked which penal agent might most satisfactorily achieve the purposes of the penal authority. Would, for instance, either retributive or deterrent expectations be better satisfied by leaving the matter in the hands of parents, employer, or any other relevant and interested penal institution, than by using the formal processes of the criminal law? In taking this perspective we are confronted by a range of policy alternatives, which may appear more or less appealing, yet deserve at least serious debate.

The general exercise being referred to here is, of course, in one form the staple diet of penology, 'the scientific study of the prevention and punishment of crime'[26] (we shall consider the role of penology more fully in Chapter 4), in that penologists are typically concerned with the operation and relative effects of measures taken to deal with criminal offenders. But the discipline of penology has been largely predicated upon the phenomena of criminality (wrongdoing as identified by the state) and the employment of state power (procedures and measures of criminal law supplied by the state). Even when penologists consider alternatives to the traditional penal process – for instance, the use of cautioning of offenders in place of formal trial, conviction, and punishment; or the use of 'administrative' as distinct from fully fledged criminal offences – the enquiry still takes place within the confines of the state legal system. Cautions are administered by the police or other enforcement agents appointed by the state. 'Administrative' or 'regulatory' sanctions, *Ordnungswidrigkeiten*,[27] or however they may be termed, are applied as part of the state's legal order. Only occasionally have penologists strayed into the zone of non-state sanctioning, as, for instance, when Willcock and Stokes carried out their interviews of a sample of young men as potential offenders in the 1960s and asked, among other things, what would worry them most if they were apprehended after committing a criminal offence.[28] Their tabulated responses provoked this remark from Nigel Walker: 'There are several striking features in this table. "What my family would think" is far and away the most important consideration. Next is the possibility of losing one's job. Considerably less important was public exposure in court, and slightly less important than that was the official penalty. The other items were relatively negligible.'[29] This suggests that sanctions conceived of from the point of view of the state authority as operating indirectly or secondarily – those in the area of family life, employment, and relating to social status – may be highly significant in the process of being dealt with as a criminal and that, to an extent, the specific penalty supplied by the state may be beside the point. There is clearly an important lesson in all this for those who construct policies of deterrence.

But even that particular foray beyond the limits of state-based penalties reveals a dependence on the operation of the formal legal system. The societal reactions listed there followed from the use of formal procedures: being charged by the police, prosecuted by the state, and tried in a court of law. Penology has yet to consider on any large scale the operation of non-state penality *independently* of any process being undertaken within the legal system. Such a study would have to consider, for example, the effect of juvenile violence being dealt with by parental or school authorities instead of within the legal system; or similarly the consequences of criminal damage on university campuses being the subject of university procedures rather than a criminal prosecution.

Let us be clear as to the nature of the argument here. We would contend that such a study of the social impact of differential penality would be important in its own right. In so far as it might indicate a range of competing penal agents as regards the implementation of general social norms in order to determine which would be the 'best', then further factors would need to be considered. For the efficacy of penality is only one element within what might be properly thought of as the overall enquiry. Punishment of drug traffickers by competing criminal gangs or of 'muggers' by 'vigilantes' may be very effective, but this cannot by itself determine the social and ethical rectitude of such processes.[30] Factors of predictability, uniformity, and due process may also be regarded as important.[31] Nor, within the psychology of the social group in question, may the interchangeability of penal agents be an easy matter. As we shall later discuss, within some societies, the allocation of 'punitive guilt' may be an important issue.[32] The point remains, however, that, given the existence of a number of punitive groups within a society, their interaction and interrelation is an important, though often difficult, question that merits further study.

PUNISHMENT ACROSS CULTURES AND OVER TIME

Since one of our overriding concerns is to achieve a better understanding of the nature and limits of penal activity, it becomes axiomatic that we should seek to avoid any ethnocentric or temporal limitations in our discussion. It is a mark of insularity, often presented in the guise of a self-conscious sense of progress, to dismiss forms of punishment as not relevant because they belong to a different time or different culture. Not only does such an attitude impede an understanding of the full range and possibilities of punishment; it also enables a definitional exclusion of phenomena that are not approved on moral or cultural grounds, leading to the assertion that they should not be viewed as punishment or should be relegated to the level of 'secondary' or 'non-standard' instances of punishment. We will consider this argument with reference to a particular range of phenomena that would, in the view of some people, have a problematical association with punishment: torture and physical mutilation (both of which represent an extreme form of action on what may be considered one of the most basic objects of punishment, the subject's body; see further the discussion in Chapter 10).

The practice of torture now attracts widespread condemnation, in spite of (and perhaps as a reaction to) evidence of its frequent use in the late twentieth century, particularly its use by state authorities.[33] Definition of torture has been a matter for debate;[34] the common perception that it is essentially a procedure for eliciting information or evidence often thereby distinguishing it from the practice of punishment. Sometimes, however, a wider view is taken, according to which torture is seen as an unacceptable infliction of pain and suffering by public authorities. Article 1 of the United Nations Declaration on Torture, adopted by the General Assembly in 1975, states for instance:

> For the Purposes of this Declaration, torture means any act by which severe pain or suffering, whether physical or mental, is intentionally inflicted by or at the instigation of a public official on a person for such purposes as obtaining from him or a third person information or confession, punishing him for an act he has committed, or intimidating him or other persons.[35]

This approach dispenses with a hard-and-fast definition of torture and, apart from the specific requirement that it should be an act of public authority, is content to list the principal contexts in which such methods are likely to be used, so emphasizing that what is objected to is the means rather than the end. On this wider view, torture may then be seen, in one of its manifestations, as an employment of punishment that entails severe physical or mental suffering. Indeed, in some instances it may in practice be difficult to separate punitive and interrogatory uses of torture, as for example when an imprisoned offender suffers both.

In this wider sense torture may therefore be regarded as including certain forms of punishment that have an inhumane quality: they involve a degree of pain or suffering which is viewed as morally intolerable. Let us clearly admit that, in social actuality, the infliction of great pain and suffering may be a significant practice of punishment. To say that does not commit us in any way to accept or approve such practice, but may impel us to ask more vigorously why it happens. Such a descriptive task in no way commits us, of course, to a doctrine of ethical relativism. It remains possible to condemn certain forms of behaviour as wholly unacceptable, but the nature and content of such moral judgements will not be addressed here beyond making the point that ethical doctrines are matters that deserve rather more solid foundation than simple wordplay or ethnocentric prejudice. Our main concern here is rather to confront certain practical difficulties thrown up by questions relating to penal practices that attract moral condemnation.

Many penal practices, whether described as 'torture', 'cruel' or 'inhuman punishment', or whatever else, are now widely condemned as unlawful, usually on grounds of violating the guarantee of basic rights of individuals under either national legal systems or international law. Yet it is also recognized that such attempts at legal control are problematical. It is difficult both to achieve wider agreement as to how far such practices should be condemned and to secure effective methods of enforcing those obligations which are agreed upon.[36] It would be useful to admit openly that there are two major difficulties to overcome. Firstly, that there is in practice a significant level of disagreement as to what is or is not acceptable in this respect,[37] and such differences may be more easily reconciled by an attempt to understand their origins and sustaining forces. Secondly, that there are formidable practical obstacles in achieving the eradication of forms of punishment that may be generally outlawed. One or two examples may serve to emphasize the general point being made here.

In western society, corporal punishment is now viewed with disapproval and even distaste (see Chapter 10). Flogging has for the most part been proscribed and mutilation is strongly condemned. The use of a penalty such as the amputation of limbs, as under some contemporary Islamic penal systems, therefore gives rise to feelings of dismay and revulsion.[38] On the other hand, it is quite conceivable that the western preference for long terms of detention, with its attendant mental and psychological pressures, or the loss of social status and sense of disgrace which is an important ingredient of much Western penality, could be viewed as unduly severe from another cultural standpoint.[39] We should not be surprised at these different interpretations of the acceptability of particular penalties and in an increasingly interdependent global community it is important that we attempt to understand such differences. We need only point to the familiar example of the multiracial community to emphasize such a need. Nor is this simply a cultural problem. There is still much room for disagreement of this kind in a relatively homogeneous community: witness, for example, the debate under the European Convention on Human Rights as to whether techniques of sensory deprivation amounted to 'torture' or 'inhuman treatment' (*Ireland* v. *UK*).[40] The fact that the European Court of Human Rights could decide that such methods amounted to the latter but not the former ('torture', in the Court's view, emerging as an aggravated form of 'inhuman treatment')[41] illustrates the scope for argument within the confines of a single ideology and culture, and also demonstrates the tendency within international documents to tackle difficult problems by resort to definitions.

Assuming, however, that the stage is reached where a general condemnation of certain practices is agreed upon, it would again be simplistic to believe that on the word of general-level decision-makers (heads of governments, legislators, and the like) the practices in question will disappear. An important question in any discussion of punishment is that of 'who punishes?', and to say in reply, for instance, 'the state' is to provide only a partial answer. As we shall go on to argue (see Chapter 8), it may be important to distinguish the penal authority and the penal agent and it may be wrong to assume that the former will always control the latter. During the 1980s the Chinese government, for example, has begun to admit to a major problem within its political organization – the tendency among police, local Communist Party officials, and informal neighbourhood security groups to succumb to the 'stubborn disease' of employing torture against criminal suspects, political detainees, and convicted prisoners. In 1987, the Department of the Chief Procurator of the People's Republic had a backlog of over 30,000 allegations of torture and illegal detention and imprisonment to deal with.[42] Clearly, even an admitted concern by the state (or, more accurately, some of its representatives) is insufficient to deal with a widespread practice itself previously encouraged by higher state policy, during the 'Cultural Revolution'.

Taking a view of punishment that traverses cultural and ideological boundaries should therefore enable us to appreciate more clearly the complexity of penal issues, whether discussion focuses upon ethical or practical considerations. In particular, there is a need to be wary of definitions incorporating assumptions that are taken for granted in some cultural or ideological systems, but not others. A study of all forms of punishment, whether approved or not, as in other areas of comparative evaluation, is a key to understanding the choices made within one's own group or society.

4

LORE AND DOCTRINE: FROM A REFLEXIVE TO A REFLECTIVE EXPERIENCE OF PUNISHMENT

It will be clear by now that a major element in our analysis of punishment is a disengagement from the parameters of debate customarily employed by much of the existing discussion of the subject and in particular from the preoccupation of western writers with the use of punishment by the state. In order to present our own arguments in clearer relief it may be useful at this point to recapitulate the main lines of discourse, the stated objectives, and the perceived achievements within the philosophical and sociological traditions of debate on punishment. Indeed, this may appear to be a necessary part of our critique since more needs to be said about the existing arguments in order to clarify both our points of departure and our points of convergence. For it also has to be admitted that our own enterprise is only possible through what has already been achieved by much of this earlier discussion and it would be useful to explain what we have drawn from it and how we have been influenced by it. As we have tried to make clear, the thrust of our argument is to open up the debate, establish it on a broader basis, and so provide different perspectives and thereby helpful insights. But to do this we must to some extent draw upon the argumentation developed by philosophy and the empirical discoveries of sociological work.

But this is not intended to be only a summary of previous work, a catalogue or expanded bibliography. Let us rather scrutinize the serious ('academic', 'scholarly', 'scientific', or whatever) discussion of punishment as a subject in its own right. In itself this would stand as a relatively novel exercise. To a large extent, both philosophical and sociological discourse have been taken for granted by their own participants, certainly in the area of debate on punishment. The history, development, and distinguishing features of these modes of discussion have not been extensively considered. Recently, the possibilities of such an enquiry have been hinted at (for instance, by Garland and Young)[1] and a major impetus has been provided more generally by historians of knowledge and ideas, notably Foucault.[2] Yet a fuller history and analysis of the development of penal discourse remains a major project yet to be undertaken. For the present, however, we can at least attempt to identify the main lines of development within this body of knowledge, if only to place our own arguments more clearly in context.

TRADITIONS OF DISCOURSE

We have already spoken, in general terms, of the division between philosophical and sociological discussion of punishment. This is probably an inevitable classification in terms of the self-perception of most of the participants, and it also serves to identify significant traits in methodology and approach to the subject as well as the objectives that inform the discussion. While the distinction between a philosophical and a sociological analysis of the subject is not, of course, absolutely rigid, it will be seen that it does reflect an important division in academic practice. In addition, we need to consider a line of enquiry that is of relatively more recent origin, that which takes an avowedly historical view of the subject. This area of work is more difficult to classify, since, while on the one hand the specific methodology of the historian has to be employed, it is also true that such studies draw upon the existing body of knowledge provided by philosophical and sociological enquiry. Social histories of punishment – typically, those that investigate phenomena of crime and penality in a particular area within a certain period – inevitably employ the sociological as well as the historical method. On the other hand, studies that are more concerned with the less-visible area of policy and theory in relation to historical penality need to draw upon the philosophy of ideas and political thought to gain a fuller understanding of their subject. Finally, within the sociological tradition, there has developed the technical and specific subject (sometimes 'science') of penology, concerned with the examination of particular penal measures in practice and an assessment of their effects. To a large extent, penology bases itself on the methods of sociology and psychological enquiry, but is, in its more specific purpose, a 'service' discipline, often reporting back to those who employ the penalties in question and sometimes ambivalent about the implications of its own critical stance.

PUNISHMENT AS A TOPIC OF MORAL PHILOSOPHY

Let us first clarify the sense in which we are using the term 'philosophical' to describe a certain kind of discussion about punishment. To be more exact, the philosophy here referred to comprises the branches of the subject known as 'moral philosophy' or 'ethics', which is concerned with the study of the principles and effects of human conduct, and 'political philosophy', which is concerned, in part at least, to relate such issues to the question of government. Having described it in that way, the connections, or possible connections, with both law and social analysis, soon become evident. Since human action rarely occurs in isolation, it produces social consequences that may require regulation or control (the subject of law) and will also deserve examination and assessment (the subject of sociology). Punishment as a social phenomenon and the product of human action is thus clearly a topic within a number of disciplines, but what then is the distinctive contribution of the 'philosophical' tradition of discussion?

The function of the philosophical discourse is to provide, in the words of Hart's neat summary, 'a morally tolerable account' of the subject,[3] or, to put it another way, which conveys the general point but begs questions about the terms used, to investigate the issue of when it is right or appropriate to use punishment, and how much of it and in what form. The gist of philosophical discussion, therefore, has been to provide a moral evaluation of penal activity and suggest ethical guidance for those involved in such practices. The results of this endeavour have been of interest especially to jurists and lawyers, who are often in the position of having to exercise some control over punitive initiatives, particularly those of the state. There is an intriguing critical aspect to all of this: the whole exercise is based on an assumption that the use of punishment gives rise to a moral problem (because it is usually seen as involving the deliberate infliction of unpleasantness; as Bentham noted,[4] it is in itself an evil) and there is therefore an overriding need to justify penal practice. But there is customarily in this kind of discussion also an assumption that a convincing moral justification serves as an explanation for a number of basic social facts: not just a widespread preference to use punishment rather than other possible methods of social control but also the origins of the punitive impulse. There is no explanation of why human beings are punitive animals, although there is a defence of them as such. This illustrates the limits of the usual 'philosophical' endeavour. It is rather like deploring the fact that human beings are carnivorous, but saying there are some good reasons for them to eat meat, yet not investigating the origins of the tendency towards carnivorous eating. The concern expressed is moral rather than sociological, but even so, 'moral' in a limited sense, since there is a hesitation to impugn the fundamental need for the practice in question. As Honderich freely confesses: 'Answers to the question of why we punish, where that is not the question of what reasons we can give, but rather a question about causes, are no part of my concern.'[5] The state of this art is usefully indicated by Garland and Young when they comment that the task of philosophical analysis appears to begin with 'the (stated or unstated) recognition of a universal necessity to punish and control' and is concerned mainly to establish a rationale or justification for the 'right to punish'.[6] It is especially this disinterest in the roots of penality which marks off the philosophical from the sociological enquiry.

The contribution of philosophical analysis to the discussion of punishment should not, however, be underestimated. It has served in particular to clarify motivation in penal practice and supply cogency in arguments concerning the extent of punishment. The main problems that have been tackled in this discourse are those of definition, justification, and distribution, although these are issues that are often seen as closely interrelated. Definition is obviously helpful in clarifying how key terms and concepts are used in discussion and also in categorizing different manifestations of the phenomenon of punishment. When objection is made (as we have objected) to categorization into 'standard' and 'sub-standard' instances of punishment (e.g. by Flew, Benn, and Hart),[7] it is the ranking process and the failure to recognize similarities as well as differences that is at issue, not the identification of different types or contexts of punishment, which is a useful exercise. The danger of definition, as Hart recognizes,[8] is that it can be used to close areas of debate and rule argument out-of-play: 'That's not what I understand by punishment, so you cannot use that sense of the term against my argument.' But 'definition blockage' is also a by-product of this kind of discourse which, because of its intellectual, abstract qualities and its lack of reference to empirical data, has a certain limited potential and room for manoeuvre.

But probably most energy in this area has been spent on the subject of justification; and here we are confronted with the 200-year-old debate in western jurisprudence centred upon the contest between 'retributive' and 'utilitarian' justifications for punishment. The moral basis for our resort to punishment has been variously asserted as an imperative of justice (e.g. Kant:[9] it would be unjust not to respond thus to wrongdoing), as an element in a beneficial calculus (e.g. Bentham:[10] reduction of crime, removal of criminality, and protection of society), or as an amalgam of these backward- and forward-looking considerations (e.g. Hart).[11] This debate has spawned an enormous literature in the jurisprudence of the English-speaking world and great energy has been expended to show that either a retributive or a utilitarian justification is not convincing. Yet a cursory view of this writing conveys more than anything else a sense of argumentative virtuosity generated by academic ritual. If an uninformed reader, plunged into the middle of this debate, were to enquire 'What does it matter, anyway?', he would have to work quite hard to extrapolate a clear answer to that simple but important question. Indeed, much of the writing in this area is self-consciously prefaced by reference to difficulties and obscurities. Hart mentions 'the mounting perplexities which now surround the institution of criminal punishment'.[12] Grupp, introducing an anthology of this literature, remarks that the conflict of 'punishment ideologies' is 'submerged or unrecognised and is not brought to the surface for a healthy airing and open debate'.[13] And Honderich begins by saying that he wishes to address himself to defences of the practice of punishment and also 'persistent obscurities' which 'are principally the work of a succession of moral philosophers'.[14] Do such comments not suggest that years of work have been to little avail? Or, more cynically, should we assume that the philosophical enterprise of retributivist arguing against utilitarian has become an end in itself? What lies at the root of all this argument?

Scanning the academic jousts, some important and intractable issues *may* be extrapolated and offered as some justification for all this intellectual effort. For instance, the frequent argument presented against the utilitarian justification is that its objective of securing the good of the greatest number may lead to unfair treatment of a few. For instance: terrorism is a major problem for society as a whole; it is felt that it may be successfully contained by extreme measures of deterrence; we are not sure that X is in fact responsible for a terrorist outrage; but we badly need to make an example and proof is difficult to find; therefore we deal severely with X, even though he may be innocent. Undoubtedly, that situation contains a moral dilemma. Or, to take an example of utilitarian attack: to support punishment simply on the ground that X has committed an offence and therefore deserves punishment presupposes that X is fully responsible for his conduct, but this, in the light of expanding psychological knowledge and determinist argument may be an untenable assumption.[15] As Hart quite rightly stresses in much of his work, the question of human responsibility should make us consider carefully our use of punishment. But, because we recognize the existence of such questions and problems, does that necessarily commit us to lengthy argument concerning the fundamental weaknesses of either retributive or utilitarian logic? In other words, is it not possible to explore these questions without having to declare loyalty and all-out war? Indeed, this is what Hart seeks to do in his account – avoid 'much confusing shadow-fighting between utilitarians and their opponents'[16] – by locating the role of retributive argument at the point of what he terms 'distribution' of punishment, while allowing utilitarian aims to justify resort to punishment in the first place. Although by no means a final answer to all the points raised in the philosophical debate and in itself open to some criticism, this approach does at least have the merit of focusing attention on the important but often relatively overlooked question of distribution of punishment.

Here the term 'distribution' is a convenient shorthand reference to a complex of difficult but practically significant issues in the practice of punishment. In summary, we are interested here in two major questions, concerning who is the subject of punishment and what kind or quantum of punishment is applied. (The other major question of who punishes – who acts as penal authority or agent – is defined away by Hart when he insists that the 'standard' case of punishment is its use by the state.) Distribution of punishment is a major aspect of Hart's treatment of the subject and he is concerned to show that retributive argument, drawing upon ideas of personal responsibility and proportionality of response, is important in the working out of these questions. Or at least he shows convincingly that western moral philosophy has evolved answers that are retributive in character, reflecting the western view of human individuality. But perhaps

Hart's major contribution lies in his presentation of a significant analytical tool in the concept of distribution as a limiting or controlling factor, providing a moral restraint on the practice of punishment. For the significant problems of justice which arise in relation to punishment do so in relation to its application to individual cases: in practice we tend not to question the justice of penal action generally, but to challenge its fairness as applied to X, or as used in a particular form or amount. And it may be seen that the two enduring moral dilemmas referred to above – punishment of the innocent for the sake of deterrence, and the elusive attribution of personal responsibility – are properly located as distributive problems, concerning the moral acceptability of using punishment in relation to certain categories of person.

We shall consider further the substance of retributive and utilitarian notions about punishment at a later point. For the present, we may summarize this overview of the philosophical contribution to the subject by arguing that its distinctive achievement lies not so much in the details of its identification or opposition of retributive and utilitarian 'theories of punishment' but in its provision of a juridical framework for an assessment of the application of punishment. In so far as most western systems of criminal law embody ideas of personal responsibility as a basis for liability and of proportionality of punishment, this reflects the underlying principle, which Hart has termed 'retribution in the distribution of punishment'. That other systems may not always have been so steadfastly retributive in their methods should stimulate a more wide-ranging enquiry which may provide some insight into the underlying impulses of western penality.

THE SOCIOLOGY OF PUNISHMENT

As an intellectual discipline the 'sociology' of punishment would appear at first sight to have a shorter history than punishment as a topic within moral philosophy. 'Sociology' is a relatively modern description, originating with Comte, and as a subject, especially with its empirical emphases, has a modern image. Yet, as historians of the field are quick to point out, the absence of a specific label does not indicate the non-existence of that type of reflection on and analysis of the social world that we now usually term 'sociological'.[17] Indeed, many pre-Comtian writers, from Plato onwards, did turn their thoughts towards social analysis, although their work will more commonly be described as philosophical, historical, or whatever else. In a number of cases, both historical and contemporary, it may be difficult to categorize work definitively as either 'sociology' or 'social philosophy'. To suggest two notable examples: is the work of either Durkheim or Foucault on punishment to be described as 'sociological' or 'philosophical'? And when we begin to list the various sub-ologies of sociology – penology, criminology, social psychology, social anthropology, the sociology of deviance or of anything else which counts as a social phenomenon – it should become apparent just how pointless any exercise in categorization may be. Therefore we shall not claim to be definitive in our description of any analyses that go under the broad heading of sociological, although it will still be useful to point out an important difference in emphasis in so far as philosophers and sociologists talk about the subject of punishment.

We have already discussed some of the significant themes in the analysis of punishment as a subject of moral philosophy. A reading of a sample of that body of literature will convey soon enough its hermetical character. Although it refers ultimately to perceived difficulties in the practical domain of penal activity, there is at the same time an assumption that ethical problems can be extrapolated from the morass of social actuality and then resolved at the level of theory. In this way, the situations and examples which are used to test argument are hypothetical or at least factually refined. Indeed, there would seem to be an implication that this is a necessary method: only by standing back from the mess of real life and discussing these problems in their essential terms can they be satisfactorily resolved. What can be broadly distinguished as the sociological approach to the subject, however, operates in the opposite direction, seeking to find out as much as possible about the mess of reality, so as to achieve a fuller and better understanding of it. Hence, the recourse to empirical research in much sociological work. The sociological method works with facts, quantities, perspectives, and interpretations and concerns itself with what is happening (or has happened) in society. The philosophical method (as identified above) tends to detach itself from the social manifestation of the problem and the resolution of the problem becomes an intellectual experience, since the answer depends on argument and logic, not on facts. Find more facts and it will make no difference, although the discovery of new data may have tremendous impact at the sociological level. It is rather like the difference between pure mathematics and physical science.

The justification for our distinction between the philosophical and the sociological discussion of punishment is based on the way in which two sets of people ask different questions about the same subject. This may be clearly seen by comparing the enduring question of the philosophical debate, 'How can punishment be justified?' with one of the most basic sociological questions about punishment, 'Why do people use punishment?' The first question assumes the existence of penal practice and seeks to subject it to ethical critique. The second question observes the use of punishment and seeks to discover why it is so used. The hallmark of the sociological analysis is therefore its resort to observation or interpretation of determinate society to achieve an understanding of human action.[18] Man is not endowed with any qualities in advance; the whole business is to discover and prove these qualities. What then has sociological analysis of punishment told us about the phenomenon? An overview of such discussion will require more organization than one of the philosophical debate: the whole field of penal activity in practice may be divided and subdivided to such an extent that there are, and have been, numerous potential lines of enquiry and specialist investigations. For the sake of exposition, however, we may perhaps identify two principal approaches to the subject in the sociological field, although, as with much of this discussion, hard-and-fast distinctions may crumble at the edges.

For convenience, we could describe these two approaches as 'systematic' and 'empirical', although care should be taken not to apply these terms out of context. Those writers who take the systematic approach are interested in extrapolating from social data concerning punishment perspectives, explanations, and relationships in order to construct a general theory of the subject. Usually such work is at least one remove from any direct observation of the practice of punishment and the sources are therefore largely secondary, in the form of written records or accounts supplied by other persons. Put in metaphorical terms, this is 'library' if not 'armchair' reflection, and not 'fieldwork'. Provided that the data used in this way are reliable (a question-begging concept, but let that pass for the moment), relevantly selected and cogently employed in working out a theoretical picture, this approach may provide important insights into the penal phenomenon. A large number of writers would fall into this category, from Durkheim through to Foucault (and, of course, ourselves). Nor need such writers be 'academic' in the conventional sense. There is, for example, a significant body of 'theoretical' discussion that has been produced by penal administrators, based largely on their own involvement in penal practice but discussing the process of punishment in general, systematic terms. The tradition of scholarly writing on the part of leading British penal administrators in the later nineteenth and earlier twentieth centuries provides us with a good example of this kind of contribution to the subject.[19]

Another feature of some of this 'systematic' writing on the subject is that treatment of the topic of punishment may be incidental rather than the writer's pincipal objective. A good deal of sociological theory of punishment has been thrown up by writers dealing in more general themes such as state power, crime and deviance, social control, or sanctions theory. The subject of punishment, in the view of Garland and Young: 'has formed an empirical area, tangential to the main sociological enterprise. . . . There are few sociological analyses which have begun with the phenomenon of "punishment" as their main object of analysis.'[20] This observation is supported by the tendency in exposition of the subject to use the term 'theory of punishment' as a description of the philosophical kind of writing discussed in the previous section. The principal area of sociological activity where punishment has been treated as a subject for investigation in its own right is the historical investigation of penality. This is a burgeoning academic field, with some pedigree of its own. Rusche and Kirchheimer's major study, *Punishment and Social Structure*,[21] was published in 1939 and during the post-war period, the history of crime, punishment, and social control has become a significant academic sub-discipline in both Europe and North America, integrating the skills of the social scientist and the historian. Much of this work in recent times has had a Marxist, or at least a 'revisionist', flavour (revision, that is, of earlier 'progressive' interpretations) and much of it is also concerned with the role of incarceration and transformations in patterns of social control: for instance, Rusche and Kirchheimer (1939), Foucault (1977), Scull (1977, 1984), Ignatieff (1978), Melossi and Pavarini (1981), Cohen (1985), Garland (1985).[22] A further significant feature of much of this historical work is the way in which it is self-consciously carried out in the hope or expectation of providing insight into penality in general, for the present and future as well as the past. As Garland explains this method: 'a historical analysis has the advantage of providing the material for an examination of the original programmes, struggles and objectives which lie behind the formation of our present-day institutions and give them their distinctive character'.[23] Interestingly, therefore, it is this field of social-historical endeavour that has produced some of the most important theoretical and systematic discussions of punishment as a social phenomenon.

It should also be mentioned at this point that a particular kind of historical investigation has emerged in the form of the more specific study of crime, punishment, and social control within narrowly drawn limits of space and time. It is axiomatic that an acquaintance with historical actuality requires a study of contemporary records in some detail, and so we find for example in recent years: accounts of sex-roles and crime in late-Elizabethan Hertfordshire (Weiner), of crime and courts in Surrey in the mid-eighteenth century (Beattie), of Bedford Prison between 1660 and 1877 (Stockdale), of crime in seventeenth-century Essex (Sharpe), of Exeter Borough Prison during the middle years of the nineteenth century (Forsythe).[24–8] The problem is how far this detailed, highly focused form of study should be taken at the expense of wider perspectives. As J. L. McMullan remarks, 'the pursuit of the parochial is no guarantee of an informed conceptual framework',[29] and the latter is required to provide an overall sense of order and direction in such study and avoid description and quantification for its own sake. Moreover, the preference for official and legal records as source material in this kind of work runs the risk of reproducing an official experience and interpretation of crime and punishment. This tension between a 'macro-' and a 'micro-' approach to criminal and penal history reflects important underlying problems in the overall investigation and interpretation of penal practice, which also come to the surface in connection with more technical penological research.

THE EMPIRICAL MODE OF DISCUSSION

Let us turn now to the other principal approach in the sociological discussion of punishment, that which we have for convenience referred to as 'empirical'. This term is used to convey the idea that the researcher goes into the 'field' to acquire a direct impression of penal actuality, which can then be recorded for information, use in argument or in further research. The results of this kind of research may have considerable impact, most obviously when a 'real' but unsuspected state of affairs is revealed to a concerned audience or readership. Conversely, there may also be a risk of attracting derision for painstakingly establishing the already-suspected or what may be thought of as obvious. But generally, as with the micro-historical studies, there is a comforting sense of coming closer to the 'reality' of the problem.

There is a well-established tradition of such empirical work in the penal field. In the days before there were 'sociologists' as such, concerned observers of the penal scene were busy informing themselves and then the rest of the world about what was happening 'on the ground'. Howard in the late eighteenth century and Mayhew and Binny in the middle of the next century are both examples of reporting work on the British penal system, which publicized a great deal of otherwise inaccessible information and achieved a noticeable critical impact.[30-1] Such works were based on the assumption that a better-informed state of knowledge is a powerful tool in achieving a shift in policy, and were an important component of the reform movement of that earlier era. They were doubtless also an inspiration for the more 'scientific' penological research that developed with the growth of statistics, sampling techniques, and the like, which rendered penal practice more susceptible to quantification and surveillance.

The term 'penology' came into use sometime in the middle of the nineteenth century and may loosely but conveniently be used to describe the empirical studies of punishment now under discussion. Penological work would appear to fall into two main categories: firstly, the 'scientific' study of crime prevention and punishment, and secondly, and more specifically, analysis of the management of the penal system, particularly its institutional aspects, such as imprisonment. As an area of intellectual activity, it has a number of distinguishing features. Firstly, its scientific or technical character: here what is usually being referred to is an emphasis on fact-finding, quantitative assessment, and rigorous methodology, and overall a concern with the practical operation of penal measures. Secondly, the essential field of discussion has comprised the armoury of penal measures, processes, and institutions set up by the state to deal with infractions of the state's system of criminal law. Thirdly, there would seem to be two principal objects of study: the impact of particular penal measures (usually, the extent to which they result in a reduction

69

in crime) and the practical problems of organizing and putting into effect such measures. Finally, penologists themselves have historically come from two principal backgrounds: either an environment of penal reform, being concerned with the improvement or replacement of existing measures, or involvement in the administration of such measures, especially imprisonment. Only in the post-1945 period has there emerged a separate and more specific profession of penologist, often working within research or academic institutions, and employed or indirectly funded by the state.

Returning to the pioneering penological work during the middle and later nineteenth century, it may be seen how this was for the most part the product of either penal reformers or penal administrators, although often there would be an overlap between these categories, since those in the best position to be critical about the operation of the penal system were usually those who had some experience of its management. In Britain Mayhew and Binny, Dickens, Galsworthy, and other literary commentators occupy one end of this spectrum, being themselves concerned though detached observers whose main occupation was not penal reform as such.[32-4] There were then a number of writers who were centrally involved in the work of penal reform, such as Mary Carpenter and William Tallack (secretary of the Howard League) who had a close though unofficial involvement with the state penal system.[35-6] But there was, in particular, an impressive body of penological writing produced by a range of people with differing official status within the penal system, such as Frederic Hill, a magistrate; Burt, Clay, and Morrison, all prison chaplains; Chesterton, a prison governor; and Jebb and Du Cane, senior prison administrators, to name just a few.[37] Some of this writing was of a theoretical as well as an empirical character; a striking feature of much of this literature was its relation to arguments about penal reform – often the motive for empirical investigation was to inform such arguments. Thus, at the end of the nineteenth century, we find two British commentators, Sir Edmund Du Cane and W. D. Morrison, both resorting to the same data concerning rates of crime to argue against and in favour of change in the prison regime.[38]

This tradition whereby penological research serves to provide information for discourse on penal reform has continued to the present time. During the mid-twentieth century, penology has evolved into a distinct professional enterprise with full-time researchers examining the deterrent and corrective efficacy of penal measures and the problems of their practical implementation. Increasingly, however, such work is commissioned and funded by the penal system itself and there is often an implicit acceptance in such work of the essential role of the state in providing for penal responses. Since the 1950s a central theme of this penological enterprise has been, firstly, a critical evaluation of traditional measures, and of the reformative and deterrent potential of imprisonment in particular, and then the comparative evaluation of new options as the latter have come increasingly to dominate state policy in dealing with crime and the 'crisis' in the use of imprisonment. For the most part such work is content – because it is often funded on this assumption – to accept that the central problem is to discover more effective methods in the 'battle' against crime, as defined by the state's legal system.[39] These characteristics of penological work have led Garland and Young to describe it (at least in Britain) as a 'technicist endeavour', the scope and range of which is 'limited by, and tied to, quite specific demands emanating from the requirements of governments, the penal bureaucracy itself and the activities of charitably-based reformers (later to be social workers proper) . . . when definite ideas of policy are promoted, they become subordinated to the details of the internal workings of organisations'.[40] Much penological work may therefore be seen as an element of the state penal establishment and is essentially concerned with the ongoing operation of the latter.

Retrospectively, therefore, penological activity may be viewed as so far having moved through two principal phases. The initial period was one of discovery, the first uncovering as methodology became available of the factual phenomena of the (state) penal system. As the present century progresses, this enterprise enters a new phase, in which it becomes less haphazard, less dependent on the initiative of interested individuals and increasingly co-ordinated as an official, continuing process of scrutiny for the information of the state itself. Within the last twenty years it is perhaps possible to identify a further phase of penological activity. With the emergence of radical criminology and the social history of crime as significant academic disciplines, often employing Marxist and structuralist critiques, an independent strain of penology has began to evolve, much more questioning of the state's involvement and of the tacit acceptance of the base fact of criminality.[41] Admittedly, some of this recent work departs also from the conventional empirical line of investigation, to which extent the use of the label 'penological' may need to be qualified. Yet what is often at issue in such work is a reinterpretation of empirical direction and of the character of the phenomena under investigation. In particular, the thrust of this kind of study is to present new perspectives on familiar processes within the legal and penal system, such as pre-trial procedures, and to question how established policies should be understood (for instance, benevolent reform reinterpreted more sinisterly as social control). In short, the new message is 'All is not as it seems – take nothing for granted' and commentators are assuming a more detached point of observation. It may be that we have now reached the stage where we are witnessing the final exhaustion of the optimism that has for two centuries sustained the endeavour of penal reform. More cynically now, there is an increasing tendency to view the motives and language of penal reform as a justification, either unconscious or concealed, for further state action. It is at this point that we come up against those disturbing metaphors of the 'punitive city'[42] and the 'carceral archipelago',[43] suggestive of penal totalitarianism. It is, of course, this very pervasiveness of the penal option, although from a different angle, that we are especially concerned to illuminate here.

Before leaving this discussion of empirical enquiry into the practice of punishment, we should also note two other fields of investigation, which have supplied some important insights into the broader spectrum of penal activity with which our study is concerned and have certainly informed some crucial aspects of our argument. The 'fieldwork' and other research carried out by social anthropologists provides a considerable body of data relating to the practice of punishment,[44] especially in the context of 'stateless' societies, kinship groups, families, and educational institutions, and these findings may be of great value both in understanding punitive impulses and purposes and in achieving a more balanced perspective of the totality of penal practice.

Also, penal activity has been examined by psychologists and again the findings of such studies are highly instructive. Early behaviourist psychology laid great stress on the pleasure/pain stimulus, suggesting a scientific basis for the operation of these factors that had figured so large in utilitarian philosophical debate. Doctrines of 'socialization' based on the internalization of external social pressure brought into prominence the role of punishment in the process. Freud, too, considered within his wider psychoanalytic theory the role of punishment, particularly parental punishment, in the formation of the human character.[45] Freud pointed out that punishment can be a potent factor in the production of conflict and can be a potent tool in the generation of psychological disorder, as evidenced for example in his well-known case history of the 'Rat Man'. Freud's theory has not, of course, been immune from criticism and nor has the controversial work of B. F. Skinner, who also stresses the adverse effects that he believes to be inherent in the practice of punishment.[46] For Skinner, punishment as an aversive stimulus does not take away the impulse to perform the act that has been punished: 'A child who has been severely punished for sex-play is not necessarily less inclined to continue; and a man who has been imprisoned for violent assault is not necessarily less inclined towards violence. Punished behaviour is likely to re-appear after the punitive contingencies are withdrawn.'[47] Punishment, he urges, may lead to behaviour that attempts to avoid the aversive stimulus, but avoidance of the act forbidden is only one method of punishment evasion; others may cause individual neurosis, still others social dysfunction. In these ways Skinner produces a thorough-going critique of the punitive society.

It is not our task here to evaluate these or other psychological theories, nor yet to review the empirical studies that have been undertaken within the discipline of psychology. Clearly, we shall have cause to refer to psychological investigation at various points during this survey, although always with the trepidation of non-experts and occasionally armed with no more than an a priori hypothesis. Our point at the moment is simply that, within the discipline of psychology, we find another distinct *locus* of discussion concerning punishment.

THE PENAL CONSCIOUSNESS

It would be useful, finally, to locate these discussions of punishment in a wider context since it will not have escaped the notice of most readers that the bulk of this chapter has been concerned with the work of writers on the subject over the last two hundred years and within the framework supplied by what may be loosely described as western culture. What we have referred to as lore and doctrine – the accumulation of ideas about and insights into penal activity, the moral analysis, and the technical assessment – is characteristically the product of modern western society. This is not to assert that there is little or no discussion of the use of punishment to be found elsewhere or at other times. But the reflective and critical intellectual tendency to view punishment as a *problem*, requiring justification, analysis, and study is predominantly reflective of an *angst* that appears to have developed in Europe some two or three hundred years ago and has resulted in an intellectual industry that has achieved an established place in the centres of research and policy-making in the western world. In other words, we are here doing no less than contemplating the origins of our own motivation to discuss the subject in this manner. What can be said about the cognitive development that has stimulated both the writing and the reading of a work of this kind, not to mention all the others which have been referred to?

This is not the place to attempt an explanation of this intellectual phenomenon. At a superficial level, such explanation may seem not too difficult to present. Enough work has been done on the idea of progress in human societies to establish with some confidence the view that, from around the sixteenth century onwards, there was a kind of 'take-off' in European culture and thought, static notions of human existence gradually giving way to the belief that the present could be improved upon and that it lay in humanity's power to bring about revolutionary and far-reaching changes.[48] It requires no great imaginative leap to associate these general tendencies in thought and ideas with the positive strategy that emerges clearly during the eighteenth century: that if certain aspects of human behaviour appear problematical, the modification of these may be a realizable goal. There would be different methods to try, such as outward compulsion (deterrence) and inward persuasion (reform), but the overall possibility was grasped in an especially significant fashion.

It may be objected that such reflection on the different possibilities of punishment was neither new nor peculiar to western argument in the modern period. Could it not be said that the penal codes of other cultures, both historical and contemporary, and earlier penal phenomena of the western world, such as the Christian system of penance,[49] are equally based upon theory and considered methodology? Those who have worked out penalties elsewhere and at other times clearly had in mind objectives of reform or deterrence; similarly there was critical observation at times of the operation of these punishments.[50] However, what may be put forward to distinguish the modern western discourse on punishment is the adoption of a radical critical position, which challenged not only the operation of specific

modes of punishment (e.g. corporal penalties, unregulated imprisonment), but more fundamentally, the normative framework within
which punishment was carried out, the authorities entitled to employ
it, and its very logic. What emerges is a comparative evaluation, the
perception of differences, and the idea of a goal or ideal in penal
endeavour. There is, in short, a transition from the reflexive to the
reflective resort to punishment. The traditional authority of the
sovereign, the leader, the head of the family to use punishment is no
longer accepted as an inevitable fact of social organization; the use of
punishment is felt to be in need of justification, its objectives clarified
and its methods scrutinized for their efficiency. Hence the debate
between retributivists and utilitarians, the concern about the role of
the state or dominant classes in the use of punishment, the insertion of
the topic into discussion of social control and power relations, and all
else which has served to make punishment the subject of an epistemo-
logical as well as a practical field. We can summarize this process by
saying that, within modern western culture, punishment has become
the subject-matter of a sphere of knowledge in addition to forming an
important element of social practice.

A number of factors may be seen as contributing to this transform-
ation of the subject, although we are here as yet moving in the realm of
hypothesis rather than established theory. Predominant among such
factors may be listed European expansionism and confrontation with
other cultures; the potential for technical development and control
suggested by rapid advances in technology and scientific knowledge;
and the concept of the individual in post-Renaissance Europe. The
latter, in particular, supplied a dual idea: that of the individual both
as an infinitely operable subject of punishment and at the same time
as an autonomous juridical and political entity capable of asserting
himself within the realm of punishment. Gains in scientific knowledge
served to open up the psychological elements of humanity to penal
possibilities, so allowing a significant development away from the
corporeal modes of punishment.[51] At the same time – and contributing therefore an important tension – the emerging independence and
integrity of the individual in western society tended to produce at the
level of discourse a resistance and a more deeply critical response to
the use of punishment.[52] From such a dialectic it was possible for a
new body of knowledge to develop.

5

PUNISHMENT, RULE, AND SOCIAL ORGANIZATION

We have seen how widely spread the practice of punishment is and how deeply it is embedded in a whole variety of social structures and substructures. It is necessary here then to attempt to relate the concept of punishment to the ideas of social organization in general and social rules in particular. One way in which this might be attempted is the conceptual approach adopted by some analytical jurists who have written in this area. This would involve us in a series of definitions of key concepts, such as 'punishment', 'social rule', etc., which would provide us with a theoretical structure of their inter-relationship. Such a structure might be more or less enlightening, more or less attractive in its expository power, but would stand in no need of empirical verification – a definition for the sake of analysis is neither true nor untrue, it is a definition. The observations offered here are, however, intended to be measurable against the reality of social fact, as generalizations from the evidence of human experience. As such they are open to challenge should they fail to correspond with such evidence. This is not to suggest, of course, that the approach here offered is a theoretically neutral account drawn from a pure spring of empirical fact. It is not necessary to go so far as to accept the impossibility of objective truth to appreciate that the material here assembled must inevitably, by the very process of selection and presentation, have been subjected to theory. But this is a truism of any form of discourse; it is mentioned here simply to indicate that our approach is in intention a descriptive one. A failure clearly to distinguish between conceptual argumentation and empirical observation is a flaw of at least one major commentary in this area.[1] Accordingly, we consider it important to make the distinction at the outset in the hope that, in so far as the method of our approach is concerned (even if in no other respects), the reader may consider us to be clearly wrong but at least to have been wrong clearly. If the observations made here are considered by the reader not to correspond to the nature of things within the real world, we shall not enjoy the luxury of being able to retreat beyond a definitional stockade.

This form of approach, however, results in certain consequences. We shall perforce have to content ourselves with certain generalizations. The concept of universal characteristics of social existence, even if philosophically tenable, attracts certain problems when it comes to the gathering of evidence! Recognition that we are considering generalizations, however, will alert us to the fact that there will be, in addition to cases that clearly fall within the framework here offered, other cases that are, we concede, not so easily accommodated. We must allow of some grey areas, some matters of degree, if our attempts to make any statements that seek to explain the nature of certain social ideas across immensities of time and space are to be at all tenable. Such humility would perhaps be taken as read by many, yet it is seldom vouchsafed to readers of standard works of jurisprudence. Such works, which may produce theories that are most satisfying in their dovetailed conceptual analyses, are recommended to readers who are likely to be annoyed by the timidity of our ensuing discussion. It is freely conceded, however, that insights from traditional analytical jurisprudence will be drawn upon here where they are, in our opinion, supportable by observation.

THE SOCIAL GROUP

It is necessary first to offer a few comments about social organization in general. Clearly, save for instances of self-punishment, to which we shall return later, punishment involves more than one individual. In addition, the instances of the practice with which we have been concerned in our examples suggest a certain idea of social order as a precursor to an idea of punishment. Discussion of the issues of private retaliation, which seems to lack a context of social order, will again be postponed until a later point. Punishment is, we would suggest, a practice associated with a breach of prescriptions, often the rules or norms of a social group. One could, it is true, describe a mere aggregate of individuals as a social group; but we prefer to use this term to describe in this context something more than simply an idea of incorporation by enumeration. The distinction to be drawn here is between a football club and a football crowd, based on grounds of organization, which characteristic, as will be seen, is one that we consider to be significant for an understanding of the idea of punishment. However, we may note that there may be within that football crowd members of collectivities of this second sort, such as a supporters' club or a 'hooligan' gang.

Let us stay for a moment within the confines of a football stadium, for this will enable us to illustrate a number of further points. Firstly, it is perhaps obvious that an individual may be at one and the same time a member of more than one group and that the norms of these groups need not be mutually concordant. Members of the 'hooligan' gang may, for example, also be members of the supporters' club, and members of both will, we may assume (although this factor was not adverted to earlier), be members of and subject to the jurisdiction of a nation-state. This complex of social groupings may be of considerable significance, it will be shown later, for an understanding of some problems connected with punishment. In addition, to return to the distinction between the crowd and the club, it is clear that the latter is characterized by more than simply the coincidence of geographical location, or indeed of purpose, that is to be found in the former. Indeed, it is clear that that social organization which we conceive as being a key to the understanding of penality may be maintained without physical geographical proximity, although clearly this may result in genuine difficulties of communication. The problem of whether a community of purpose is a necessary, though insufficient requirement for the existence of a social group in the sense in which we would prefer to use the term, is rather more complex. A. M. Honoré, in discussing the idea of a social group in this sense, maintains that there may be a necessity for a 'shared common purpose',[2] but the search for any simple 'purpose' in the group that forms the membership of a complex modern nation-state, or, indeed, in that which comprises a tribal grouping, is likely to prove difficult. It may therefore be possible to dispense with this requirement.

What does seem to be necessary for the existence of a structured social group, a social organization, is a certain predictability of action, a certain shared understanding. Honoré, writing from within the tradition of analytical jurisprudence, suggests the following formulation:

78

It is a matter of degree whether the shared understandings of individuals are firm, numerous, important and lasting enough for them to count as a group. Subject to this qualification, a group may be described as a collection of individuals who share a fairly definite understanding of what is to be done by one or more of themselves in given circumstances, or how the question what is to be done in those circumstances is to be decided.[3]

Simon Roberts, having reviewed the anthropological evidence, contends:

At the root of everyday life in any society there must necessarily be some patterns of habitual conduct followed by the members, providing a basis upon which one member will be able to predict how another is likely to behave under given circumstances or how his own actions will be received.[4]

Clearly such understanding, such acceptance of the idea of predictable response, will necessarily imply a restriction on the absolute liberty of individual members of the society. This need not in every case, however, be a restriction experienced as irksome, indeed may not even be noticed by the majority of persons subjected to it. Theoretically at any rate it is possible that such restriction, indeed the predictable pattern of conduct itself, need not be articulated or even inculcated but may arise and continue merely as a display of coincident behaviour. But typically, in practice, social groups will be obliged to recognize some modes of behaviour as 'proper', or at the very least as 'usual', for the purposes of instructing their children in the techniques of life in society, and for recognizing and responding to those individuals whose behaviour steps outside the understandings that support the continuity of the social group.

It is in this conception of the 'proper' behaviour of members of the social group that we begin to approach the notion of a social rule. As the social psychologist S. E. Asch observes: 'The presence of men in the same surroundings sets definite requirements for ordered relations between them. The first function of social rules is to establish paths of action and clear expectations . . . rules limit the area of the unknown and unpredictable; they become the ground of stable orientation.'[5] We would assume too much, however, if we were to think that in all societies such rules were articulated. As Roberts observes:

Although in any society understandings shared by members must underlie many of the regularities of behaviour which can be observed, human groups vary a great deal in the extent to which these understandings are translated into explicit rules which members talk about. Some peoples talk freely about their rules, quote them constantly in everyday life and furnish detailed inventories for anyone who may ask about them. Others find it difficult to think and speak in terms of rules (i.e. in terms of how people 'ought' to behave) at all. But it does not follow that because people do not talk about rules they are unimportant. Norms of fundamental importance may be accepted tacitly and rest implicit in the basic organisational features of a society.[6]

Such social rules, by which we mean simply general statements of behaviour understood to be proper, are clearly of great importance. The generality that is a feature of the rule is an economical means of communication when set beside a series of individual *ad hominem* or *ad rem* statements all in the same form.[7] As Roberts suggests, it may be that in some societies it is possible for a rule to be unarticulated, its existence being deduced only by observing behaviour when the boundary of 'proper' conduct has been transgressed. Such an apparently illogical position, that the rule may only be discovered when its breach has been identified, may seem very difficult to maintain. It should be pointed out, however, that this idea is similar to that which lies at the root of the ideology of the Anglo-American common law, under which system the judge, faced by a dispute over the applicability of a rule, 'discovers' what that rule has always been. Clearly the process that we are describing may reveal rules in a similar way, by dealing with their infractions, yet it may not be either so artificial in its technique nor so normative in the language associated with it.

Before expanding further on the nature of a social rule we may perhaps briefly address ourselves to the question of whether any particular content is necessary in the regulation (explicit or tacit) of behaviour within a social group. From the features we have earlier identified it would seem that one rule, as Honoré has recognized, cannot stand if a social structure is to be maintained in this way – that is, the rule 'Everyone is to do as he [or she] likes'.[8] As to whether any positive content is necessary within the regulation of social groups (and at this point we are concerned with those groups that are centred around, amongst other things, the most basic functions of life – what we may term 'total society groups', as exemplified in certain contexts by the tribe or village – rather than, for instance, the squash club), then this is a question the answer to which may be suggested by an empirical investigation as to the universality of their observation. So it has been suggested that some regulation of violence and of sexual relations is to be found in all such societies. The anthropologist I. M. Lewis suggests that 'in principle all societies recognize that human life and property, whatever price is placed upon them, have to be protected, and that their violation constitutes a wrong or offence which has to be rectified or punished. Beyond this the elaboration of substantive law is largely a matter of material technology and cultural sophistication.'[9] Let us leave aside for the moment the distinction that Lewis draws between rectification and punishment and also the question as to what is meant here by 'law', and content ourselves with mention of one qualification. That is, that it is clearly not a necessity for continued group survival that the regulation should extend to all members of the group. So, for example, social collectivities may still display the features of group understanding and regulation notwith-standing that they may contain a number of slaves who may be killed at will and without any social censure from the group as a whole or may employ a system of human sacrifice. To take a concrete example, among the Eskimo at one time in certain circumstances infants could be killed without attribution of blame or imposition of sanction and such action was frequently taken when twins were born. Those who were old or invalid might also be assisted to end their lives once they had made known their wish so to do.[10] Evidently competition for resources in a harsh environment will explain such attitudes and practices. Less intelligible was the Comanche husband's absolute right to kill his wife with or without 'cause'.[11] If any general principle, such as the protection of human life, is found to be universal in all human societies, examples such as those given above must be under-stood as marking the parameters of the rule within a particular society rather than negating its existence.

To those whose background lies in analytical jurisprudence, the above discussion will evoke memories of an aspect of the legal theory of H. L. A. Hart. Hart has suggested that certain forms of regulation are dictated by certain 'truisms' about the nature of man and the world in which he lives. It is in such speculation that Hart discovers his 'Minimum Content of Natural Law'. Hart's own armchair observations on this subject are not necessarily compelling.[12] The question of whether there is a basic universal content to social regulation may be more satisfyingly answered from anthropological investigation. Such investigation should include, however, alongside a scrutiny of 'healthy' and settled societies, those also in which the social bonding is placed under stress, such as that described in C. M. Turnbull's disturbing study of the famine-stricken Ik of Uganda.[13]

SOCIAL RULES

Let us return to our consideration of social rules generally, and our consideration of such rules will not be restricted to their operation within the context of the 'total society'. We have suggested that the idea of a rule is one that we may use to describe that state of affairs where conduct in certain circumstances is not only considered usual but also proper. The ambiguities and nuances within English words such as 'norm', 'custom', and indeed 'rule' itself, hint at, for some purposes at least, a broad cultural correspondence, at any rate within the tradition that employs these terms and, we would suggest, beyond it between antiquity and rectitude. Although this correlation is evidently far from total there may well be elements in many cultures of a way of thinking which runs as follows: 'We have always done this. Our predecessors have always done this. It is right that you should do it.' In such reasoning normativity is linked with settled expectation in defiance of David Hume's famous observation as to the impossibility of deriving an 'ought' from an 'is'.[14]

Whatever their origin, it is clear that we must examine the nature of social rules in more detail, for it will be argued shortly that an understanding of social rules may well prove to be a key to the understanding of punishment. Yet again, we turn to the work of H. L. A. Hart, for although we may doubt his conclusions, he has recognized the importance of the discussion of social rules. Hart contends that a rule consists of two elements, one being the external regularity of behaviour (in itself indistinguishable from mere habit), the other being what he terms the 'internal aspect' of the rule. In Hart's own words: 'There is . . . one point of similarity between social rules and habits. In both cases the behaviour in question must be general though not necessarily invariable.' But in addition, for something to be described accurately as a rule: 'what is necessary is that there should be a critical reflective attitude to certain patterns of behaviour as a common standard and that this should display itself in criticism (including self-criticism), demands for conformity and in acknowledgements that such criticisms and demands are justified, all of which find their characteristic expression in the normative terminology of "ought", "must" and "should", "right" and "wrong"'.[15] In so far as this viewpoint is intended to represent a statement from empirical observation there are some points to be made. As has been mentioned earlier, the overt use of the language of normativity is not necessarily to be regarded as a *sine qua non* of the existence of patterns of conduct considered to be 'proper' within a social group.

Secondly, it is clear that Hart's analysis cannot explain the nature of all social rules even if it will account for some. As Hart's critics have recognized, legal rules in a complex modern state are not necessarily of this order. Rules of this kind may, for example, be honoured more in the breach than in the observance, and such breach may result in no popular criticism nor yet, in some cases, official criticism. In a legal system that has no notion of desuetude, examples such as the British regulations on Sunday trading or domestic video and audio taping make it clear, as Hart himself recognizes in other parts of his work, that rules need not be expressions of a genuine social sentiment.[16] Whilst rules may be such expressions within certain small societies and almost by definition in acephalous ones, in other cases rules owe their existence to the fact that they are created by a certain person or body recognized as having the capacity to create such rules for the society. Indeed, we shall see later that there may exist a very important tension between 'official' norms (those, that is, created by such a recognized authority) and 'popular' norms (those supported by community sentiment). Such tension may on occasion be revealed by examining the respective views of the norm-creating agency and the community as a whole as to which punishment is appropriate for breaches of proscribed patterns of activity.

The last sentence may perhaps have given the reader some hope if he or she had begun to despair of returning to the question of punishment. The point, however, that we wish to develop is that punishment is connected with rules and in his identification, albeit that the analysis is underdeveloped, of an 'internal aspect' of a rule, Hart is indicating the point of intersection between social organization and punishment. For it is clear that the rules that we find in all societies and in the social groupings within these societies imply by their existence that deviation will be regarded as improper. It should be pointed out that we refer only to that class of rules which seek to control rather than to facilitate behaviour; in Hartian terms: 'duty-imposing' rather than 'power-conferring' rules.[17] It may be that the feeling of impropriety is experienced by the generality of members of a society. This is likely if a rule concerns behaviour that is regarded as important by that generality. On the other hand, in a more complex social structure such as the modern industrial state, rules may be established by the recognized rule-creating authority, breach of which may result in the feeling of impropriety being experienced by only a few, possibly only the officials of a system. At its furthest remove from general group support a rule need not have any genuine popular support at all *qua* rule of behaviour, although that support may attach to it *qua* rule in the sense of a regulation of the appropriate authority. It will be the case in such an instance that the rules tend to have the appropriate response in the form of a sanction built into them at the formal level. So, for example, the Sunday trading instance is a law that contains its own sanction even though it may be but seldom invoked.[18] Again in this example the tension between the official rule and its popular observance is notable, although 'the law' or 'the rule of law' may attract a popular support which its individual regulation may not. But the point remains that the notion of a rule implies impropriety in the non-observer, a breach of the 'understanding' that the rule signifies, although the extent of the feeling of impropriety will vary with the nature of the rule and its significance within the society.

In complex societies it may be, as in the example given above, that the rule laid down by the rule-creating authority (*de iure* or *de facto* – it is not the purpose of this study to analyse the principles of legal legitimacy) will have incorporated within, or attached to, its formulation the steps to be taken in the event of non-compliance. On the other hand, rules that rest simply on social acceptance may leave the appropriate post-breach response unstated. But whether stated or not it is clear that the notion of punishment has its essence, we believe, in the feeling of impropriety that all rules carry as the reverse side of their prescribed or proscribed conduct.

Now it is clear that since we talk in such broad terms, of rules generally, that the impropriety may be registered in a fleeting and trivial fashion. So, one who lies in order to avoid a dinner invitation may, on account of this breach of a general, though imprecise, social rule that one should be honest in one's dealings with one's fellows, simply be passed over on a future occasion if the host discovers the subterfuge, or the host may avoid the company of the invitee for a while. At the other extreme, the reaction to breach of a rule may be much more severe. As we shall see, human life and the body are generally available objects upon which social sanctions may operate, whilst the support of the rest of the group, property, or reputation may also be items of enormous significance, which may be, significantly, withdrawn. It perhaps should be observed that the dishonesty exhibited within our first example might be viewed more seriously and acted upon differently in other cultures.

Whilst it is clear that most people would be happy to apply the term 'punishment' to describe these latter cases there may be objection to its use as descriptive of reactions of the former kind. This, it might be argued, is to cast the net too wide. Yet the difference between a group of workmates 'sending a colleague to Coventry' for a breach of a rule of the workplace and a group of Eskimo abandoning the persistent offender against tribal custom to a lonely death by desertion during the night, is clearly only a matter of degree.[19] If punishment as a term is felt to be appropriate for application only selectively to some adverse social responses to the breach of rules, then drawing the line along the scale of infinitely variable reactions is of necessity an arbitrary enterprise. It is true that in some cases a breach of a rule known to the social group as a whole or to that part of it charged with the determination of the sanction will attract not even the smallest social censure. This may be the case where the breach may be regarded as too trivial or as justified by other rules or exceptional circumstances. Yet in none of these instances is it necessary to abandon the link between rule-breach and sanction entirely. The first of these objections – the lack of social censure because of the triviality of the infraction – would be critical only if no breaches of the rule were met with adverse reaction. If this were true it would be difficult, we feel, for persons to maintain that a rule exists at all, unless, of course, it was a rule of the type described above, which owes its existence not to social acceptance but to its being derived from the appropriate rule-creating source.

The second proposition, that breach of norms need attract no censure because justified by exceptions, is used by R. N. Moles as an argument against Hart's conception of rules.[20] Yet we would repeat a contention that we made earlier, that justification of breach would seem to us to indicate the limitations of the applicability of the rule, to mark its boundary, rather than to cast doubt on the idea of censure as being significant to the rule in the first place. In stating this we are not seeking to define such instances out of our conception of a rule, to rely on dogmatic stipulation, but rather simply to suggest that this is a perfectly feasible way of interpreting the evidence. A further argument made by Moles against Hart, namely that the 'reflective critical attitude' of a rule is not, properly speaking, constitutive of that rule but is rather only evidence of its existence,[21] similarly need not concern us here – the social consequences are the same no matter which interpretation is applied, and it is the social consequences of rule breach with which we are here concerned. However, if certain rules are not identified by social activity on breach as expressive of a certain psychological attitude then it is difficult to appreciate how a rule is to be identified in circumstances in which this cannot be done by reference to a specific rule-creating authority but only by social acceptance.

Certainly, then, we would maintain that punishment forms part of the range of flexible response to rule breach and covers a vast variety of behaviour. We would by preference use the term to describe responses that share certain key features, while recognizing that, in English at any rate, the word may be used in senses which lack some of the elements to which we here draw attention. A casual listening to those most accomplished of linguistic experts, sports commentators, will reveal a host of uses – 'the marathon is being run at a punishing pace', 'United's square defence was punished by a fine goal', 'the bowler's waywardness was punished by some agressive batting' – in which we may discover analogies with cases of 'punishment' that contain these elements. To other such cases in which the English word is used but which lack some of the features to be discussed here and which seem, to us at any rate, to be instances of rather different social practices we shall return in our discussion later.

The first point to stress, then, is that we shall consider and use the term 'punishment' to describe certain responses to the breach of social rules. The responses are those which are considered objectively (for we must take into account the existence of the occasional masochist) to be unpleasant. As such we shall distinguish punishment from what we shall term 'positive sanctions' which will be discussed shortly. But the practice we are describing will also involve some sort of communication of the unpleasantness to the party in breach of the rule. So, for example, the diminution of peer approval implicit even in such apparently non-afflictive actions as the 'growling' that in Australian aboriginal terminology accompanies taboo breach would indeed be considered by us to be a form of punishment even if followed by no further action.[22] On the other hand, a reaction to a rule breach that carried no such objective unpleasantness – where, for instance, the members of a social grouping had immediately forgiven the rule-breaker – could not comfortably be described, we feel, as an instance of punishment. Yet in the understanding that we have of the practice it would seem that the communication of the unpleasantness need not be accompanied by explanation to, nor even knowledge on the part of, the rule-breaker of the fact of punishment. So, a man might have his property taken or his reputation denounced while he is out of the country or he may be shunned by his colleagues for a rule of infraction that he has committed of which he is unaware. We feel no unease in asserting that such actions are intelligible as examples of a consistent social practice of punishment and we shall consider such cases in due course.

The second element with which we are here concerned is the connection between the punishment and the rule. So, if someone who has broken a rule suffers an objective unpleasantness but the two are unconnected then we would not generally employ the term 'punishment' to describe that unpleasantness. If a man lies to his colleagues and they, in ignorance of this lie, decide to have no more to do with him simply because they do not like him, then this cannot be understood we feel as a punishment for the lie. It might, of course, be so for other earlier breaches of group norms or, on the other hand, simply evidence of an increasing personal distance in which there is no sense of rule-breaking (it is not argued here that all withdrawal of friendship or support is explicable in punitive terms). A requirement of a casual connection between the rule breach and subsequent unpleasantness has led many philosophers to discount instances of 'naturally occurring' affliction as cases of punishment – the burglar, they say, who breaks his arm in climbing the drainpipe is not being 'punished' for that burglary since that 'punishment' is not by a human agency nor causally connected to the rule breach as opposed to the activity which that comprises. Robert Nozick makes the point well when he observes:

If S wrongfully shoots another in a canyon and the sound of the shot causes an avalanche which maims or kills S, then this happens to S because of his wrong act but not because of the wrongness of the act. Since an act's moral qualities, qua moral qualities, seem to lack causal power, if something is to happen to someone because of the moral quality of his act this must occur through another's recognition of that moral quality and response to it.[23]

Now this may strike us as admirably sensible but it is firmly based in our cultural norms and by no means represents universal thought about the agency of punishment, as Nozick himself, it should be conceded, recognizes.[24] Quite apart from the more remote issues of eternal torment that inhere in eschatological religions there are many peoples throughout the world who confidently believe, as we shall see later, in immediate punishment on earth by supernatural agency. To give one example, though many others could be cited, the Eskimo who violated one of many highly complex dietary taboos would fall ill because vapour would envelop his soul.[25] That such belief systems are widespread and indeed that illness as a result of wrongdoing does result on occasion is not to be doubted. As to this latter phenomenon the sceptical advance the notion of psychosomatic response: it is not our task to judge the reasonableness of anyone's religious beliefs. In such instances the causal connection of the unpleasantness with the rule breach is integral to the belief system and the issue simply becomes one of punishment by a non-human agency. In such a context, it will be discussed in Chapter 8.

Modern western religions are in themselves not immune from such speculation. At the time of writing a debate rages as to whether the disease AIDS is a 'punishment' by God for the activities of homo-sexual or promiscuous conduct or of drug abuse, which activities, the proponents of the argument contend, are contrary to religious norms.[26] Flew, arguing against similar contentions, maintains that disease may be described as a penalty of promiscuity but not as a punishment for that conduct, the basis of his reasoning being the necessity of punishment being administered through human agency. But even, he argues, if we do allow of the notion of divine punishment, then a problem arises. For, his argument runs, 'guilty' persons may escape without contracting the disease (if their partner happens not to be infected) whilst 'innocent' person may suffer (in the AIDS context, even those who speak in terms of 'guilt' in respect of the types of behaviour mentioned earlier would presumably acquit the unborn child or the haemophiliac of any such fault).[27] Though this will certainly require explanation by those who argue for this way of explaining disease, it is not of course incompatible with the idea that such consequence is a punishment. We have argued that in conception punishment is linked with rule but in distribution all human systems at any rate run the risk in practice of punishing the innocent and overlooking the guilty. Quite why an omniscient power would suffer the same problems when His traditional role in western penal systems has been the correction of human error is a problem which those who espouse this view must confront. The whole question of whether a Superior Being does, or would wish to, behave in this way is ultimately a question of faith or belief.

One of the problems of any such argumentation is that of the content of the rule, the deviation from which is regarded as grounds for punishment. Again, at the time of writing, attitudes towards homosexuality within the Church of England are diverse and questions of consensus on any religious or moral rule concerning it are considered within that body to be not free from dispute.[28] Certainly, all rules may have problems of interpretation but there may be causes in which at any one time it is difficult to establish whether a rule exists or not. In certain structured systems, such as western legal systems, the questions can be answered in many cases by reference to criteria of validity – promulgation by the appropriate rule-creating authority, for example. However, in cases such as are to be found in acephalous societies or in other societies in which some rules, for example moral rather than legal ones, are set by community sentiment, it may be difficult to ascertain whether a rule exists or not. This is significant, for we shall see that there are a number of psychological factors to be considered when 'rule' or 'punishment' are at issue. Since punishment for breach of rule is widely regarded as legitimate, then it may be that the rhetoric of punishment, with the element of justification it contains, may be used to cloak acts of private malice or expediency. So, for instance, the terrorist who kills a political enemy or the leader of a coup who executes a member of a former government may claim to do so on the grounds of 'crimes against the people' even when no other offence against the positive legal system may be found. Indeed, such acts are frequently explained by their perpetrators by appeal to some 'higher law', which stands in direct contradiction to the operating legal system. The rhetoric of punishment, with its associated psychological overtones of justification, would accordingly seem to be regarded as important by the 'punisher' as explaining his conduct.

The traditional stress on the 'internal' equation of wrong and punishment, which is emphasized by 'retributivist' discussions, may be seen as perhaps unwittingly underpinning such an attitude. For in these theories the stress is upon the connection between and internal justice of the punishment and the wrong rather than, it often seems, questioning the justice of the rule, breach of which is being punished. As to the existence of 'higher norms', of the access of persons to them if existent, and as to their conferment of any 'right' to punish (and if so upon whom, by whom and in what way), these are matters which will not detain us here.

PUNISHMENT AND OBEDIENCE

In linking the notions of punishment and rule we must not be seen as suggesting that the sanction is the reason why rules are obeyed, for clearly there may be many reasons for obedience. Whilst there is no doubt that there may be many cases in which the presence of the punishment may be the deciding factor as to whether the rule is to be obeyed or not, other reasons may predominate in other cases. Reasons for obedience may vary, for example, as between different people *vis-à-vis* the same rule or the same people *vis-à-vis* different rules. Among such reasons, indolence, deference, sympathy, reason, and the innate desire for order have been suggested as material.[29] Clearly much in this area will depend on the role of socialization in securing the response of members of society to the content of particular rules or to the attitude towards rule-creating authorities. Such matters will form part of a society's culture, concerning which the anthropologist Lewis has remarked: 'Its component elements are absorbed in the first few years of life largely unconsciously and later more deliberately by informal and formal learning processes. Socialization inevitably takes place within and through the medium of a particular cultural tradition.'[30]

It comes as rather a surprise in this context to find one commentator describing societies in which obedience to rules that have the status of law is secured by education as 'not so well organized' as those in which obedience is secured by punishment.[31] For indeed it would seem to be a paradox that whilst early jurisprudential thought may have tended to overestimate the role of sanctions in maintaining social cohesion – a consequence of having seized upon the notion of sanction as a factor that would distinguish 'law' from 'custom' – early anthro-

90

pologists tended to underestimate the significance of sanctions.[32] It was this view of the blind obedience of 'savage' peoples to custom which led to Malinowski's famous and pioneering study of social solidarity among the Trobriand Islanders. He redressed the balance of anthropological opinion by maintaining that: 'the threat of coercion and the fear of punishment do not touch the average man, whether "savage" or civilized, while on the other hand they are indispensable with regard to certain turbulent or criminal elements in either society'.[33] If the two disciplines have moved closer together in their assessment of the significance of sanctions, this would seem to be a wise convergence. Indeed, we would maintain that any wholesale distinction between a 'sanction-motivated' and a 'socialization-' or 'education-supported' society is a dangerous one. For we shall maintain later that punishment intrudes at a fundamental level into techniques of socialization and education, although we would not hold that this is by any means the only method used within these functions.[34] The distinction may not, however, be one that can be drawn perhaps as widely and as glibly as many authors seem to feel. In this way we may understand that though a particular social rule may be obeyed by a particular individual not out of fear of a sanction, but out of some highly complex psychological response, that response may itself be partially due to the application of earlier independent sanctions. We would not go so far as to assert that punishment is the most important factor of socialization or of social organization, but clearly when the layers of significant factors are peeled away it is surprising how often we find punishment to be integral to them.

Indeed, it may be that an instructive connection can be drawn between the nature and extent of punishment utilized by society as a whole and by family groups within that society. The family unit occupies a highly significant position in most societies, yet in the frame of analysis offered here it is clear that the family performs a rather complex role. Firstly, as is true of any grouping, it may have its own particular norms (governing the roles of members of families generally in that society as a whole). Secondly, it may have its own peculiar norms (relating to the behaviour of individuals within that individual family). Thirdly, it may enforce and foster, as a key agent of socialization, the general social norms of the total society, punishing for example violent or dishonest behaviour. In most societies this socialization function is particularly associated with child-rearing and in centralized nation-states the punitive *function* for breach of general societal rules, in so far as it exists at all, will generally end with the child's transition to adulthood, although the punitive *response* (e.g. familial ostracism for a socially deviant act) may still be forthcoming. In other communities, as we shall see, the family grouping remains vital as the primary means of enforcing general societal rules even amongst adults.

To return to the instant point, however, it is clear that the nature of and attitudes towards punishment within the family may both influence and reflect the nature of and attitude towards punishment in a society as a whole. LeVine's illuminating comparison between two East African societies, the Nuer and the Gusii, both similar in many aspects of their socio-political organization, may be instructive in this respect.[35] The Nuer, generally described as an 'independent' and 'egalitarian' people, avoid judicial decision-making and centralized punishment, but use more interpersonal violence, particularly based around the blood-feud. The Gusii, on the other hand, are a very 'authoritarian' people, using centralized punishment rather than interpersonal aggression to settle their disputes. It is found that Nuer fathers are much more demonstrative and much less disciplinary with regard to their children than the more distant and punitive Gusii fathers (Le Vine maintains that the father's position is the important variable, for both societies are strongly patrilineal, with men occupying all positions of authority). On the other hand, Nuer children are encouraged by their parents to be more aggressive in dealings with their peers.

Now, it would be tempting to see child-rearing techniques as a possible independent variable in social attitudes towards the questions of what agency of punishment or what form of punishment will be employed by a society. Such reasoning would, however, be clearly illegitimate. As LeVine himself concedes: 'Child training may be a cause with respect to the behaviour of individuals but it is effect with respect to the traditional values which aid in the maintenance of social structures.'[36] Our point is rather to indicate the connection between attitudes towards punishment, which may be found within societies as displayed in the practices and values of a group as a whole and within the activities of its primary agencies of socialization. But if such connection may be seen as simple within some societies the picture may obviously be rather more complex in those which are less homogeneous. So, for example, the Newsoms' classic study of child-rearing practices within Britain displayed significant variation

92

between modes of parental punishment across socio-economic groups. They conclude that: 'On the issue of enforcement of obedience by smacking or by other means there is a significant overall class difference, rising to a peak between middle class and working class mothers.'[37] Similarly, it may be the case that practices in this respect will vary over time.[38]

To the issue of the role of punishment in forming social attitudes generally, we shall return in the next chapter. Our aim here has been to link punishment with the ideas of social organization and social rules. To the question of why it is so linked we must now turn.

6

THE PURPOSES OF PUNISHMENT

THE DIFFICULTIES AHEAD

The discussion so far has proposed that punishment is rooted in the idea of conduct that is considered improper by the community (using that term in a sense wide enough to include a vast variety of groupings but excluding arbitrary aggregates of individuals) as a whole or those to whom its power is delegated or by whom it has been appropriated. The wholesale incidence of the practice of punishment both through-out and across societies makes it important for us to suggest reasons as to why punishment is such a widespread phenomenon, what purposes it serves. For it would seem *prima facie* likely that unless punishment has its origin in a wholly arbitrary spontaneous response to wrong-doing coincidentally in all the societies in which it exists, or has been slavishly copied from some remote historical archetype, its present existence being simply a result of unthinking and unfeeling tradition, then punishment must serve, or at least must be seen to serve, some purpose or purposes. Although we maintain that tradition is a most potent force in this area we would not assign to it an influence as profound as this. The question of purpose, then, will help us to understand why punishment is in so many cases the response considered natural or appropriate to much disapproved conduct.

Yet as soon as we begin any realistic enquiry as to the purposes of punishment, we are struck by the presence of enormous difficulties. Firstly, we must explain what we mean in this context by 'purpose of punishment'. Let us begin with the obvious point that an act may be said to acquire its social meaning from the way in which it is perceived. Those involved in an instance of punishment, the punisher, the punished, and other people (who may be split into a greater or fewer number of discrete subgroups) may conceivably all view the infliction of unpleasantness differently and may all ascribe a different 'purpose' to the same social fact. To the observing scientist it may be difficult to select any one of these interpretations as being the 'correct' one. It seems *prima facie* attractive to suggest that the material viewpoint is that of the body or individual who authorizes or inflicts the punishment. Yet even if we leave aside for a moment certain practical difficulties – ascertaining the punisher's reason for punishment, which may be distinct from his *motive* for punishment (which may not have the quality of rationality), and also from his articulated rationalization of that punishment – it remains far from clear that it is solely with the punisher's purpose that we should concern ourselves. For it is clear that the use of punishment has important social effects, functions that seem important in the externally observable operation of the community and in the psychology of its members. Such matters – the termination of dispute, the confirmation of conformity, etc. – are, we believe, important factors to be considered in any investigation of the 'purposes' of punishment generally. Yet such broad sociological ends may not be clearly visible in each individual manifestation of penal activity. On the other hand, it would not, we think, be legitimate wholly to ignore expressed reasons for the administration of punishment nor yet (if these are conceptually different) the rationalizations which support it, and concentrate wholly upon broad social consequences. The former material too is of importance in understanding the punitive complex.

This is only the tip of the iceberg of our difficulties and hints at a much greater mass towards which, Titanic-like, we appear to be steaming. For we have conceded that an individual application of punishment may have different meanings for different persons, and we have embraced the concept that both immediate individual purposes and sociological and social psychological effects are of importance in investigating the punitive technique. If we then add that different applications of punishment may have different *raisons d'être* and different effects we encounter yet again a problem we have already considered – namely, is it possible to class these various aspects of punishment together at all with any coherence? So, for example, it may be objected that the purposes of punishing a 5-year-old child by sending it to bed early because it has refused to put its toys away are so wholly different from those which underlie the public execution by firing squad of a deserting soldier in wartime as to

95

indicate that any search for purposes applicable to punishment as a whole is either simply doomed or is intellectually misconceived. Our reply may seem to partake more of an affirmation of faith than a review of evidence, but we must repeat that the two manifestations of punishment are united by certain important features. The appreciation of the totality of punishment may, we believe, inform even those who, with commendable regard for their own academic credibility and their mental health, choose to concentrate on more discrete areas. Again, we return to our understanding of punishment as an associate of disapproval of rule breach, as the dramatic manifestation of that disapproval. Seen in this perspective, there are, it seems to us, a finite number of purposes that may credibly be related to this concept. If such a claim is found to be suspect, then at the very least we may adopt the coward's approach and maintain that in common discourse, with which we are familiar, only a relatively few purposes are generally associated with punishment.

The objection may be made, however, that individual punishers may have a variety of individual purposes in administering punishment and that in so far as we cannot exhaustively discuss these then our search must be doomed. So, the schoolteacher who exercises his discretion to beat a boy who has broken the school rule (assuming a time and place in which such action is regarded as legitimate, indeed as proper) may be doing so because he detests red-haired children, or because the child reminds him of his hated uncle, or because he obtains sexual gratification from so doing (*le vice anglais*, as the French of the nineteenth century characteristically called it but in fact a deviation that was recognized at least as early as the writings of Quintilian).[1] Yet we feel justified in excluding such material from our analysis, and not simply on the grounds that it is our intention only to make statements of what we consider to be of general application. For in these cases it may be urged that the breach of the rule, rather than providing the *reason* for the infliction of unpleasantness provides instead only the *occasion*. Whilst it would be dogmatic to close completely discussion of such motivational factors on the ground that their satisfaction is not really a punitive purpose (for in a sense it clearly is) we nevertheless feel justified in affording to material of this kind a secondary place in our discussion.

In seeking the purposes of punishment we must further concede that there are dangers both in the silences and the statements of the punishers themselves. Often punishment may be administered with only the briefest of explanations, or none at all, of the purposes which that punishment is intended to serve – the child may simply be told 'Go to your room', the criminal 'You have done wrong and the law must impose the proper punishment'. Obviously an investigation as to the purposes behind such instances will involve us in some rationalization of the brute social practice. What is worrying here is our residual fear that a full understanding of such activities must necessarily involve a fuller appreciation of the principles of group psychology than that contained within this chapter. The problem of making sense of social practices is further compounded when the evidence of very different cultures is examined, for here the dangers of ethnocentricity are added to our other difficulties. Often it is the case that the anthropological evidence we have examined, though detailed on the actions undertaken by people in different societies, and though instructive on some of the belief systems those activities may reveal, give us few clues as to why persons are thought to be punished within those societies rather than simply detailing the wrong for which those persons are punished or the form which that punishment takes. Similarly, discussion of abstract notions, such as a particular society's conception of 'justice', which may inform our understanding in this area may be lacking in the literature.

The position is not necessarily any more promising when a body of information does exist giving explanation for instances of punishment. Fitzmaurice and Pease, investigating the process of choice of sentence by judges within the British criminal justice system, explain that it may be difficult when assessing reasons given for decisions to speak with any confidence as to the real motivating factors.[2] Though full reasons may be given for a particular sentencing decision these may, the authors argue, turn out to be no more than *ex post facto* rationalization. They point out that judges who offer very different verbalizations as to why they have selected one particular sentence rather than another may yet reach in that sentence strikingly similar results.[3] The rhetoric of punitive purpose, in other words, even in cases where there is no hint of a cloaking of personal or improper motives (as there was with our earlier sadistic schoolteacher) need not represent reality. However, the rhetoric of punishment may be a most important subject, as we shall see, for it must in itself be acceptable within the context in which it is used. It may also be a potent force in reducing guilt, both the individual guilt of an individual punisher and the collective guilt of the constituency in whose name the offender may be punished. Fitzmaurice and Pease found that no matter how complex the process of judicial reasoning appears to be from judicial verbalization the most significant predictors of sentence length are simple (and, as we shall, see widely accepted and very traditional) factors – the perceived gravity of the offence and the previous behaviour of the offender.[4]

We would pause at this point to indicate that the same process may be seen in operation on a large scale when we consider the sequence of different initiatives and philosophies attached to, for example, the use of imprisonment at various times in its history. To assert this is not to claim that these changing philosophies had no impact at all in the real world, any more than we are committed to the idea that any punisher's utterance is necessarily useless in determining the 'real' reason for the infliction of punishment. But it is remarkable how many things about imprisonment have remained constant, not least that it has been regarded as the appropriate repository for a fairly constant stream of fairly similar persons, whilst its purported *rationale* has changed dramatically.[5]

One final word is necessary for those who approach this work from the background of that traditional body of discourse which concerns itself with the justification of criminal punishment. We shall consider in the following pages a number of the notions which appear in that context – we shall have to refer, for example, to what is termed 'retribution', and to ideas such as deterrence and reform. Clearly, our discussion of such concepts will be of a very different nature from that of theorists of those disciplines, for we are concerned to produce a descriptive account of what purposes punishment may, or may be perceived to, serve rather than a prescriptive ethical doctrine of why states are justified in punishing. It would, no doubt, be erroneous to see the discussion of the justification of punishment merely as another form of *ex post facto* rationalization of a socially determined phenomenon, but we must not forget Eckhoff's criticism of such justificatory discourse already referred to in Chapter 1.[6]

Because we shall discuss such concepts in a very different context from that of the debate about justification, we should at the outset concede that many of the clean lines which can be drawn in philosophical debate are not so easy to describe in enquiring, for example, into what we take to be some of the psychological effects of punishment. For here we suggest that the edges between, let us say, 'deterrence' and 'reform' are not easy to separate, and even a comfortable distinction between a backward-looking retributivism and a forward-looking consequentialism may be elusive in at least one general significant purpose of punishment.[7] Again the traditional justificatory discourse, restricted as it is to the penal activity of the state in response to criminal acts, may elevate some functions of punishment to a prominence in discussion (e.g. protection of the public) to which a more broadly based descriptive survey, such as our own, which concerns itself also with punishment within the school or the family, would give relatively less attention. Indeed, the question arises within this wider perspective as to whether the justifications offered as tenable for state punishments of crime are applicable, in the views of their proponents, to punishment more generally. Are sophisticated arguments about retribution or consequentialism applicable to the home or the schoolroom, to the practices of the Eskimo or the Australian Aborigine, or are these not intended as justifications of punishment as a whole but culturally and/or contextually specific? It may be, of course, that the protagonists would return to the argument that the different instances and contexts of punishment to which we refer are so diverse as to be not at all the same things. For ourselves, we can only stress the uniting, linking feature of the deliberate infliction of an objective unpleasantness on the grounds of a transgression of conduct regarded as proper, where proper conduct is delimited by the existence, explicit or tacit, of a rule or individual prescription. Again, we would maintain the advisability of examining the genus rather than starting with the species, but the applicability of much of the discussion of justification of punishment to these extended horizons remains obscure.

RULES AND THE COMMUNICATION
OF DISAPPROVAL

Let us begin our discussion of the purposes of punishment with the idea of breach of rule and the disapproval of the community or of the rule-enforcing agency for that breach of rule. May we not say quite simply that the principal or a principal role of punishment is in the communication in dramatic form of that disapproval? Indeed this is, we believe, a useful starting-point for our discussion, but it begs some rather important questions. For this formulation leaves us to explain *why* it is that the disapproval is communicated, rather than, for example, being internalized and resulting simply in unexpressed

99

feelings of condemnation and anger. The further point that the bare formulation given above leaves unclear is why disapproval needs to be communicated *by punishment* as opposed to, for example, by mere verbalization.

This second argument may be understood in two distinct ways. The first is that the forms of conduct that a society approves or disapproves may be inculcated in ways other than by punishment. This is clearly true. It is no part of our thesis to maintain that all social learning about prescribed conduct is carried out by punitive reaction to a breach of a rule concerning that conduct. Other techniques, such as example and verbalization, in the sense of statements concerning the propriety of rule obedience that are not in the form of an objectively unpleasant reaction – for instance, a general exhortation to obedience or explaining to a child why his behaviour was wrong – are, of course, of vital importance in the socializing process. The relative weighting of punishment as against other socializing factors we leave to the psychologists.

The second formulation is as to why punishment does not always take the form of verbalization if its purpose lies in the communication of disapproval. This latter argument has been brought up in the literature in other contexts. For often, in the philosophical arguments concerning the justification of punishment we find that this question arises, although we would stress again that it is an explanation of, rather than a justification of, the practice which is being attempted here. So, for example, the eminent British judge Lord Denning once propounded the view that 'the ultimate justification of any punishment is not that it is a deterrent, but that it is the emphatic denunciation by the community of a crime'.[8] To this, C. L. Ten, after noting other objections to this 'theory', counters with the observation that 'the most fundamental objection is that Denning's theory does not explain why the denunciation of crime should take the form of imprisoning or even executing offenders rather than merely denouncing them verbally'.[9]

A number of points may be made arising out of this observation. Firstly, we suggested in the previous chapter that reactions of disapproval, albeit in verbal form, are quite capable of being construed, and we would suggest quite properly so, as punitive – they are and are intended to be objectively unpleasant and may be particularly effective in producing feelings of shame or loss of prestige. Indeed, that a verbal denunciation may be properly viewed as an instance of punishment is accepted by Ten himself.[10] We have only to consider the treatment of children within western culture to appreciate how often 'a good telling off' is used as a sanction both in the home and the school. The question, however, remains why verbal denunciation is not used in all cases to signify disapproval of a wrongdoing individual. It must be recognized that the proportion of wrongs punished by verbal means rather than by other forms of unpleasantness is variable between cultures. Indeed, as the Newsoms' work, referred to earlier, on the social-class differentiation between verbal and physical techniques in child discipline testifies, it varies possibly even between subcultures. The difficulty here is in knowing whether the Newsoms are talking about verbal punishment or more generally of verbal socialization techniques; the text is ambiguous, as often, we shall see, the action will be.[11]

Certainly there are many societies in which verbal punishment techniques are by no means restricted to the treatment of children or to minor forms of offence. So, amongst the Kapauku of New Guinea, public shaming for offences, the denunciation of the wrongdoer, is considered worse than the infliction of any sanction save death. Pospisil quotes one Kapauku, publicly rebuked for seven days on account of his embezzlement, as saying of the rebuke and consequent ostracism: 'If they would beat me and take away my belongings it would be better than this.'[12] Similarly, amongst the Eskimo, the process of 'naming' the malefactor – calling a kayak thief 'Kayak' – was regarded as being worse than a transitory beating.[13] In Chapter 10 we shall consider this penal technique as part of the range of punitive response.

For the present, however, we shall be content with the following comments. Firstly, it is clear that whereas, as we have seen, the constant factors that are available to be affected adversely by punishment – the body, and, to a lesser extent, property – have a weight in all communities, the objects of verbal punitive technique, those things, in other words, that will be affected in a way considered objectively unpleasant thereby – dignity, prestige, conscience, etc. – are not cross-culturally anything like as standard in value. We may hypothesize tentatively, but not, we think, unrealistically, that personal prestige is more likely to be at a premium in relatively small societies, simply on the grounds that the anonymity of the crowd is unavailable and also, it might be supposed, in societies that are largely self-contained and/or hierarchical, where reputation may not be obscured by moving easily into a different community or subculture. It should perhaps be pointed out that we are not thinking here necessarily of tribal or traditional societies – examples of the importance of 'personal honour' that spring to mind would include the clichéed vision of the disgraced nineteenth-century army officer disappearing behind a locked door with a loaded revolver muttering 'I know what to do, old man', or the eighteenth-century aristocratic duelling classes.

It may be that in larger communities, such as that typified by the modern nation-state, such a 'personal' matter as reputation plays a less central role in the signification of disapproval of actions, particularly those that are regarded as especially grave. Paradoxically, the 'shrinkage' of large communities, which has been accomplished by developments in the dissemination of information, may once more establish reputation as a most important punitive object even in large modern states. So, for example, it is often said that offenders may worry more about 'getting their name in the papers' than appearing in court, while at the time of writing a Scottish television company has revealed plans to list on its broadcast programmes the names and addresses of persons convicted of driving with excess alcohol in the blood.[14] Similarly, a local authority in the city of Wolverhampton was considering, again at the time of writing, a plan to publish the names of convicted 'kerb-crawlers' in its free newspaper distributed to households.[15] Clearly, such measures indicate that reputation may still be an object that may be acted upon in modern societies even in its attenuated form (where reputation means little more than simply being law-abiding). The notion may be one of much greater complexity and sophistication in smaller societies.

The social significance of those qualities of the wrongdoer that may be 'attacked' by punishment thus differs across societies. But this does not explain of itself why punishment in many cases extends beyond verbal denunciation – even the Kapauku know of capital punishment.[16] At this point then we must turn to the question of why disapproval is being communicated. An understanding of this issue may explain why the communication takes certain dramatic forms.

Although the question phrased in the above manner may seem to suggest that the further purposes we are about to consider are subordinate to, or constituent elements of, the communication of disapproval of a prescribed act, they may also be postulated, certainly at the level of reasoning behind particular sanctions, but also at the level of general discourse, as independent but related purposes. Such lack of clarity at this point of the analysis may be felt by some to be deeply offensive, but it is difficult when speaking generally of complex social behaviour to identify one 'real' purpose or a serial ordering of purposes, particularly when, as we have seen, the 'real' reasons for actions may be hidden behind *ex post facto* rationalizations.

THE CONFIRMATION OF RULES

Let us return then to our basic position that punishment is an expression of the social disapproval engendered by breach of a rule. Considering this a little more closely, it becomes apparent that the breach has implications for both those who have not themselves broken the rule and for the individual who has. Both the former, whom we may designate the 'conformists', and the latter, the offender, will have an interest in the single punitive act.

We will concern ourselves here with the function of the punitive response, which we may characterize as the reaffirmation in dramatic style of the norm that has been breached, for the benefit of the conforming members of the social group. Such confirmation of the 'norm' is a feature not only of punishment – it has been argued that a contemporary display in London of waxwork-style representations of persons with physical abnormalities (a relic of the Victorian freak-show) serves to confirm and comfort the observer in his or her own normality.[17] With regard to punishment, it is not surprising that this factor has been identified by anthropologists as of importance: it is a feature of sanctioning that is related to the functioning of the group as a whole, and the solidarity that it maintains is externally observable. A. R. Radcliffe-Brown maintained that this was a feature of utmost importance when sanctions were investigated, observing that

> in a consideration of the functions of social sanctions it is not the effects of the sanction upon the person to whom they are applied that are the most important but rather the general effects within the community applying the sanctions. For the application of sanctions is a direct affirmation of social sentiments by the community and thereby constitutes an important, possibly essential mechanism for maintaining these sentiments. Organised negative sanctions, in particular . . . are expressions of a condition of social dysphoria brought about by some deed. The function of the sanction is to restore the social euphoria by giving definite collective expression

to the sentiments which have been affected by the deed . . . or by removing a conflict within the community itself.[18]

In such a fashion the rule is dramatically restated for the benefit of the conformists. The psychology that underlies the process may be rather more complex the more closely it is examined. It will not be the case, for example, that the conformists will form a monolithic community, but may themselves contain a whole variety of attitudes towards the norm and its breach. This truth was recognized by J. Toby when he suggested that: 'conformists who identify with the victim are motivated to punish the offender out of some combination of rage and fear. Conformists who identify with the offender albeit unconsciously may wish to punish him for quite different reasons.'[19] Leaving aside for a while other factors, the resolution of the ambiguity of the conformists *vis-à-vis* the conduct in question by the dramatic registration of disapproval may be of considerable importance. Freud in *Totem and Taboo* stressed, from his basic standpoint of social repression of individual urges, the ambiguity that may, (he insisted that it does) exist with regard to the prohibited conduct. 'If others did not punish the violation', he urged, 'they would perforce become aware that they would want to imitate the evil doer.'[20] The restatement of the rule, then, confirms the conformist and does so by stigmatizing the wrongdoer, by marking him out as different from the conformist.

Social stigma is often referred to as a subordinate form of punishment, but it will, we hope, have become apparent that by seeing the roots of punishment in the notion of social disapproval we rather take the different view, namely that all punishment is to some extent a dramatic indicator of stigma. This marking-off of the offender as different in type to others is most clearly expressed by measures that confine him to a specific appearance or location within the community (the prison, with its uniform) or, even more clearly, by putting the offender outside the community altogether by ostracism. This latter term we can use to describe both the interposition of geographical distance between the offender and the community (the Eskimo leaving the wrongdoer behind when they strike camp, the medieval felon being obliged to 'abjure the realm') or distance of other kinds, such as the withdrawal of communal protection (outlawry or, in religious contexts, excommunication) or support (the refusal of other persons to have any dealings with the offender).[21] While such

104

physical ostracism may be an extreme form, it is true to say, in a sense, that all punishments, in that they register the desire to mark out the wrongdoer by stigmatizing him as different from the conformist, savour of ostracism no matter what form the punishment takes.

A brief reflection on the vocabulary applied to crime and criminals in Britain will indicate how keen is the desire to separate 'us' and 'them'. Offenders may be linguistically identified with other species – a sex offender becomes a 'beast' or a 'monster', a violent football crowd become 'animals'. On the other hand, membership of different 'tribes' may be ascribed, street offenders becoming at different times in the nineteenth and twentieth centuries 'garotters', 'hooligans', and 'muggers' which names have their origins in visions of other cultures, 'hot-blooded' Latins, Irish, and black Americans respectively.[22] On the other hand, self-styled conformists may use deliberately vague or integrative language to describe their own wrongdoing, for it is important for the maintenance of stigma that stigmatizer and stigmatized should be kept distinct. So, for example, persons taking home material from the workplace may describe themselves as doing a whole variety of things rather than 'stealing'. So they may say that they are 'having their perks' (which implies entitlement) or 'working a fiddle' (implying reward for intelligence) or 'nicking' (simply a less 'official' and therefore less formally divisive terminology). 'Perfectly respectable' (in their own eyes) people who commit the highly socially dangerous offence of drinking and driving are appalled by any suggestion that they might be 'real criminals,' and may at least comfort themselves by their reflection that their punishment will take the form (in part at any rate) of 'disqualification' or 'having their licence taken away', an inconvenience that might have been produced by failing eyesight as much as by moral turpitude.

Stigma, then, reaffirms the rule, reaffirms the conformists as conformists, and separates off the wrongdoer who has broken the rule. But in small societies such imposition of stigma, such social division as is made apparent by the imposition of punishment may in fact be disadvantageous. In these societies it may be more important that the social division is glossed over rather than pointed out, for mutual co-operation may be vital for the maintenance of the community. It is this feature, we suggest, that accounts for those systems in which disputes are routinely settled by mediation or negotiation rather than by an adjudication that one party is clearly wrong. In addition, grievances are redressed by a rebuilding of the link with the wider community by, for example, the offer of compensation, rather than the affirmation of division by condemnatory punishments. To a discussion of these types of system and the way in which our own understanding of punishment relates to them we shall return in the next chapter.[23]

PUNISHMENT AND ANGER

The function of confirmation of rule is, we feel, of major importance in understanding punishment as a social practice. Yet we have still not shown why it is that simple denunciation of the wrong will not in itself always be used to fulfil this end. Let us consider other factors. We may, by suggesting that confirmation of the rule is of such importance, have perhaps given the impression that those who use punishment are in some way only marginally committed to the rule concerned and that the ambiguity towards the prescribed conduct, which Freud maintains is so important, is inevitably near to the surface. Now, this may be true in some cases but clearly there are many instances in which the conformists are very committed to the content of the rule and such ambiguity as there is lies at a very deep level. For the majority any ambiguity towards and desire to imitate such behaviour, if it exists at all, is very effectively suppressed. In these instances we see punishment being used for the purpose of expressing anger at the wrongdoer or frustration at his perpetration of the wrongs. Such feelings may be appeased by the flexibility and potential gravity of afflictive punishment, yet may not, in many societies, be adequately satisfied by a public denunciation of the wrongdoing only.

Such a characterization of popular cries for retribution may invoke the unsavoury spectacle of the mob howling for revenge, but to ignore its existence would be ludicrous. Of course, such feelings of anger and frustration will not apply to the same extent across the whole range of behaviour that happens to be proscribed by a particular social group but will vary, it may be suggested, with such factors as the gravity of the offence and, for other reasons (notably the elements of contempt for social norms that may be evidenced), the frequency of the offenders' wrongdoing.[24] So, the angry mobs still seen on TV news reports shouting outside courtrooms as the police van containing the suspected child-murderer speeds past the camera tend not to administer the same treatment to the man charged with driving with a

106

defective exhaust pipe. It is not, however, simply at this total society level that punishment, or least particular forms of punishment, may reflect a mood of anger or frustration. The Newsoms' research on child discipline showed that mothers from all social classes were more likely to smack their children when the mothers themselves were angry. A woman described as a lorry driver's wife put it this way:

> I start off speaking kindly to them; but I end up shouting like a maniac! I've got to be a bit het up over something; then I will land one at him. I feel sorry straight away; I always regret it afterwards. I don't really believe in smacking; I don't like it; but I think everybody gets to that pitch sometimes when they've just got to smack them.[25]

Of course, the dangers of using punishment as an expression of frustration or rage lie implicit in the very idea – the mob outside the courtroom is not far removed from the lynch mob, and the words 'I just lost my temper' could be used to explain both a routine disciplining of a child at home and a gross instance of child abuse. Punishment is an important tool in the settlement of disputes, as a reaction to grievances. In so far as it partakes of and reflects anger, frustration, or revenge, punishment, the infliction of unpleasantness on another individual, runs the risk of creating grievances, of protracting disputes.

This danger will help to explain two features that are very frequently to be found whenever social groups apply punishments. These are the ideas of proportion and of the 'marking-off', the depersonalization, of the reactive response of punishment from personalized acts of aggression. The idea of proportionality, with its assertion of both a positive ('correct', 'proportionate') response and a negative ('incorrect', 'disproportionate') response is something that will be considered shortly. We shall simply mention at this point that, even across communities whose actual penal practice differs widely, there is a general finding of rules of proportion, that a 'punishment' which goes beyond a certain normative limit is 'wrong' and in itself deserves criticism or a more extreme manifestation of disapproval. The notion of proportionality, we shall argue, serves to restore a popular conception of fairness, an equilibrium. This feature is valuable not simply in itself but also, it is hoped, as drawing a line underneath the grievance, as settling the dispute.[26]

Indeed, Robert Nozick goes so far as to use this idea of

proportionality as marking off retribution, explained by him as 'punishment inflicted as deserved for a past wrong' from revenge. 'Retribution', he maintains, 'sets an internal limit to the amount of the punishment, according to the seriousness of the wrong, whereas revenge internally need set no limits although the revenger may limit what he inflicts for internal reasons.'[27] We shall offer our own thoughts on the distinction between revenge and punishment shortly. Whilst we would hesitate to urge any necessity for proportionality in punishment, at least in all its manifestations – Nozick, of course, is writing within the context of philosophical explanation ('trying to explain how it is possible that retributive punishment sometimes is appropriate or demanded')[28] rather than an empirical overview of penal systems – yet such a doctrine is a most useful one. In so far as punishment may express similar sentiments of anger and rage as an act of personal revenge, the functional connection of punishment with social rules, with rules, that is, of social cohesion or control, will argue against its being in itself routinely generative of grievance and disorder. A proportionality principle will be of great assistance to this end.

Similarly rage may be voiced through punishment yet controlled through its depersonalization. A judge in the modern western penal system, who states when passing sentence, 'This court must reflect the deep sense of outrage and disgust felt by the public at an offence of this nature', is, in that process of 'reflection', interposing a mirror between the rage and the unpleasantness inflicted upon the wrongdoer in its name. More important for our purposes is the fact that individuality is submerged at all points – those persons who feel genuine personal anger have become subsumed within 'the public' and, most significant of all, the unpleasantness is not inflicted by specific individuals. This is done rather by 'the court' or 'the law', whose personnel in their wigs and gowns and (in times gone by) whose executioners in their masks and with their requests for forgiveness from the condemned man transcend dangerous, inflammatory, personal rage. Paradoxically this very depersonalization, which controls rage, will also assuage guilt, not only in those who administer the punishment (the hangman, and, less immediately, the sentencing judge) but also in those who may be likely to be personally affected by the rage, the victim, his friends and family, and 'the public' generally. It may also explain, as we shall see, several of the circumstances that surround the issue of 'who punishes' to be considered in Chapter 8.[29] Even within a thoroughly 'depersonalized' judicial system, however, it may be that a personal sense of responsibility for the offender's suffering and the guilt thereby engendered may not be wholly expunged. Such a proposition is consistent with the findings of Sherman and Dowdle. These writers found that subjects may agree with the severity of prescribed punishments for crimes yet prove 'either somewhat reluctant to apply these punishments themselves or inconsistent in their application'.[30] It is clear, however, that elements of anger at rule breach and guilt in punishment must involved many variables and will neither jointly nor severally be held by the same or different persons to the same degree. The variables will differ also in relation to the different types of rule transgression at issue.

We have seen that the important element of expression of anger within punishment is controlled by elements of proportionality and of depersonalization. It may be seen that proportionality is a general element in penal practice, a point to which we refer again shortly, but it may be thought that it is only in the modern state that the line is drawn between depersonalized, legitimate punishment and inflammatory, angry response. This is, in fact, not the case, depersonalization being possible even within societies where no obvious buffer exists between the punitive agency and the aggrieved party, as, for example, in societies in which the kindred grouping is responsible for the visitation of punishment. There are, it is true, peoples amongst whom the pendulum of blood-guilt as dictated by the structure of the feud will swing backward and forward for an indefinite and often protracted time.[31] These we may term 'vendetta societies'. But even in these instances killing in feud is regarded as different in kind from other forms of homicide. In the normal run of events social pressure will be brought to bear upon the parties to settle the feud by negotiation and/or the offer of compensation. Alternatively, other techniques may be used to arrest the escalation of violence. Amongst the Eskimo, a recidivist homicide might be killed with the consent not only of the rest of the community but also with that of the wrongdoer's own kin in order that the feud be avoided.[32] The point here is simple, namely that violence done as punishment within a social order is regarded by members of that order as being different from a simple act of anger, even though it may express anger. The existence of, even the persistence of, retaliation in a feud system should not blind us to the structure that lies behind, indeed is expressed directly through, the feud machinery itself.

Clearly this degree of depersonalization is visible at this level of punishment within a total society but it may be thought that there are penal contexts in which it cannot apply. But even within schools or the home (where the fear of escalation of the dispute is more readily intelligible in terms of the alienation and hostility of the child rather than retaliation), anger is often 'depersonalized' by reference to the rule infringed. In addition, there may be rituals, not simply the elaborate 'bogey man' usages to be described later,[33] but the being 'sent to the headmaster's office' or the waiting 'till Father gets home', which will indicate that what is happening, though it expresses anger, is based on an acknowledged transgression rather than personal malice. A simple blow, or other punishment, unaccompanied by reference to the rule, or by a ritual setting, is, of course, highly ambiguous, particularly to a child whose inability to extrapolate the norm transgressed from the penal conduct may result in confusion. Of course, at this level the norm itself may invite confusion, for 'not annoying one's parent or teacher' may be in itself considered to be a norm for breach of which punishment may be considered appropriate.

JUSTICE AND RETALIATION

The confirmation of the existence of the rule, the restatement of that behaviour considered to be 'right' within the group, together with the expression of anger at behaviour categorized as 'wrong', may be seen as constituent elements of what may be termed the 'retaliatory urge'. These elements need not both be present at the same time or in the same quantities. We have stated earlier that there will be instances of rule breach that will move no one to any genuine anger yet nevertheless will attract punishment. It is also possible to conceive of other cases, where persons are punished for a technical breach of a rule as an excuse, or as a token act when a regulation has, or is acknowledged to have, fallen into desuetude. In such cases restatement of the regulation would not seem to be a genuine aim of the punitive action.

Another feature of the response of popular retributivism where it is found to exist may be described as the restoration of the balance of fairness and equity, the notion of serving by retaliation of a punitive kind an idea of justice. It is not meant to imply by this (perhaps it is here that the term 'urge', which may conjure up dark visions of automatic and inevitable responses, may mislead) that popular retaliatory reactions must be necessary responses, still less necessarily intemperate responses, to rule breach. A popular notion of justice to be found within many societies may include a demand that equity be restored by the punishment of the wrongdoer, but this is by no means the same thing as asserting that that is the *entirety* of that conception of justice, other aspects of which may predominate in particular instances.

Whatever rationalizations are offered for the practice of state punishment the existence of this popular retributivism seems to be accepted by writers in the area. The origins of this notion of retaliatory justice cannot be stated with total assurance. Certainly the talionic equivalent involved in the 'eye for an eye' philosophy has a certain basic intelligibility, at least for some types of wrong. Revenge, a sentiment akin to anger and frustration, which we discussed earlier, contains the additional element of 'getting even'. A. A. Ehrenzweig, one of the few writers to have applied psychology to the investigation of state penal systems, considers revenge to be of vital importance in understanding punishment. He maintains that 'we rarely admit, and hardly ever face the overwhelming impact of that "unofficial" motor of much of our criminal law, our retaliatory urge'.[34] Ted Honderich, in a postscript to his book on the supposed justifications of punishment, turns at one point from abstract philosophical reasoning to observation of the 'facts of life' and recognizes that: 'The truth of retributivism . . . in absolute brevity, is as follows. First, harmful actions give rise to what can be labelled grievances, which is to say certain desires for the distress of the agents, desires whose only and full satisfaction is in the belief that the agents are being distressed or made to suffer.'[35]

Even those concerned with justifying the 'institution' of state punishment on non-retributivist grounds may find themselves obliged to take account of this widespread retributivist strand in the popular consciousness. The utilitarian R. M. Hare draws a distinction between the intuitive level of moral thinking and the critical level. While some moral intuitions, he maintains, which may amount to no more than 'the received opinions' may be anti-utilitarian, this is by no means determinative of our response to the practice at a critical level.[36] Nicola Lacey goes so far as to concede that such intuitions will have to be taken into account by the utilitarian theorists: 'intuitions may be a rough guide in making assessments of utility: they must also be taken into account in any utilitarian calculus since they are in themselves relevant effects which if ignored may prevent optimal consequences being achieved overall (for instance because of loss of respect for the system and resort to self-help)'.[37] Such popular basic retributivism, then, seems to be recognized as a social fact even by those whose concern is punishment theory. One of its constituent elements, we have suggested, lies in a common conception of justice. This asserts that punishment of a wrong in some way restores an upset balance of fairness, in some way adjusts a disequilibrium. A lack of evidence prevents us from stating exactly how common such a conception might be – even where punishment structures are well charted by anthropologists the contents of beliefs as to the nature of justice are less often explored in ethnographic literature.

Again, at this point, it may be useful to refer to orthodox punishment theory. For writers such as Herbert Morris, J. M. Finnis, and Jeffrie G. Murphy, the restoration of an equilibrium achieved by countering the wrongdoer's unfair advantage with an imposed disadvantage is the basis of the justification of punishment.[38] It is not for us to consider these arguments save to say that whether or not such restoration of equilibrium does justify punishment it would seem that, for many, a belief in such an idea does exist, although it may receive little in the way of articulation. Whether or not it has any potency as a moral argument, it would certainly seem to have potency as a moral force.

This conception of 'fair return' would seem to underlie the widespread notion of proportionality or even of direct equivalence within punishment practice. The former at any rate is, as we have said, very prevalent and does not seem to be restricted to current western penal systems. The pragmatic benefit of proportionality, for which we have argued above – the resolution of dispute rather than its prolongation – depends for its efficacy on an idea of fairness or justice of the sort discussed here.

It will be appropriate here to mention a concept discussed by the great pioneer of anthropology, Malinowski, which may be of some value in explaining the content of popular notions of justice across temporal and geographical boundaries. Malinowski introduced the idea of 'reciprocity' into the discussion of tribal economic and social relations.[39] How far we may extend this notion, which Malinowski himself considered to be highly significant, is unclear. It has been suggested that it may indicate no more than the correlation of right and duty.[40] Others, however, have taken the idea further. A. W.

Gouldner suggested that reciprocity as a general norm of social interaction may include a notion of retaliation, although he conceded that the hypothesis demanded empirical investigation: 'Only research can resolve the question whether a norm of retaliation exists in any given group, is the the polar side of the norm of reciprocity or is a distinctive norm which may vary independently of the reciprocity norm.'[41]

Whilst our own observations can hardly be seen as the empirical validation of the 'negative reciprocity norm' hypothesis as a universal, it is, we would maintain, a general feature of social organization that an offence against social norms will demand a reparation of the social dysphoria, and that harm done to an individual or community will meet with demands for either compensation or punishment to restore the balance of fairness. Such a notion would seem to be an immediately accessible one; the importance of a positive equivalent reciprocal act in many social circumstances would seem to be well established and, abstracted, could be characterized as a concrete manifestation of a conception of equity, justice, or fairness. There is certainly no more conceptual difficulty in a negative reciprocal norm than in a positive one – 'If you poke out my eye, I shall poke out yours, similarly look to your teeth!' makes up in immediate intelligibility as a principle in equity for what it loses by virtue of its barbarous literalism. Nor is the step from such 'homeomorphic' equivalence to a 'heteromorphic' equivalence (the terms are not ours)[42] such as imprisonment, fines, etc., any more difficult to understand within such a theoretical structure than it is in the case of positive equivalence (your gift of a red shell necklace, to use material from Malinowski's own researches,[43] is the equivalent of my gift of a white shell bracelet). This is so notwithstanding that the reasons for the existence of the heteromorphic equivalent and the particular form or forms that it takes may be the result of complex and culturally specific factors.

The claim we are making here is not an ambitious one, indeed it may seem transparently obvious, namely any social grouping that allows of notions of 'right' or 'wrong' – any social grouping, that is, that has a normative structure – will recognize the disequilibrium occasioned by rule transgression. It is not improbable that the element of restoration of the equilibrium, the re-establishment of a 'fair' distribution of benefits and burdens will provide some satisfaction. Piaget, in his study of the development of morality in (western) children, argued strongly that such a response was a natural one. 'It cannot be denied', he urged, 'that the idea of punishment has psycho-biological roots. Blow calls for blow and gentleness moves us to gentleness. The instinctive reactions of defence and sympathy thus bring about the sort of elementary reciprocity which is the soil that retribution demands for its growth.'[44] It should be pointed out, however, that Piaget allowed that conceptions of justice are not static within the development of the moral conscience, which will accommodate considerations of justice over and above a simple return of a mathematical equivalent of the blows that have been received.[45] To return to the issue of negative equivalence, we would not assert that this is a universal rule, but we would regard it as being no less likely to be a cross-cultural phenomenon than the sorts of positive exchange relations that are well documented in many societies. It is hoped that the reader will not think that we are trying to have our cake and eat it when we say that, in many societies, this notion of the re-establishment of a just order may not formally be articulated. This need not deprive it of its status as a potent factor in the psychology of individuals or groups.

Let us say again that we do not maintain, even where such an element is found to form part of a conception of justice, that this 'internal' question of transgression and restoration is the overwhelming or exclusive characteristic of that conception. So a harsh, substantively evil rule imposed by a dictator may result in punishment being administered for its breach in which the vast majority of persons within or outside the particular society would be hard-pressed to find any, or any real, conception of the restoration of a just equilibrium. The point may perhaps be made here that many retributivist theories that seek to justify punishment in terms of its internal relation to a breach of the (invariably criminal law) rule structure often ignore the fact that such rule structures in their totality (to the question as to whether there is any necessary core of social regulation we have adverted earlier)[46] are defined by social rather than natural forces. It may well be then that any token 'justice' involved in the restoration of 'fairness' *vis-à-vis* the breach of a particular rule is outweighed by other considerations that might be included under an abstract conception of justice, or even one prevalent simply within the particular society.

Whilst the temptation to ignore this complexity is a seductive one for retributivist theory, we should concede that those writers whose names we have mentioned earlier are all aware of the problems that such blinkered preoccupation with the 'internal' equation can produce. Morris restricts his theory to punishment for cases of breach of the 'core rules of the criminal law',[47] whilst Murphy indicates that inequalities in living conditions and opportunities call into question the very credibility of the argument based on 'restoration of fairness'.[48] Finnis considers the issue of punishment from the standpoint of a Natural Law theorist, for whom the justice and morality of a legal system as a whole is a paramount theoretical requirement.[49] It becomes clear then that the 'internal' equation as represented by the equilibrium theorists is not a sufficient determinant of justice in itself. Nevertheless we are content that it is not improbable that such a notion should play an important role in many popular conceptions of justice.

PUNISHMENT, RESPONSIBILITY, AND DISASTER

It is possibly a similar idea to this notion of the intrinsic rectitude of the punitive act as satisfying a conception of justice which will explain a most interesting use of punishment. We have mentioned earlier that in many societies there is a strong belief in witchcraft or sorcery, a belief that in some social groups, such as the Zande, extends so far as to ascribe all misfortune to invocation by a hostile human agency. Where such beliefs are prevalent the punishment of the supposed malefactor may be seen as both dramatically asserting responsibility and also, by restoration of justice, as bringing misfortune to an end. In this way, sense may be made of the otherwise apparent awful arbitrariness of the world, malice being a much more comfortable concept than chaos. In Europe too, the urge to find responsibility for natural calamity has led to quite appalling instances of 'punishment' – if identifiable minority groups could be held responsible for disaster than they often would be. Wholesale massacres of both Jews and lepers in the fourteenth century were occasioned by the onset of plague, which had been caused, it was held, by the poisoning of the wells.[50] Indeed, reaction to the Black Death as indicating the balancing forces of wrong and punishment is fascinating and many-layered. For, though the Jews might be considered agents of the disaster and therefore punishable, there was paradoxically little doubt also that the pestilence was God's will and was a punishment for man's sins. The growth of the Flagellant movement, associated earlier in the Middle Ages with other disasters, which accompanied the Plague, was an attempt to 'buy off' God's punishment by mass self-punishment.[51] God's punishment was a familiar cry in that period and is still to be heard as we shall see. Giraldus Cambrensis believed the Norman Conquest to have been God's punishment for selling children into slavery in Ireland.[52] Punishment may dramatically explain, and may restore as it explains, even the most catastrophic natural or historical occurrences in such a psychology.

It would be tempting perhaps to consign this psychology to other days or 'primitive' cultures. Yet research carried out in the USA within the last twenty years reveals a similar drive to maintain belief in a just and fair world in which suffering is deserved – and deserved suffering is the essence of punishment. Melvin J. Lerner examined in a paper published in 1970 the reactions of those who witnessed the suffering of an objectively blameless (relative to the suffering) individual. He observed that:

> When the person becomes aware of a victim who is clearly innocent of any act which might have brought about the suffering, he is confronted with a conflict. He can decide that he lives in a cruel unjust world where innocent people can suffer or that the only people who can suffer in this world are those who deserve such a fate. The evidence supported the hypothesis that most people will persuade themselves that 'innocent' victims are sufficiently undesirable people that their suffering may be an appropriate fate.[53]

Punishment 'evens out' wrong in a perception of justice based upon fairness, and Lerner's conclusions support the hypothesis that so interwoven in the psychology of persons within at least some cultures is such a sentiment that 'wrong' may become implied so that arbitrary suffering may be interpreted in some cases at least as 'punishment'.

RETRIBUTION, FACT AND THEORY

Our observations above have considered some of those elements that may be useful in understanding the desire of groups to punish wrongdoers. We have spoken of an idea of 'popular retributivism', which may be used as a term to encompass several of these strands. Yet such a term is a potentially dangerous one, for in the language of the justificatory theorists the hallmark of retributivism is that the relation of punishment to (again the limited sphere) crime is 'backward-looking', and does not include – or at least the justification does not, or need not depend upon – beneficial social consequences for the future that are promoted by that punitive act. Yet again, our admiration for those who can speak of such divisions within the sphere of justification, in which forum such definitional categories are quite acceptable, without the most insultingly perfunctory investigation as to the psychological and social functions that punishment actually serves of the kind offered here, is immense. Our own problem is not only that, as we have seen Lacey arguing earlier,[54] a consequentialist may need to consider popular retributivist beliefs in any drawing up of any utilitarian table of social benefits and detriments, but goes rather deeper. For it is by no means clear whether the gratification of the function served by punishment as restating and confirming the rule in the minds of conformists is to be seen as a retributivist ('backward-looking') or a utilitarian ('forward-looking') concept. While such a clear distinction is, we concede, legitimate in the language of moral philosophical discourse, it is wholly inappropriate, we feel, when actual social practice is examined. Certainly punishment as fulfilling the social function indicated here can be forced by theory into such compartments and presumably would be held to be consequentialist, but we do have difficulties with such a formulation, which obscures the element of vindication of an existing rule.

Now, clearly we do understand that the 'ought' and the 'is' occupy different worlds, that the existence of a practice is not the same as a justification for that practice, or that the gratification of those psychological purposes that may be served by such a practice is its justification either. What we do assert is that the justification of a social practice must exist against the background of the real world if it is to be more than a sterile academic exercise. It may need to be appreciated that the stark opposites of moral argumentation may converge in the deep pool of popular psychology.

PUNISHMENT AND DETERRENCE

Deterrence, that archetypally utilitarian aim/justification of punishment, is often an expressed purpose in the application of the technique. Although we have stressed that the articulated justification for the application of punishment even by the punishing authority may not correspond to the 'real' reason for its application, there are no grounds for assuming that deterrence is not a genuine motivation in the infliction of punishment in at least some of its applications. Our observations concerning the generality of popular retribution as a reason for the application of punishment in no way commits us to abandoning the reality of a consequentialist motive for and function of punishment in other, or indeed the same, applications of punishment. Indeed, the element of deterrence may be an integral part of that complex function of punishment that we have characterized as the restatement of rules for the benefit of conformists – the restatement in itself identifying and reinforcing the potential for suffering as a result of breach in the minds of conformists. The principle involved in deterrence is a very simple one, which contains a self-evident element of truth – that in many cases I am less likely to do something if it will have an unpleasant consequence than if it will have a pleasant or neutral one, all other things being equal.

In this context it may be important to restate some of the suggestions as to the potency of sanctions in determining behaviour that have been advanced by psychologists. It will be recalled that for one school of thought the response of the individual towards the experience or anticipation of reward and punishment is the crucial element in human learning processes.[55] B. F. Skinner's development of the controversial theory of 'operant conditioning' maintained that things might be rather more complex – that unpleasant consequences need not reduce tendencies towards punished conduct though they may suppress that conduct, whilst the process of suppression may involve its own forms of socially harmful 'pollution'.[56] Other authors have viewed variables such as proximity and intensity of punishment, and the role of vicarious punishment as determinators of the efficacy of penal acts, as deterrent forces. For a discussion of these various studies the reader is referred elsewhere.[57] Leaving the complexity of psychological theory behind for a moment, however, it seems clear that the threat of suffering may influence behaviour.

It is customary to view deterrence in punishment as applicable to two potential 'constituencies' – the wrongdoer himself (individual deterrence) and the rest of the group (general deterrence). The theory centred around this notion and the evidence of its efficacy in at least the sphere of the operation of criminal law have been extensively considered elsewhere.[58] We shall restrict ourselves here to a few general comments, some of which are occasionally overlooked in discussion. Firstly, let us indicate that, presumably because of its association with the justificatory theories of the nineteenth-century penal reformers such as Bentham, it may be thought that deterrence is in some way a 'modern' notion. The simplicity of the idea as briefly stated earlier, however, should alert us to the fact that it is unlikely to be an exclusively recent phenomenon, and even when the British penal system alone is investigated we find avowedly deterrent penal measures as early as the thirteenth century.[59] Nor, we suspect, is deterrent theory likely to be found only in a western context, although it is conceded that anthropological studies are often silent on the expressed grounds for the application of a sanction. Where no such grounds are advanced (or, of course, where the grounds advanced are no more than *ex post facto* rationalizations of a different psychological reality) we are obliged to enter the realms of speculation. Certainly the theoretical work of psychologists seems based on the premise of the general rather than a culturally specific influence of threats of sanction as behaviour modifiers, although they would concede presumably considerable cultural or subcultural variation in application, or even conceivably, effect.

We may also offer an observation upon the division between individual and general deterrence. Firstly, of course, the latter is a concept that is really applicable only where there is a 'constituency' to be influenced who are in the same or a similar position to the object of punishment. Clearly then, an only child who is sent to bed early for not putting away his toys is unlikely to receive punishment motivated by general deterrence. It is possible that the parent intends to make a dramatic announcement of the sanction to children of the neighbours, as we shall see, for example, happening in an interesting case from the Hopi Indian culture.[60] It is also possible that we might construe the punishment as being self-regarding and thereby deterring in some way the parents from sloth. Yet neither of these formulae would seem immediately likely in this case, although we have stressed the general importance of the latter kind of reasoning above. Individual deterrence, on the other hand, is not, we would maintain, so distinct from another frequently cited aim of punishment (again discussed principally in the context of the criminal law), namely rehabilitation, as is often assumed. By this we mean not simply that the end result of a transgressor who, once punished, fails to repeat his transgression is the same whether we, or he, choose to ascribe the conformity to rehabilitation or deterrence. Rather, the socialization process – the original 'habilitation', which the punitive process is supposed to restore or reinforce – is itself the result of many techniques, amongst which the deterrent effect of punishment has quite probably played a significant part. To this point we shall return later, but for the moment we shall simply state that we would feel happier if this type of question were more often addressed in the literature about punishment, which still seems to operate largely with clear and dogmatic categories.

The next point to be made is related to this and is that 'deterrence' will not have a constant role to play within punishment but must be viewed against the background of a series of variables that will determine both its actual and its perceived efficacy. These may have a bearing on its importance as a social and psychological function of punishment. Firstly, it is clear that a key variable lies within the personalities of those within the deterrable constituency. This formulation may in itself alert us to an interesting point. For it is notable that deterrence is something done to other people – it points out a distinction between the norm-protectors, the administrators of punishment, and 'the rest', the potentially deviant class. The language most commonly used in deterrence administration is that it will act as a warning 'to others', whether they be naughty schoolchildren, cowardly soldiers, or convicted robbers. The authority issuing such an articulated premise seldom if ever includes itself within the deterrence constituency, although we have suggested that the confirmation of norms, which will have importance for all members of the conforming group, will contain perhaps a notion associated with deterrence within it. This latter function of punishment is one that is, on the evidence we have examined, however, seldom articulated. But to return to the variables within the constituency it would seem *a priori* reasonable to assume that some people will prove easier to deter than others depending upon variables within their personalities and circumstances.

One thing is very clear: different social wrongs will also be differentially amenable to deterrence. Indeed, if we again refer to traditional justificatory argumentation in the context of the criminal law we find that a, somewhat belated, recognition of this fact has led to criticism of utilitarian penal philosophy, which, by ignoring this factor, fails, it is urged, thereby to account for the principle of proportionality.[61] For, the argument runs, many murders, as momentary and highly specific acts of passion, are not rationally deterrable, as is parking on a double yellow line, and the more severe punishment of the former is therefore unjustifiable on consequentialist grounds. Again, it is no part of our brief to enter into discussion of utilitarian defences and counterclaims to this assertion – to add yet another furrow to an already well-ploughed field. We shall offer merely one comment, since it fits with our present strand of reasoning: Bentham's classic account, which includes the argument 'where two offences come in competition, the punishment for the greater offence must be sufficient to induce a man to prefer the less',[62] is clearly based on an erroneous premise. For, as Ten affirms: '[It] is very doubtful that there are many offenders who survey the whole gamut of crimes and punishments and then choose one rather than the others in terms of the relative leniency of its punishment.'[63] The different disposition of offenders towards different sorts of offence – the fact that a man is more likely to park on a double yellow line than to commit murder and will not see the range of social wrongs between these points as equally appealing save for their different punishments – may indeed itself be related to the deterability of the various types of social wrong. But it may be the case that those offences that an individual is least likely to commit, the very gravest, such as homicide, are those that are least likely in some manifestations (e.g. passion murders) to be open to the kind of rational weighing process Bentham envisages the potential criminal undertaking before carrying out his antisocial act.

Ehrenzweig, following Freud's observations on a possible dualism, goes so far as to suggest two different forms of criminal conduct, which he terms 'oedipal' and 'post-oedipal' crimes.[64] 'Oedipal' crimes, such as murder, require the actor to overcome the strongest, because earliest, repression:

> Such an oedipal crime [maintains Ehrenzweig] can thus occur only due to an abnormal absence of repression or due to an overpowering urge. In either case, fear of punishment will be ineffective to act as a rational deterrent to both the actually and potentially tempted. It is too weak both to replace the normal oedipal repression and to compete with urge strong enough to overcome it. Moreover in so far as the process of repression remains unconscious, it is inaccessible to conscious motivation.[65]

Such principles are not applicable to 'post-oedipal' offences, such as theft, the repression of which urge is weaker and is wholly or partly conscious. These crimes are accordingly susceptible to rational deterrence. He supports this argument by reference to the well-known instance of the withdrawal of the Danish police under German occupation. 'Oedipal' crime, he suggests, was hardly affected in terms of the frequency of commission whilst 'post-oedipal' crime increased enormously.[66]

Now, it is not necessary for us to accept Ehrenzweig's rather simple dualism, still less his nomenclature, to grasp the element of truth underlying such assertions. That truth is that the impact of deterrence in punishment in fact is subject to a great many more variables (in terms of individual or group psychologies and the relative potency of the restraints on conduct conferred by the general processes of socialization) than its use in the discourse of justification or the *ex post facto* rationalization of the imposition of penal sanction would sometimes lead us to expect. Nevertheless, the frequency of the expression of deterrence ideology in such contexts in, at least, the Anglo-American penality sphere is evidence of the attraction such a theory holds. And let us repeat that we are not sceptical as to the infliction of punishment with intent to deter in many cases, nor yet as to the deterrent efficacy of punishment in many cases. To see such a simple and valuable notion merely as a rationalization would be unfair and would underestimate the role it plays in social reality. At the same time, we might observe, its rather 'scientific' and 'civilized' nature – gazing into the Future Good and bearing no taint of atavistic primitive revenge and separating neatly those who form the deterrence constituency from those who order the punishment – has made it a very attractive ideology for the task of justification of individual punishments or of 'the institution' generally. For those who themselves are involved in the administration of punishment such an ideal might serve possibly as a potent method of mitigating any guilt felt on account of the infliction of unpleasantness.

EDUCATION AND THE FORMATION OF MORALITY

If the language of general deterrence may not be over-prevalent in some punishing situations, such as the family (although we are satisfied that it is not uncommon even there), then the language of individual deterrence may be, and it is linked, as we have argued earlier, with another professed aim or function of the technique of punishment – education. When we talk of this function as applicable to adult criminal offenders, at least within the British tradition, the words 'reform' or 'rehabilitation' are generally used. This latter term, in common use in this context, is particularly interesting in its suggestion of a restoration after a lapse from a hitherto untarnished state. Here, it might be suggested, is the Benthamite calculating criminal, fully formed, with no competing subcultural norms, no inadequate socialization, and no pre-existing fault given linguistic credence within this terminology.[67]

'Education' is the word we tend to use in this context almost exclusively with regard to the young as if the acquisition of knowledge and understanding can come only at a particular age, like puberty. We have linked this process to individual deterrence and, since the boundary between the two is not one, we believe, that can be easily drawn, a few words are necessary, for most accounts in traditional debate on this area tend to have no difficulty in establishing this dualism. The difference, it is affirmed, lies in the reason for the future conformity with the norm on the assumption that this will not come about without the use of punishment. Deterrence, it is said, occurs when the individual is induced to obey by virtue of fear of a penalty to be inflicted in future, reform is where the motive is an internal acceptance of the norm. Now, these may be distinct psychological states but again concentration on the adult criminal offender may be responsible for an over-simple view of the world, and a dualism that may there seem theoretically sound may be less supportable elsewhere. For when the process of socialization of the young is considered the withdrawal of approval or other forms of punishment may well, we might argue, be a potent form of inculcating acceptance of the norm, of 'forming a morality'.

It is difficult for us to speak with confidence of the detailed processes involved in socialization and the development of morality. But it is not necessary to view socialization only in the crudest 'carrot and stick' terms to accept that the disapproval of actions (the dramatic display of which is the essense of punishment) by others and the fear of discomfort engendered thereby may well be a critical component (amongst others, such as explanation, emulation, and ratiocination) in the development of moral sense. If this is so, and others will know this better than we do, then the individual's external compliance out of trepidation and his conscientious conversion are not as totally distinct as may elsewhere be presented. It is an overstatement to suggest that the difference between rehabilitation and deterrence of wrongdoers boils down to a difference in the efficacy of punitive techniques and the age at which they are employed, but there is a grain of truth in the suggestion.

Nor need this ambiguity of penal purpose be restricted simply to techniques of child-rearing. In criminal justice history the gallows might be the stage for the performance of a drama not simply about the location of power or about deterrence. The condemned eighteenth-century criminal's confession to the crowd would be, like some of Hogarth's engravings, in the nature of an elaborate moral fable. Those who attended, adults as well as children, were there not simply to be terrified, or to connect crime with a particular response, but to heed a lesson about how minor vice led to greater crime and ultimately to the gallows. Moral example, an educative purpose, was as potent a force in the drama as any other.[68]

The common English expression used with regard to both children and adult criminal offenders, that the punishment will 'teach them a lesson', is capable, by its splendid inherent ambiguity (what is the lesson being taught?), of describing both of these (and possibly many other) punitive functions. At a sociological level, of course, such a distinction is of secondary importance – if the norm is preserved then the conformist's reason for not breaching it is possibly not vital – yet it may be more comforting, less guilt-inducing for the punishing community, to feel that the deviant can and will be induced to agree with them rather than submit through fear.

In this chapter we have suggested certain functions, sociological and psychological, that may be served by the practice of punishment. We have considered only some functions for, as we have said, the range of aims that punishment may serve in individual cases will be very diverse, as the range of applications of the punitive sanction is enormously wide. The functions we have considered here are, we suggest, those most often associated with punishment. It is clear, however, that in describing the function that the practice fulfils we need not necessarily be describing the purpose for which a punishment is professed to be applied, nor yet are we suggesting that all of the above functions are served in all applications of punishment. It may be difficult to determine, for example, whether a deterrent effect has been served by a particular punishment, even if this is the only avowed and (we shall assume the only intended) purpose of those who administer the punishment. It cannot, of course, be maintained that this will be the only purpose served by that punitive act, nor indeed (unless the punitive administrators are entirely coincident with the whole society) can it be said that the purpose for which it is consciously imposed will be the same as that for which it is seen to be imposed by others examining the situation. The chameleon aspect of punishment, which allows it to perform so many functions – actual and rationalized, conscious and unconscious – is an important feature of its nature. We have restricted ourselves here to a discussion of some of the ends that may actually be served by punishment in the social circumstances in which it is most frequently encountered. In so doing we have perforce come across references to familiar expressions from the language of 'justification theory'. Again, it must be noted that our task is to attempt to describe what may be accomplished by the infliction of punishment rather than what justifies that particular infliction or the system that does the inflicting. Whilst it seems to us quite proper to deal with these as distinct matters it seems quite staggering how much discussion of the latter question has been accomplished with such scant regard for the issues raised by the former.

7

SIMILARITIES, COMPARISONS, AND CONTRASTS

It is necessary at this point to distinguish the practice of punishment from certain other social practices, which may either serve by different means the same ends as does punishment or which appear to have other points of similarity. We shall also attempt to relate such practices to the technique of punishment. Again, it should be pointed out that we are concerned to identify and interrelate practices that we consider to have some genuine sociological, anthropological, or psychological differences from what we have taken to be instances of punishment rather than to rely on the purely nominal difference resulting from a stipulative definition. It is perhaps advisable at this point briefly to summarize the position we have reached so far. Punishment, it has been suggested, is intimately connected with the nature of prescription or rule, for rule implies disapproval of contrary conduct either by members of the society subject to the rule as a whole, or, where the rule is identified by criteria other than popular acceptance, disapproval of the rule-creating or -maintaining authority. Where in the latter case the sanction will be typically identified within the rule itself, or by reference to the rule-creating or -maintaining authority, in the former case this disapproval will be felt by the society as a whole or a socially significant section of it. It is when this disapproval is 'voiced', translated, that is, into words or, more clearly, actions, that are unpleasant to the actual or supposed rule-transgressor or an acceptable representative of that transgressor, that we feel justified in using the term 'punishment'.

Though, clearly, the further we proceed along either or both the axes of organization and severity in penal application the more obvious it becomes to use the term 'punishment', its roots lie in the simple notion of disapproval of breach of a rule or of a particular prescription. Moreover, we have indicated that the use of the technique of punishment may have a variety of different aims and different consequences, some explicit, some not so. So punishment can be a way of restoring societal harmony, of making sense of the world, etc. Now we must investigate other techniques that may be used to serve at least some of the purposes for which the elastic practice of punishment is used. For it has at no time been suggested that, fundamental though it is in deriving so closely from the very essence of the rule breach, punishment is the only method of securing those particular objectives with which we have seen it associated.

It is tempting to refer to punishment in this context as simply one method of 'social control', and it is in these terms that many writers have looked at the role of the penal sanction together with other measures with particular reference to modern states.[1] However, 'social control' begs too many questions if we seek to use it as a term to describe the aims of those who utilize the instrument of punishment in general. Whilst it does no violence to language or to reality to describe an action taken by a tribal group to heal a potentially damaging internal dispute as a method of 'social control' (indeed, in many ways the expression is ideal) the unstated questions of 'by whom?', 'how?' and 'why?' may be the important ones to examine. Moreover, the phrase also conjures up associations from its use in much contemporary writing that may unconsciously suggest inappropriate answers to these imporant questions. Let us investigate, then, various other social practices that may be related either in aim or (a rather different point) that may be similar in appearance to punishment.

REWARD

Just as punishment can be seen as having a role to play, in actuality or perception, in ensuring compliance with social rules, so too can reward. Because of its utility in this respect reward has been described by some philosophers and anthropologists as a species of sanction, sometimes with the qualifying adjective 'positive'.[2] It is evident that reward, like punishment, may be a potent motive for obeying rules or prescriptions, and both are used in the process of socialization. But it seems clear that not all of the multiplicity of functions of, or aims of, punishment may be discharged by reward. Reward would seem incapable of referring back to a breach of rule and therefore of supplying the retrospective qualities that inhere in the notion of punishment, for example the healing of social dysphoria. Of course, it might be argued that the denial of reward when a social rule is breached would perform the same function and, particularly in cases where the 'reward' being denied is not a superadded benefit of social life but is conceived of as an expected or even essential element thereof, then this would be an alternative means of viewing punishment. So when Malinowski described the web of reciprocity that supported the social interaction of the Trobriand Islanders he showed that the man who refused to join the fishing team was not given any fish.[3] This might be variously categorized as the denial of a reward for action, a punishment for inaction, or the failure to qualify for an entitlement, which latter idea will be discussed shortly.[4]

Ultimately, of course, it becomes possible to discuss all sanctions as the denial of reward, all expressions of social disapproval, that is, as denials of social approval. Indeed, in the case of punishments such as ostracism or outlawry it makes more sense to discuss what has been removed rather than what has been imposed. But if we leave aside this 'negative reward' characterization and return to the positive formulation we must appreciate that, although it may be an important method of guiding human conduct, reward does not seem to be capable of filling all the roles that punishment is called upon to play. Honoré, arguing *a priori*, suggests that since it is a characteristic of rules to restrain action, it is normal to find social interaction depending upon negative as well as positive sanctions, and observation would seem to support this suggestion.[5]

COMPENSATION

In the light of the importance attached within this text to the infliction of punishment as a consequence of rule breach it is obviously of great importance to consider those societies in which breach of even the most important norms of social interaction gives rise not to a demand for an afflictive punishment to be imposed on the wrongdoer but rather a claim that he should compensate the victim for his loss. Such societies are many both in recent and earlier times. The Nuer of East Africa, the Ifugao of the Philippines, the Yurok of North America, and the Anglo-Saxons in early medieval England all serve as examples of cultures in which compensation rather than punishment was central to the dispute-settlement technique.[6] This method also has an important role to play in the contemporary smoothing over of disrupted international relations.[7] Indeed, so numerous are these systems that Lewis takes this method of dealing with wrong as characteristic of non-centralized societies. 'On the whole', he suggests, 'whatever the social distance of the parties attacks on property and persons in uncentralised societies tend to be treated as wrongs demanding reparation (if necessary in kind) rather than as crimes demanding punishment.'[8] To certain of the assumptions contained within this statement we must needs return presently but its substance certainly gives cause for thought.

Neither is such a system lightly discarded if the evidence of the Nuer is in any way typical. This people, though no strangers to interpersonal violence, used centralized afflictive sanctions only in the relatively infrequent action taken against 'public enemies' (witches and ghouls). Other cases of hurt, homicide, or other wrongs, were regarded as matters for compensation between the parties concerned. The legal system imposed upon the Nuer by colonization, which involved sanctions such as imprisonment, seemed not to be understood by the indigenous population, imprisonment being imposed only under pressure from the authorities. The Nuer themselves would ask for fixed penalties to be laid down so that they might absolve themselves from the responsibility of imprisoning by pointing to the instructions of others. In this way their own distaste for afflictive penalties might be, it would seem, assuaged.[9]

This enormous body of information on compensation-based systems, so often wholly ignored by western jurisprudential writing, could, of course, be conveniently disposed of definitionally. We could simply maintain our commitment to discussing only systems of punishment and thereby consign these other systems themselves to outer darkness (in the context of this commentary – they do not so easily disappear in the real world). Alternatively, we could simply say that the payment of compensation is the 'punishment' for breach of a norm and indicates the disapproval of that breach, thereby consigning the sociological and psychological differences from our 'standard model' which these systems reflect into the same darkness. Clearly neither of these alternatives is satisfactory and some, albeit limited, investigation of compensation-based systems is necessary.

Not only do we find that in some societies even those offences that we would categorize as the most serious, such as homicide, are amendable but also that complex and highly structured scales of compensation are laid down. This was true for the Nuer and was also true for the Anglo-Saxons. The earliest material that we know to have been written in the English language, the early-seventh-century 'dooms' of Ethelbert of Kent, speak, as do later Saxon enactments, in very precise terms as to the amount of compensation payable. This will vary even according to which of a number of teeth is broken: 'For each of the four front teeth vi shillings, for the tooth which stands next to them iv shillings, for that which stands next to that iii shillings and then afterwards for each a shilling.'[10]

Two points may be made before we continue. The first is to note the idea of proportionality in this as in other compensation systems. Different injuries are accorded a particular weight as measured by the physical harm involved, characterized in this Anglo-Saxon example by the utility of the tooth lost for purposes which, other evidence suggests, would include fighting capability.[11] In addition, the gravity will be determined by the relative status of or degree of proximity between the parties, and again, Anglo-Saxon evidence and contemporary anthropological sources, such as the homicide provisions of the *diya*-paying Somali nomads, would serve as examples.[12] This relative weight will be reflected in the amount of compensation payable. We have already commented on the typicality of proportionality in the context of the exaction of punishment.

The second feature is discernible from the Nuer evidence and may well be found in other societies employing the compensation model. The Nuer, like the Anglo-Saxons, had detailed and elaborate scales of compensation, which, in the case of this East African people, were set in tradition. However, in practice only in the case of homicide was full compensation likely to be paid; in other cases the sum was modulated by the social context, the code forming a starting point for negotiation that would allow other variables, such as, for example, the mental state of the wrongdoer (ignored in the traditional scales) to be given bargaining weight.[13] Similarly, factors outside the formal scale of payments might influence the sum settled upon as compensation amongst the Ifugao.[14] This too, whilst it may not have direct parallels in punitive practice, will remind us that systems of punishment may also allow of amelioration of sanction on the grounds of 'popular sentiment'. This is obviously the case in small-scale societies and compensation-paying societies tend to be small also. Yet such ideas may also have some residual impact, as we shall see, even in the penal practices of centralized modern states.[15]

These apparent points of contact apart, however, it does seem *prima facie* as though social systems that rely on compensation to mend the social fissure caused by one party's wrongdoing differ fundamentally from those that employ punitive techniques. But a closer examination of the evidence may suggest that the dichotomy between the two methods of dealing with an overstepping of permitted behaviour is not so profound, at least in so far as some of the societies we might look at are concerned. Firstly, in the case of both the medieval Anglo-Saxons and the Nuer, as well as in other social groups, the payment of compensation operates against the background of the blood-feud. In this context, the payment of compensation may be characterized as the purchase of an exemption from the prosecution of the feud. Indeed, Einzig goes so far as to suggest that the use of money was initially developed for this purpose.[16] The feud is a social framework for the administration of an afflictive, retributive penalty. It is none the less punitive for being imposed by the family or kinship group rather than the 'state', this confusion being, as we have seen, a constant feature in orthodox discussions of punishment. This is not to maintain that compensation is in any sense merely a secondary form of dispute-settlement that is in essence subsidiary to the 'real' punitive sanction. The issue of primacy of a group's modes of social regulation is to be determined by the practices and attitudes of the members of that group rather than by our analysis. So, if societies do indeed exist in which a wronged individual, as a result of his socialization, routinely considers his injury as being predominantly the occasion for a claim of compensation rather than for condemnation, retaliation, and the infliction of harm upon the wrongdoer, then we would be fully justified in seeing the former as the primary factor.

This formulation suggests another point, namely that in any one society it is at least possible that systems of compensation and punishment may co-exist, the same behaviour being both stigmatized by popular opinion (or being subject to other sanctions) and giving grounds for compensation. So in his investigation of the Nuer, Howell pointed out that, in addition to those actions against witches and ghouls mentioned earlier, reprobation, unpopularity, loss of respect of neighbours, and the loss of privileges (social, political, or economic) also operated as sanctions. Moreover, in certain cases misconduct might attract a spiritual penalty manifested in illness, which might in itself need to be 'bought off' by spiritual purification.[17] Such sanctions may seem *prima facie* more nugatory in substance or in organization than the indemnity tariffs (although, as we have mentioned, such

131

tariffs may in fact be modulated by the apparently diffuse social pressure, which incorporates notions such as the communal appreciation of moral responsibility) but they should not, we have urged, be ignored for that reason.

The third point that needs to be made in relation to the connection between compensation-based and punishment-based systems is related to those above. We have seen that in some compensation systems at least the offer and receipt of the indemnity leads to exemption from feud. This leads us to consider the wider question of what is to happen if compensation is not paid. Lewis, who is keen to keep compensatory and punitive systems conceptually distinct, concedes that 'the ethnographic literature is often disappointingly vague on this point',[18] but he gives a number of examples, all of which involve community action against life, property, or social status. He states:

> among the Somali nomads the recalcitrant member of a diya [compensation]-paying group who refuses to pay an internal fine or to contribute his share of an outgoing due is liable to be seized summarily by his peers and tied, none too gently, to a tree while several of his most coveted livestock are slaughtered under his eyes to feast the elders of his lineage. This sanction is also applied amongst the Gurage and in certain neighbouring Galla communities in Ethiopia.[19]

Whether we characterize the breach of rule being sanctioned here as the original wrong or a subsequent wrong (the failure to pay being understood as a sort of contempt of due process) we find the same thing. That is that, as with a system based on reward, a system based upon the voluntary reciprocation (even though that voluntariness may be socially expected or even demanded) implicit in the notion of compensation will, if faced by intransigence, typically (it is tempting to suggest inevitably), fall back upon punitive measures in order to support the rule.

The above observations invite one further comment concerning orthodox terminology within this discourse, yet it is one that, since it requires some psychological evidence to support it, evidence that we do not have, we put forward with some timidity. Writers faced with compensation systems often use the terminology of 'private' wrong when discussing such procedures. So, Howell, writing of the Nuer says: 'homicide is not a wrong in abstract either against God, mankind in general or society but only against the dead man's kin' and other writers use other formulations to suggest that such wrongs are considered as such only as between the parties.[20] Now, either this is simply a shorter way of explaining a compensation system or it risks confusing social attitudes towards wrong with the agencies of rule enforcement (either by feud or compensations). So, whilst we know nothing specifically about the Nuer attitude towards the taking of life, we would stress that it is by no means a necessary conclusion to draw from the practice of any people that their communal abhorrence of homicide, or abstract respect for life is in any way diminished by the fact that the enforcement agencies are kinship groups rather than independent agencies of the society as a whole.

Before leaving this vitally important area a few further comments are necessary. Lewis, who correctly identifies the issues as concerned essentially with the settlement of disputes, points, as has been seen, to the compensation-based system as being typical of uncentralized societies. Yet he also points to a connection with more centralized societies. 'In total refutation of the erroneous speculations of both Durkheim and Maine', he contends, 'as centralisation develops so does the range of wrongs that are redefined as crimes against the state, for which punitive rather than restitutive measures are required.'[21] Save in so far as this statement is seen as maintaining an over-exaggerated distinction between the occurrence of the two types of technique, and save in so far as the final clause might be taken as annexing punitive measures solely to state systems, our own understanding would be in line with the general tenor of this statement.

A brief review of historical developments within the English system, whilst not laying any claim to being in itself typical of the process of movement of societies generally, may be interesting at this point. Early Anglo-Saxon society was supported in its dispute-settlement technique by the blood-feud. Enactments enshrining compensation, such as that of Ethelbert of Kent mentioned earlier, have been explained as modifications of an unrestricted feud procedure. A. W. B. Simpson argues that the moral changes resulting from the adoption of Christianity may lie behind the legislation.[22] W. W. Lehman has argued for a more secular cause – the scattering of kinship groups in the invasion of England, which would jeopardize the operation of the feud system on its own.[23] Whilst either, or indeed both, of these views may be correct it may also be the case that feud and compensation developed side by side from the outset, for we have

133

seen that they are often intimately connected. However, it is possible that social changes within the early medieval period were reflected in changes in the response to wrongdoing. As kinship gave way to lordship and geographical community as the significant factors of social organization, and as these factors combined in the notions of kingship and state, so we may trace the decline of compensation and the growth of afflictive punishment organized by the agencies of the state themselves.[24] An intermediate stage may have been the payment of a *wite*, a type of compensation payment to the king over and above that (*bot*) paid to the aggrieved individual himself. In the times of the later Saxon kings more wrongs came to be categorized as *botleas* or unamendable and by the thirteenth century it might be argued that traces of the *wergild* (compensation) system within the common law could be found only in occasional composition agreements in royal charters of pardon.[25]

Yet we must also concede that while 'trespasses' (wrongs) thus came under the purview of the criminal law they might continue also to be brought by victims and (by different procedures) for compensation. The Anglo-American law of tort obviously still provides compensation for injury to property and chattels and in English law in cases of battery the possibility of alternative procedures has led to statutory regulation.[26] The defendant in a tort action who refuses to pay the damages awarded against him will have his property seized against his will, much as the Somali nomad, but without being tied to a tree.

The mutual interplay between the distinct but related patterns of activity that may occur on breach of rule, compensation, and punishment, is still within the Anglo-American system discernible in the practice, language, and psychology of persons within it. So, in criminal cases in England and Wales, the judge may make a compensation order against the convicted defendant.[27] A criminal who serves a period of time in prison or is the recipient of another penal sanction is often described as 'paying his debt to society', rather as in earlier times he paid his debt, monetarily, to the victim or his kin. Psychological research by Berscheid, Boye, and Walster suggests that in the perceptions of wrongdoers in their American sample compensation of the victim or the wrongdoer's own liability to retaliation were seen both to be means of restoring the inequity created by the wrongful act.[28] Consideration of compensation systems, then, and their relationship to penal activity are most important for an understanding of social response to rule breach.

CONFESSION

Just as social structures exist in which compensation is seen to fulfil the role of dispute-settlement rather than a recourse to punishment to this end or, as we have argued above, rather than immediate recourse to punishment, so too in some societies does confession. Of course, confession has a role to play in all societies but in the Anglo-American context tends to be seen, at least in so far as a response to serious wrongdoing is concerned, as a means of attributing or ameliorating culpability rather than settling the dispute. In religious contexts, even within these societies, confession is stressed as a necessary means of expiating a sin. In other societies more emphasis is placed on the role of confession, which is seemingly viewed as a less personal act than in those cultures mentioned above but one that rather seeks to satisfy the group to which confession (and presumably the public apology implicit within it) is made. It may be imagined that shame and the loss of prestige are natural, or at least typical, concomitants of public confession and, since these are features clearly associated with the use of punitive sanctions, it might be possible to ignore confession as an independent subject and view it as being simply instrumental in the punitive process. This, however, would be to do it less than justice as an autonomous means of healing social dysphoria. M. B. Voyce, studying methods of discipline within an order of Buddhist monks, considers confession to be an important social 'sanction' but argues that punishment is a concept inapplicable to the community of monks.[29] It may be, however, that a monk may be expelled from the community in certain circumstances, and here we can see confession as possibly analogous to compensation in that its requirement of voluntary action on the part of the wrongdoer marks the limitation of the strategy in the face of intransigence.

In other societies the confession, although in itself important, is supported by a range of familiar afflictive penalties. Amongst the Central Eskimo of Canada and those of West Greenland, for example, open and public ritual confession was used to expiate wrong and to cleanse the soul of the vapour that envelops it as a supernatural sanction. But persistence in and defiance of the *shaman* would be punished by, again, putting the offender outside the community by exile.[30]

Confession is, within the British experience, important in spiritual contexts and in other environments in which rules may be broken.

'Owning up', either on its own or as a precursor to further punishment, is frequently demanded within the context of family or school disciplining regimes. The Newsoms' study discovered, interestingly, social variation in the incidence of children's confession to wrongdoing; a significantly greater percentage of middle-class than working-class children in their study owned up to wrongdoing.[31] In the sphere of legal rules confession has been of symbolic importance, particularly in the context of political or religious heresy. Often within the legal environment, however, confession has been used as an appropriate factor in avoiding punishment, or at least in avoiding certain types of punishment. In medieval times a felon who took sanctuary would be allowed on leaving the church to 'abjure the realm' (go into exile) on condition that he confessed his offence to the coroner. In this way the standard penalty for felony, death or mutilation, would be avoided.[32] Within the present day an offender will, in certain circumstances, be granted an official police caution rather than prosecuted, and, again, confession of guilt is a precondition.[33] When sentence is passed on offenders after trial, those who have pleaded guilty will generally be given more lenient sentences. The traditional justification, obviously still theoretically very important, for the 'guilty discount' is that it indicates remorse. Critics argue, however, that a simple plea of guilty need not on its own indicate any such thing and that the practice is rooted in the interests of cutting down the number of trials that 'go the distance'.[34] In the other cases mentioned above we must not forget that the confession benefits also the officials. The abjuring felon and the cautioned offender have both by their confession drawn a line under the offence, the officials of the system have the satisfaction of considering the case closed.

NON-QUALIFICATION

By non-qualification we have in mind cases in which persons are adjudged not to merit, or at any rate not to be suitable for, entry into a particular role or position. At first sight this is a very different scenario from that of punishment – it may be felt bizarre to consider that one who fails to obtain the necessary examination grades to go to university has anything in common with one who is being punished. There is no rule, it will be urged, set by society as a whole or by an authorized rule-creating agency that examinations should be passed, only a hope or possibly an expectation; there is no condemnation of those who do not pass examinations. The failure to attain a qualifying standard is not the same as the falling below it once it has been attained. 'He is not suitable to practise as a doctor' means something wholly different if it is said in the context of a careers adviser's office of a person of subnormal intelligence, who faints at the sight of blood and who has beautifully legible handwriting, from its meaning in the context of an adjudication by the General Medical Council on a person already practising as a doctor who, whilst drunk on duty, has ordered an amputation as the cure for a sore throat.

It is, indeed, on the grounds of breach of rule that we feel the situations are distinguishable, but in reality the two distinct concepts of non-qualification and punishment may run together in certain circumstances. Returning to the Buddhist community discussed earlier, we may ask whether the monk who is obliged to leave the community is being punished for breaking the rules to be observed by such monks or is failing to show the qualities he must have to achieve or maintain his religious status. Is the footballer 'dropped' for a game after playing badly being punished for his poor play on that occasion or is he considered not to be showing sufficient ability to merit his place in the team? To the objection that in this latter case there can never be a rule that a footballer, even a professional, should play well but merely a hope or expectation, we may reply that this Corinthian attitude may not be shared by some football managers, whose opinions alone may be sufficient to form the basis of the 'rules' within his autonomous dressing-room kingdom. Within the highly structured ranking of Japanese Sumo wrestling, we understand, pressures to retire from the highest division can be intense on wrestlers who do not win enough bouts.

The many ways in which breach of reciprocal arrangements may be considered have been discussed earlier in this chapter in our analysis of Malinowski's example of the fishing team.[35] If there is a ground for distinction in these problematical cases it lies in how the measure is understood by the individuals involved within it. This is culturally and contextually specific, not something which can be 'solved' by the scientist. If in the language or the psychology of the culture concerned there is no distinction then we cannot impose one.

There may well be cases in which there is genuine doubt as to whether an envisaged pattern of conduct is indeed a rule, which is breakable, or only a standard to be striven towards. This is particularly so when the appropriate distinguishing feature is to be found in popular conception rather than in a more clear-cut rule-creating source. To return to the example with which we began this section, and to add a further complicating factor, whilst it may be true that poor examination results may not generally be seen as a punishment but as an indicator of education attainment they may be seen by parents or teachers as punishment in particular individual cases for a breach of wider norms. These may not be regarded by all as formal rules but may be so characterized by some – we have in mind such things as the idea that children should work hard at school. In this way a teacher's ambiguous comment 'He/she got what he/she deserved' may contain an implicit punitive reference within the notion of desert or may simply refer to the reflection of an appropriate intellectual standard.

REVENGE

Again we may see that the distinction between punishment and acts of private revenge may be clarified by reference to the notion of social rules, for although the two look similar there are, we think, differences in the social meaning of the actions involved that need to be investigated. We must be aware that, if our distinction is to be drawn at the level of social meaning rather than by dogmatic definitional fiat, we must appreciate that here too we may find situations where the distinction is obscured in real life.

Let us be clear, firstly, as to what it is we are distinguishing. Other writers, such as Nozick, have distinguished between a retributive characterization of punishment and revenge, on grounds that seem to boil down in essence to the institutional, depersonalized nature of the former.[36] Clearly it would be absurd to distinguish between 'punishment' and 'revenge' for the former, we have maintained, is a technique connected with the implementation of social rules, whilst the latter is a motive. It is possible, then, to view punishment utilized by a society in instances, perhaps in all instances, as gratifying a desire for revenge on the part of its members. But it is clear from our characterization of punishment that we regard activities done in consequence of disapproval of breach of social rules as having some material difference from those that indicate other forms of disapproval. This is the point hinted at in the context of Nozick's, admittedly very different, argument when he states that 'retribution is done for a wrong, while revenge may be done for an injury or harm or slight and need not be a wrong'.[37] He follows this observation with the example of the rejected suitor, who may be driven to revenge but could not be said to have been wronged, for the rejecter has a right to reject.[38] In our formulation we would say that no rule has been broken in such a case.

But again we must be aware that in order to seek to legitimate such acts of private vengeance the actor may invoke general norms of fidelity or friendship, breach of which he sees as justifying his actions. This argument is similar to the situation we considered in Chapter 5, to which the reader is referred.[39] Here again we see the rhetoric of punishment, with its associations with rectitude being employed to give moral colour to a blameworthy act.

A related but distinct problem may arise in the following circumstances. A burglar enters X's house and removes the latter's property. X discovers the burglar's identity, retrieves the goods, and administers a sound thrashing to the wrongdoer. All this happens within a legal system in which there are state agencies of adjudication and punishment. In this case we would not dissent from X's claim that he was 'punishing' the burglar, for the burglar has acted in breach of a recognized social rule. The significant point here is that in the social context of the example, the punishment is administered by the 'wrong' person, in the 'wrong' way, and possibly to the 'wrong' degree, and will, of course, run counter to other social rules, thereby itself giving grounds for punishment.

Of course, it is open to the reader to object that in choosing a different word to describe the activity of the jilted suitor from that of the burglary victim, we are, despite our protestations, merely restating a definition of punishment rather than justifying a distinction. To this we would reply that, although in many societies it is regarded as quite proper for the victim to impose the sanction on the wrongdoer (a point to which we shall return later), in no society of which we are aware is it permissible for individuals, except those enjoying supreme political power within the community, to determine on their own behalf the rules of conduct by which persons within that community are to be bound. Therefore, we feel it quite proper to describe the burglary victim's act as punishment whilst stressing its pathological nature in its cultural context, yet choosing a different term to characterize the actions of the deserted lover. 'Who administers the sanction?', in short, is a question of a different sort from 'Who draws up the rules?', although as we have said, there may be factors operating in actual practice that blur the distinction.

PREVENTIVE AND RELATED DETENTIONS

There are, of course, instances in which an objective unpleasantness is visited upon a member of a social group by the community or its agents where the 'victim' has not infringed the rules of that community. Such instances again would seem to be functionally different from cases of punishment as considered in this text and are generally associated with a type of punitive sanction familiar to many societies, the deprivation of liberty. We find instances of individuals or groups being incarcerated not for a wrong they have done but in order to prevent then from doing that wrong. It is true that within the traditional punitive discourse, in Britain at any rate, the idea of preventing a convicted offender from committing further crime, not by deterrence or reform, but simply by 'taking him out of circulation' (with associated arguments as to how far such action is justified) is regarded as a legitimate penal aim. The incarceration of persons who have not committed any offence is, however, again within the British system, regarded as being a different question, and one that leads to moral argumentation of a particular order. Those who seek to support it know that it will need compelling arguments if the moral objections associated with the very idea are to be overcome. Again, in the English language, at any rate, the 'morality' implicit in the rhetoric of punishment may be used to oppose this type of measure – as when the argument 'X is being punished but he has not done anything wrong' is voiced.

An associated issue, but one that seems much more remote from an accepted notion of punishment, is the deprivation of liberty from someone on grounds of their illness, physical (the quarantining of a person with a contagious disease), or psychiatric (the compulsory hospitalization of mentally disordered individuals). In addition to the loss of liberty in such cases, unpleasant actions may accompany methods of treatment: the surgeon who removes a hand for medical reasons looks similar to the surgeon removing it from a thief convicted under certain interpretations of Islamic law, whilst the administration of electrical shocks to an individual, which might in some circumstances be prescribed as part of the treatment of a mentally disordered patient, would be regarded by many, we think, as inhuman if used in a punitive context. Clearly, however, it is argued in such cases, there is no element of disapproval, no notion of rule breach, with the consequent social signalling of impropriety. This is true not only of past conduct but also (in contradistinction to the earlier example of preventive detention) to anticipated future conduct. Moreover, it is argued, in these medical examples the imposition of the unpleasantness is not the aim of the action; the aim is the restoration of health and the suffering is only incidental to the pursuit of that aim. Typically, discussion about punishment recognizes that unpleasantness is intrinsic to the idea of punishment itself, although it is conceded that some utilitarians would agree that the end state of social welfare does not demand suffering and that, should science provide alternative means of dealing with society's malefactors, which would produce the appropriate beneficial social consequences without the suffering of the wrongdoer, then punishment would become as unnecessary and improper as a major operation without anaesthetic in a modern western state.[40] To a related, but not identical, argument that 'crime' is a form of social pathology directly analogous to illness we shall return shortly.

Whatever the strengths of these points of distinction the rather too clear-cut theoretical dichotomy becomes once again obscured when we examine social practice, particularly if that examination is extended over time and space. This blurring is produced by a number of factors over and above the physical similarity sometimes visible in measures taken against the ill and the wrongdoer. This consideration is, however, certainly worth bearing in mind, for the leper colony may look very like the penal colony, and the stripes on the back of the madman who in earlier periods in Britain was whipped as part of his treatment would be practically indistinguishable from those on the back of a petty thief of the same time.

One point to be made, then, is that a society may have difficulty in separating the actions it characterizes as wrong from the symptoms of illness. What we have in mind here is not simply practices of a kind discernible in English history, such as the medieval imprisonment of lepers alongside 'ordinary' criminals for the 'offence' of having the illness, or at any rate the offence of going around whilst suffering from it,[41] nor yet the fact that suicide, nowadays characterized by the formula 'while the balance of mind was disturbed' was until 1961 a criminal offence.[42] Such instances will remind us, however, that the

141

social and legal treatment of abnormality of many different kinds is likely to be the product of a whole complex of factors; fear, super-stition, and religious beliefs amongst them. The profound philosophi-cal investigations as to why we *should* not punish the insane, whether couched in the language of utilitarian optimific calculation or retribu-tive ideas of desert, often tempt us into thinking that it is solely because of these considerations that we *do* not. Here, as elsewhere, such explicit rationalization follows the institutionalization of social practice, which contains its own internal dynamic. The legal discrimi-nation between 'sane' and 'insane', which extends as a tradition back at least as far as the thirteenth century in English law, is just as likely to have originated in fear and superstition than in the types of argument used to justify the contemporary maintenance of the distinction.

However that may be, we need only look to the operation of contemporary law in England and Wales with regard to mentally abnormal offenders to see the difficulties in the application of the distinction between wrongdoing and illness. Of course, the problem here is partially explained by the label, for such persons are both 'offenders' (who have done wrong and accordingly deserve censure for their breach of the criminal law) and mentally abnormal (they have been induced into their action by their abnormality and for this they are not 'to blame', are not 'morally guilty'). Though the theor-etical stance of the law is clear, its operation may not be. The disposition of the psychopathic offender to prison or hospital depends not on the diagnosis of psychopathy itself but of its prognosis in terms of 'treatability'.[43] Lest it be argued that this is merely a pragmatic issue of containment, which shows no real confusion between morally neutral disease and morally culpable criminality, let us take some other illustrations.

In order to avoid the mandatory sentence of life imprisonment for murder in English law, it is not uncommon for a homicide who is quite rational at the time of his act, for example a person who, acting out of some sense of 'compassion', is prevailed on by a terminally ill and suffering relative to hasten that person's demise, to be found to be suffering from 'such abnormality of mind . . . as substantially impairs his mental responsibility' for his acts and omissions under Section 2 of the Homicide Act 1957.[44] On the other hand, it may be that there are some atrocities that are considered too grave in themselves to allow of them being treated as being in any way exculpated by reference to a defective mental state, at least in so far as popular opinion, represented, of course, within the legal system by juries as well as outside opinion, is concerned. Such an assertion, which evokes perhaps the attempts to ascribe responsibility and guilt to explain disaster in the animal trials and in the tribal beliefs we shall mention below, is not one for which we can provide clear proof. Nevertheless there are examples of cases where particularly notorious offenders have been found to be 'bad' rather than 'mad' at their trial, only to be moved from prison to a secure psychiatric institution after the commencement of sentence. If it is the case that such instances may be interpreted as assertions of popular rather than technical ideas of culpability (again we must stress that this is by no means a necessary conclusion, for we are not qualified to discuss the mental states of particular offenders involved nor yet the process of reasoning employed by the juries) then we may be witnessing another example of the role of 'popular penality' even within a centralized legal system.

If there is any substance in the foregoing speculations with regard to the popular reaction to at least some actions of those who may be suffering from mental abnormality, then the distinction between blameless illness and culpable wrong may not be as pronounced in the popular psyche as our initial model suggested. Nor do we know to what extent responses to the diagnosis of illness, such as the whipping of the insane, may have reflected similar feelings of hatred and distrust, and a similar desire to distance the normal from the abnormal to those which we may find in the punishment of the wrongdoer. Certainly in some traditional societies a distinction between 'illness' and 'wrong' is much harder to draw. Amongst the Akawaio of Guyana, for example, illness is a symptom of wrong – either that of an individual, who is being punished by spirits or, if this proves an inappropriate explanation, the wrong of another community, which is employing witchcraft.[45] Similar attitudes towards misfortune are to be found in other societies, such as those of the Zande or the Lugbara.[46] Clearly for such peoples as the Akawaio no such comfortable distinction between 'illness' and 'wrong' would be feasible. The same point may be seen *a fortiori* in those cultures mentioned by Radcliffe-Brown in which illness is apparently not seen as a symptom of sin but as a sin in itself demanding expiation.[47]

Clearly, as illness is in some cultures regarded as a symptom of wrongdoing so the reader may be familiar with the argument that all crimes are a symptom of illness. Such an unabashed theory, which is

143

familiar in the well-worn debate as to whether punishment should give way to treatment, was particularly associated with a fairly recent school of thought, which, fuelled by scientific optimism, was committed to the ideal of penal rehabilitation. Today it is seldom seen in so unrestricted a form.[48] The major objection to the theory on conceptual grounds (there were many on practical grounds) was that 'crime' is a socially defined phenomenon, not at all similar to the scientifically observable objective abnormality of, say, a cancerous tumour. The argument (into which we shall not enter here) that medical conditions, or at least some of them, particularly as related to mental illness, are themselves socially defined in no way, of course, answers the objections to the treatability thesis of deviant social activity, the justifications for which have been strenuously challenged.[49]

The analogy between antisocial conduct and disease is by no means new in western jurisprudence. The 'quarantine' explanation for imprisonment, to prevent the spread of the 'contagion' of criminality goes back in England at least as far as the thirteenth century.[50] Nor again is it wholly restricted to European jurisprudence. Eskimos are reported to have reacted with disgust on an occasion when a man who had exposed a baby to die was whipped, opining 'To whip a man does not cure him', although it should be remembered that there is a close link between wrongdoing and disease in traditional Eskimo understanding.[51] Moreover, it is perhaps instructive to note how 'clinical' the process of execution has become in some cultures. In the United States some states allow for the death penalty to be carried out by injection; while the use of gas and electricity, as well as being designed to secure a 'clean' execution (with a doctor to pronounce when life is extinct), perhaps may also bear some connotations of the medical operation. For the use of both gases and electricity may possibly suggest the analogy of the use of techniques in medical contexts, anaesthesia and electro-convulsive therapy, for example.

A most remarkable case, which prompts speculation as to a number of issues, is given by Ehrenzweig.[52] The case concerns one of the most theoretically puzzling features of the Anglo-American legal tradition: the refusal to impose punishment, or at least certain types of punishment, on one who, notwithstanding his sanity at the time of the commission of the crime and at the time of trial, is found to be mentally disordered at the time at which punishment is due to be inflicted. In the context of our own discussion, of course, such a regulation is not a 'problem' to be rationalized by theory, but a social fact to be explained by investigation. In relation to the origin of this legal rule it would again seem probable that fear and superstition may have been more potent forces than justificatory theorems. The other interesting point about the case is the effort, using techniques clearly distinguished as medical in an attempt to get the accused ready for the gas-chamber (the use of the electric chair as the technique of execution would have made the point even clearer). A 34-year-old man, Henry Ford McCracken, according to the San Francisco Chronicle of 15 January 1953, 'has been given six electric shock treatments of the kind usually prescribed for insane persons' in an attempt to render the patient well enough to be killed. Recently, R. A. Duff has justified the sentence exemption on convicts mentally disordered at the time due for the infliction of sanction on the ground that punishment fails in its communicative function in such cases.[53] Yet perhaps it is the conformists who are the ones who fail to receive the appropriate communication – the gibbering madman on the scaffold is no longer sufficiently like them to confirm their conformity, and demons either literally or figuratively (in the form of guilt feelings) will be released on his death.

8

PUNISHMENT: AUTHORITIES AND AGENTS

At first sight the answer to the question 'Who punishes?' may seem straightforward, and it might appear to be simply a matter of investigation in each social situation of punishment to identify the actor taking the penal measure. However, the points stressed in our analysis of the essential elements of punishment and our insistence upon the diverse location of penal phenomena will have alerted the reader, it is hoped, to possible complexities. Moreover, before proceeding with an enquiry into the character of penal authority and agencies, there is a general point that could usefully be clarified at this stage. It follows from the view that we have taken of penal activity that breaches of the norms of one social group may, in fact, be dealt with by agencies within another group. This may come about through a substantive overlapping of norms and so of the possibility of punishment in more than one normative system – the situation we have already discussed in more detail in Chapter 3. For instance, an act of damage to property may all at once infringe rules of criminal law, family behaviour, and those of an educational institution. If punitive action is taken within just one of those systems, it is possibly also being taken on behalf of the authority of the other orders, so that the answer to the question of who punishes may be, from the point of view of the latter, the agents of another normative system. We have already explored the implications of this state of affairs and would only add at this point that we do not wish to be dogmatic (cf. Hart and others in their definition of punishment)[1] in insisting that a breach can only properly be punished by the authority of the system of norms thus breached. So to insist would fly in the face of social actuality. For that matter, a breach within one system may automatically qualify as one in another (for example, conviction for a particular criminal offence may violate minimum norms of professional conduct, so leading to expulsion from that profession).[2] There is nothing absurd or improper in this; nor does it undermine the cogency of the theoretical structure being presented here.

AUTHORITY AND AGENCY

That point apart, there are further complications in seeking to identify the author of penal action. In particular, it should be pointed out that in many social situations it is possible, and indeed important, to draw a distinction between a penal *authority* and a penal *agency*. In short, it may be seen that in many cases one person or entity will take the decision to punish, leaving the implementation of that punishment to another, and we shall use the terms 'authority' and 'agent' to convey these respective functions. Admittedly, there will be some contexts in which these two roles are vested in the same body. This fusion may well occur in relation to the punishment of relatively minor breaches, which invite a summary response: for instance, the parent or schoolteacher who reprimands a rebellious child, the master who beats his disobedient dog, the drill-sergeant who orders a fatigue. But fusion of authority and agent does not only occur in the context of minor violations, for many supernatural and 'popular' penal activities may not lend themselves to this kind of distinction. It is, in fact, difficult to be hard-and-fast in this kind of analysis. On the one hand, it would be possible theoretically to dissect the parent's summary punishment and assert that it has taken place in two stages, those of decision and implementation, although the act conveys the appearance of a mental and physical unity. On the other hand, supernatural authorities may send a plague of locusts,[3] or a Norman invasion,[4] or lynch mobs may nominate a hangman. In short, this distinction of functions may be useful as an analytical device and a tool of exposition; it has some explanatory force, but is not a definitional necessity, and therefore should not be pressed in all situations, especially when separation of the two functions would appear artificial in practice.

But since the division of authority and agency is observable with some frequency, and is also, of course, of great significance within western industrialized legal systems, it is necessary to say something concerning its prevalence. It is probable that it results from both logistical and psychological factors. Firstly, it is clear that in many situations the penal authority may be too many or too few to act as the agents of punishment. Too many, in that not all the members of the social group can administer, for instance, a flogging themselves nor would find it productive to sit outside the prison as guards. Too few, in that once a punitive authority has become established in the form of a tribal headsman or body of judges then they may not themselves have the resources to carry out the penalty as regards all wrongdoers within the society. And once such a division of labour is established, it may be seen that the skills associated with the authorization of punishment tend to be linked to the task of identifying the prior breach of a rule, and that these will be skills of a different order from those necessary to carry the punishment into effect. Moreover, a difference in social position is likely to result from this dichotomy of task. The sentencing judge may be admired and respected, the executioner hated and feared.

But this kind of argument from logistics may be less compelling when applied at a level below that of a total society and especially when the normative group under consideration is small, such as that of a family or classroom. Further explanations must then be sought. It may be, for example, that reference to an agent more distant in time and space may increase the drama of the penal communication, by producing an anticipation of the actual punishment and emphasizing its eventual occurrence by employing another person specially for that purpose. Another issue, which has been discussed earlier, may also be important in this respect. The deliberate infliction of unpleasantness is likely to be regarded by many as unpleasant in itself, even though clearly justified. Obviously, this statement begs a number of questions relating to cultural attitudes – warrior societies of both the past and present are likely to be far less squeamish in this regard than, for example, a British chartered accountant (or at least, a typical person of such a class!) None the less, particularly when the wrongdoer's body is the object of punishment, the latter may cause distress to the punitive assailant; even in societies where there is a frequent experience of interpersonal violence, such violence may be surrounded by a complex system of beliefs.[5]

In short, it is difficult to avoid the conclusion that the punitive act *may* be unpleasant for those who apply it and so give rise to feelings of guilt. In this way, it may become easier to understand those punishments to be discussed shortly, in which an animal or elemental force is used as executioner. Yet it is not only in such cases that these or

148

similar factors operate. Again, we shall shortly discuss the figure of the 'bogey man' used commonly in family situations as a deterrent penal agent – possibly so that parents may be absolved from feelings of guilt in their punitive action, possibly as an aid to holding the balance in the difficult and ambiguous twin task of discipline and nurture that the parental role entails. Such explanations are here advanced as a possible schema for interpretation: they may not commend themselves to all psychologists. Lloyd de Mause, for instance, writing a psychogeneric history of childhood, has urged that the bogey man figure is to be understood in connection with the projection of the parent's own unconscious in the parent's reaction to the child.[6]

Distaste for the inherent unpleasantness involved in penal action and possible consequent guilt are most convincing as explanations of the separation of penal authority and agency in those situations where the punishment is corporeal in character. 'Would you pull the handle?' is still a question considered significant enough to be asked in contemporary British argumentation about the use of capital punishment. There are, of course, invariably a number of people who answer 'yes' to this question (and may not even insist upon the traditional request of the hangman for forgiveness from his victim), notwithstanding that the question is posed in a society in which the slaughter of animals is carried out by specialists behind closed doors and in which even the most tranquil and natural death of human beings is ideally entrusted to the care of experts, the hospital and the undertaker. If the affirmative answer to the above question is both honest and representative of a majority opinion, then our preceding comments may be an overstatement, even as regards the society in which they are written. Certainly in earlier periods within this society there was no shortage of persons willing, and indeed eager, to witness executions taking place.[7] It was not a waning of public interest that led to the transfer of hangings in Britain to behind prison walls in 1868.[8] We find that as recently as July 1987, in Peking, 18,000 spectators were reported to have been present within an indoor sports stadium to witness the execution of ten murderers, robbers, and thieves.[9]

But, if our assertions on this point are accepted in relation to at least some instances of punishment, it should be conceded that the perceived unpleasantness and guilt potential involved in the administration of punishment is likely to be different only in degree rather than in kind when the agency is set apart from the authority.

149

Reference here may be made to our earlier discussion, where the value of the depersonalization of penal authority was indicated. Certainly in England, where the most severe afflictive punishments have been traditionally sited in courts of law, it is the 'dread majesty' of the law rather than the decision of individual human judges that is said to be responsible for the most serious penalties (and, interestingly, the identity of individual sentencers is seen to be relevant usually in cases of allegedly lenient decisions, particularly in discussion in the contemporary tabloid press).[10] It is also worth noting in this connection (as in many others) the role of supernatural judgment and punishment. For, in the medieval period, man was considered incompetent to judge his fellow man and God's judgment of fact, as revealed by a supernatural test, would be crucial, leaving only the mechanical application of the sanction to human agency.[11] Although this would seem to suggest the reverse of what was being argued earlier (that the infliction of a penalty may give rise to feelings of guilt despite its authorization), the balance would not seem to be constant across time and space. In a violent age, killing another in fulfilment of God's command (the ideology that underlay that medieval team sport known as the crusade) is unlikely to involve too much guilt on the part of the agent. In the English legal system, the accused's obligation to submit to the judgment of his fellow man was not established at law until as late as 1772.[12]

THE DECISION TO INVOKE OR DEFLECT THE PENAL PROCESS

A further problem in attempting to identify those persons who are responsible for the administration of punishment concerns the initial decision to invoke the punitive process, whoever may be in a position to take that decision. For instance, in some situations the penal authority may be rigid in its application of penalties, acting upon an inflexible legal, moral, or religious equation of offence and punishment (a system of 'fixed penalties'), and a potential case for punishment may not be referred for that reason. This preliminary decision as to referral is then, in effect, a decision as to who punishes, or, perhaps, who does not punish. Some examples will serve to illustrate this kind of decision-making and its ramifications.

Malinowski's research has shown that in a tribal society the decision to initiate a penal procedure may be of greater significance for purposes of punishment than the discovery of the commission of a wrong, since the former decision contains an element of discretion.[13] So whether or not to call for a decree of banishment is a discretionary decision; but once the penal procedure has been invoked, the tribal and ritual authority with which it is imbued leave no option but for its obedience.[14] This is, of course, generally true of decisions whether or not to prosecute within systems of criminal law or, in a different context again, a teacher's decision whether or not to refer a classroom offence to a headmaster. In each of these cases it may be felt that the decision to invoke the penal process will inexorably lead to a penal result that the referring agent may not wish for or see as appropriate.

Moreover, the character and role of this referring agent may differ from one context to another. It need not be somebody acting in an official capacity, such as a police officer, public prosecutor, teacher, or immediate hierarchical superior. In some situations this crucial role will be performed by the victim of the wrongdoing. When such an act occurs out of public view, the victim's decision to initiate penal proceedings may be crucial, and there may be a number of factors that could inhibit the desire to do so: shame or embarrassment connected with the offence, personal fear of the offender, conversely a love of or regard for the offender, or indifference to the matter, among others. In so far as ultimate punishment depends upon the victim's initial referral of the matter to others, the victim is then clearly one of the penal actors. And, it should be added, if the offender or another party can use devices such as blackmail or intimidation to deflect a penal referral, such persons also play an important, albeit essentially negative, role in the penal process. The offender also may play a positive role in this respect, for instance by 'turning himself in' to the police or 'owning up' to the teacher; we shall return to such a part being played by the offender later in the chapter.

The same point may be made in relation to later decisions in the penal process that may deflect the ultimate punishment, even though the matter has been referred to penal proceedings. This may be illustrated by reference to an important aspect of the history of English criminal procedure. At the time when sentencing for felonies was restricted to an order of capital punishment under a rigid and, at times, clearly oppressive penal code,[15] and when prosecutions were routinely brought under that code, flexibility based on a notion of popular justice was regularly introduced through the 'unofficial' action of a part of the official penal authority. 'Jury equity' would result in the acquittal of persons on charges of which they appeared guilty and punishment would be imposed by means of committal to custody before acquittal or following conviction for a less-serious offence, and the capital punishment thus deflected.[16] Recent research has suggested that this kind of popular mediation of a strict legal order may be as old as that form of centralized legal order itself.[17] But there is a tendency to stress the negative aspect of such intervention – the jury exempting the offender from the full rigour of the law – rather than its positive element in the form of an assertion of 'popular' penality (albeit that this begs significant questions as to whose 'popular' opinion the early jury represented). We shall return to this point later (see Chapter 10), where we shall discuss this phenomenon of exemption from a penalty regarded as disproportionate as in itself an application of a guiding principle of proportion. The point here, however, is simply to emphasize that the introduction of motive forces to the implementation, non-implementation, or variation of punishment prescribed by an official punitive authority is a crucial, even if complicating, factor to be borne in mind in attempting to identify the authors of penal action.

NON-CONVENTIONAL PENAL AUTHORITY AND AGENCY

It would not necessarily be useful to attempt an enumeration of all those actors who, in various contexts, take part in the administration of punishment. Such a list could include such diverse persons as parents, judges, teachers, executioners, and the 'hit men' of criminal gangs, and the list would surely be a long one with attendant arguments about categorization. We would propose, rather, to develop the discussion around certain themes, which may provide some general insights into the question of punitive authority and agency. Firstly, we wish to indicate the possibility of penal actors who are distinct from the more conventional paradigm of hierarchical and official human personnel – in particular we would draw attention to supernatural action, elemental and animal action, and the involvement of both offender and victim in the administration of punishment. Secondly, within the more conventionally familiar field of punishment by human officials appointed for such purposes, there are certain tendencies and tensions that deserve discussion. Finally, it would be useful to distinguish situations where the penal actors are more dispersed, especially in the context of 'popular' penality and of international sanctions.

Supernatural punishment

Frequently authority and agency are fused within the idea of supernatural punishment, which is widespread across time and place, although the actual beliefs that go to make up the concept of such punishment are manifold. Three main forms of supernatural administration of punishment can be considered here.

In the first place, in some belief structures the forbidden act will itself produce the spiritual punishment of the wrongdoer. In such cases no God or ancestral spirits take action and it would appear that the wrong itself directly affects the wrongdoer, often by tainting or polluting his soul. This was the way in which the nineteeth-century anthropologist Robertson Smith understood the Polynesian taboo (a form of social control) concerning the eating of certain forbidden food, consumption of which was held to cause illness.[18] 'The punishment of the impious', he argued, 'flows directly from the malignant influences resident in the forbidden thing, which so to speak avenges itself upon the offender.'[19] Such beliefs would not seem to be restricted to Polynesia, but would explain also, for example, the operation of Eskimo dietary taboos.[20]

Secondly, other systems rely on outraged ancestral spirits as both an authority and/or an agency for the punishment of human wrong. Examples of such belief systems have been mentioned already – that of the Lugbara, for example.[21]

Finally, there is the less-immediate supernatural intervention of the eschatological religions such as Islam and Christianity. Clearly, different faiths may have a different view of the punitivity of their God or Gods. Whether the tenet of many religions that man is made in the image of God is correct (and we have no power to judge) or whether Durkheim is correct in saying that religious forms are a reflection of human society (and though this may hold some truth there would seem to be no direct reflection in the phenomenology of different religions), the end result will often be the same: both God and man exercise punitive functions among their other roles.[22]

Even within societies in which the reality of the supernatural sanction is an important and unchallenged feature of the belief system, it is (as will, we hope, have become obvious) by no means the case that sanctions of this type are the only ones such societies will understand. Some of the anthropologists who have studied the Polynesian taboo system (Frazer, Marett, and Steiner) have drawn attention to the existence of social as well as spiritual sanctions that result from breach of taboo.[23] The interplay of supernatural and human penal systems in particular societies is an important and fascinating subject in its own right, but space forbids very much detailed discussion here. For example, a human sanctioning authority may purport to influence the liability of a wrongdoer to punishment in afterlife by ordering penalties of its own, such as penances.[24] On the other hand, a reminder that human punishment may be only the beginning of penal torment may provide a potent instrument of terror. In medieval Italy, convicted offenders being led to execution might have pictures (*tavolette*) of prospective punishment in Hell carried before them to concentrate their attention upon their penal fate;[25] while the artist Taddeo di Bartolo painted in the Duomo of San Gimignano in Florence a fresco of punishment in the afterlife, crowned by a defecating figure of Satan, pushing screaming sinners into his mouth, the same then emerging upside down from his anus, wearing mitres indicating the name of their sin.[26] Certainly, those who purport to speak in invocation of the punishment of God as well as that of man hold a powerful means of deterrence against those who believe in their authority to make such pronouncements.

One further example of human invocation of supernatural penality may be mentioned as demonstrating the breadth of this phenomenon. Among the Hopi Indians of North America, children might be threatened that if they behaved badly a representative of the spirit world would come to kidnap the child and cut off its head.[27] To reinforce this belief, on a certain day a man dressed as a horrible clown, armed with a knife and carrying a basket, would visit the village. A drama ensued, to which other children would listen and during which the clown would attempt to take a child while the parents would bar the entrance to the clown and would give him presents to buy off his spirit wrath. Not surprisingly, the child in question would promise to be good in the future. A number of points may be made about this penal drama. Firstly, we should note that the parents are the engineers of this deceit, yet by its operation will be seen by their child as its allies – thereby, we have suggested, reducing any parental feeling of guilt and resolving the ambiguous parental role in favour of its benign aspect. Secondly, similar results may of course be achieved through the invocation of 'bogey men' who need not be related to the spirit world and need not make a physical appearance (although the need for a staged appearance would seem to vary; it is by no means restricted to the Hopi – there is a documented example from England in 1748).[28] A glance at Western European history will show that use has been made for this purpose of supernatural beings (witches, monsters, devils, werewolves);[29] ethnic minorities (Jews, blackmen, gypsies);[30] personalities with a historical basis ['Bluebeard' (although the original had a red beard),[31] 'Boney' (i.e. Bonaparte, but the skeletal connotation probably helped)]; persons of unorthodox appearance (*le barbu* – the bearded man, the chimney sweep);[32] as well as the remote personification of state power ('the policeman') as the bogey man. A scarifying visual depiction of this penal device is supplied by the wood engraving from Heinrich Hoffmann's *Struwwelpeter* (*c.*1876) of such a bogey man attacking with a pair of shears the thumb of an errant thumb-sucking boy: 'Ah!' said Mamma, 'I knew he'd come to naughty little Suck-a thumb' reads the accompanying caption.[33]

Elements and animals

Even when a human authority has taken the decision to punish, this may be carried into effect through an agency that is both non-human and non-supernatural. So, for instance, the ostracism of a member of Eskimo society leaves the victim to face an ultimate fate that is dictated by the elements. But the connection may be closer still. A custom of the Borough of Portsmouth of about 1272 provides: 'if a woman sle a man she shall be teyed to a stake at lowe water and let the flod overflowe her at Catt Clyff'.[34] The immediate agent of punishment might even be an animal. The celebrated English Halifax Gibbet was in the form of a guillotine, which was operated by an animal pulling a rope when disturbed by the noise of the crowd.[35] This points to a suggestive situation – that the whole local community might, by making the noise, be involved in the execution of the errant member, but no single individual would bear the taint of the executioner (in the same way as it is often the custom for the members of a firing squad not to know which of them fired the fatal bullet). It is perhaps a paradox that we may see in the desire to punish animals a need to affix responsibility (see the discussion in the next chapter), while in this case the punishment by an animal would seem, in part at least, to indicate an attempt to abnegate responsibility.

The wrongdoer

The wrongdoer himself may be the agent of his own punishment in some instances. Indeed, he may act as both authority and agent, as when guilt is produced by an act the individual knows to be wrong. Such guilt, although it may attain pathological levels, may not manifest itself in any harm to the body viewed externally; but sometimes in extreme cases it may do so, at least in literature. So Oedipus, experiencing guilt at the killing of his father and his incestuous liaison with his mother, blinds himself.[36]

There have also existed societies in which we find punishing systems, under which even suicide is regarded as the socially correct way of dealing with an offence, not against self-judged norms but against norms as judged by others. Of course, such a distinction may not be easy to draw in practice, and we would not wish to make any generalizations at all about the aetiology of suicide as a whole. In the kind of case we have in mind, the individual's self-destruction may be characterized as the act simply expected or demanded of a wrongdoer in certain societies. In this way, Socrates is presented with the cup of hemlock in prison to end his own life after condemnation by the court,[37] and similarly our caricature of the army officer depicts the dishonoured man left in a locked room with a pistol and the muttered injunction 'You know what to do, old man'. Less dramatically, perhaps, the dishonoured Japanese gangster (*Yakuza*) will sever one of his fingertips in acknowledged, though not fatal, self-punishment.[38]

A variant upon this theme of using the wrongdoer as the agent of his own punishment may be seen in the practice of obliging offenders to mutilate themselves. Instead of cutting off the offender's hand or ear, the community forces the victim to do it himself. This practice is referred to, for example, in the seventeenth-century verse of 'miners' law' from the English North Midlands:

> For stealing oar twice from the minery
> The thief that's taken twice fined shall be
> But the third time that he commits such theft
> Shall have a knife stuck through his hand to the haft
> Into the stow and there to death shall stand
> Or loose himself by cutting loose his hand,
> And shall forswear the franchise of the mine,
> And always lose his freedom from that time.[39]

156

Moreover, following from the point made at the beginning of this chapter, a person may claim to be a penal actor by setting in train the operation of another punitive order. In this way, of course, the offender who gives himself up to the appropriate authority and confesses his own guilt, may be characterized as an agent of his own punishment. It may be, of course, that self-punishment, and also the infliction of punishment by 'inappropriate agencies', could run counter to the exercise of penal power by the agency that regards itself or is widely regarded by others as the primary one. Significantly, such punishment may deprive the dramatic visitation of communal disapproval of its most important actor. Sterling Rault, a convicted murderer executed in 1987, observed, two days before his execution: 'The guards have been nicer to me since they knew I was going to die. They are afraid I might kill myself and cheat the system.'[40]

THE VICTIM OF THE WRONG

It is clearly possible in some cases, where a wrong involves injury to an ascertainable individual, that such an aggrieved person may act as an agent of punishment. Where such a person acts as both penal authority and agent, it may be difficult to distinguish such action from revenge, and the reader is here referred to our discussion in the previous chapter of the distinction between punishment and revenge and our earlier observations on the value of depersonalization within the framework of punishment.

But it is still worth remarking that, even in systems that employ a distanced penal authority, an aggrieved individual may be obliged to act as an agent of punishment if the penalty is directed against the wrongdoer's body. It may be in such cases that a desire for revenge will be satisfied, although subsumed beneath the *aegis* of penal authority and so distanced from simple vengeance. On the other hand, as we have already indicated, the victim may be unwilling to execute such an unpleasant office. To illustrate both the practice referred to here and the agent's unwillingness to carry out the punishment, we may look again at an aspect of English legal history: the custom, well attested in some localities in the medieval period, of obliging the prosecutor in a criminal action (usually the victim of the offence or, where this was not possible, a kinsman) to himself execute judgment. To take the example of a custom of Romney, which does, however, allow the complainant the option of delegating his burden, we learn from a custumal of 1498 that if after a private prosecution the malefactor confesses: 'the bayleff shall fynde the galowys and the rope and, the suter [suitor] which maketh the appele shall fynde the hangman. And if he may fynde non hangman neither that he wyll noght do that same office himself, he shall dwelle in prison with the felon unto the time that he wyll do that office or else find an hangman.'[41] In other customs of this kind, the use of a surrogate is not mentioned and the obligation on the complainant would seem to have been personal.

A familiar extension of the idea of the wronged individual is that of the wronged family or kinship group. It is well known that kinship groups are of paramount importance in the phenomenology of many social groupings. An indication of the penal role of such groups has already been provided in connection with the prosecution of blood-feuds. We have also seen that in a kinship-based system a feud may, as each clan authorizes one or all of its members to avenge the wrong done to them, escalate into a vendetta, which may threaten the existence of the total society unless measures are taken to prevent this. For a literary and historical depiction of this problem, reference may be made to the theme and narrative of one of the leading works of Icelandic medieval literature, *Njal's Saga* (and note our earlier observations at p. 109).[42]

THE ART OF SENTENCING

In view of the crucial relation between punishment and rule-breaking it is not surprising to find, as we have indicated, that the person or institution who determines whether or not a breach has occurred is commonly also given the task of choosing the appropriate punishment: the criminal court or tribunal serves also, in many systems, as the sentencing body. The term 'sentence' (L. *sententia*, Fr. *sentence*) connotes an authoritative statement or opinion or a judgement and is widely used in western legal systems to describe the decision-making process whereby a punishment is determined in relation to a convicted criminal. The institution of a sentencing tribunal is now a global phenomenon and its counterpart may be found in less-centralized societies, even though the form taken there may be more akin to arbitration or a convention of community representatives or elders. There are some points to be made about this process of 'sentencing' as it occurs within state legal systems, especially in relation to the desirability of fusing the role of breach identification with that of choice of punishment.

Interestingly, the main challenge to this state of affairs has arisen from the utilitarian argument that the typical members of a tribunal tend to lack expertise in terms of penal knowledge and experience to choose the most suitable form of punishment. Implicit in this kind of claim is a view of punishment as a reformative or deterrent device, requiring individualization as regards both quantum and character in order to produce the optimum forward-looking effect in terms of crime reduction. It has been contended, for instance, that legally trained judges in the field of criminal law have an insufficient knowledge of the operation of rehabilitative programmes or of the assessment of deterrent measures to make an informed choice.[43] In defence of the judicial role in sentencing, it is often claimed (and convincingly so) that the legally trained sentencer guarantees a sense of due process and proportionality of action in the exercise of the sentencing function and may be responsive to wider, more popular feeling on the subject of criminal offending.[44]

In truth, the arguments that have urged the replacement of judicial sentencers by panels of 'penal experts' are to an extent a reflection of the developing confidence and assertiveness of the executory person-nel in the field of legal punishment: the fact that the agents responsible for putting into effect penal measures have acquired a more auton-omous and professional identity.[45] The natural interest of the penal agent in the implementation, practicalities, and impact of punish-ment may provoke a prior claim for technical over juridical consider-ations, which in turn provokes misgivings about the possibility of arbitrary punishment or the unqualified pursuit of utilitarian aims. These arguments have been rehearsed in detail elsewhere and form an important topic within the field of contemporary penology.[46] It is sufficient for present purposes to note that the dichotomy of function between penal authorities and agencies has given rise to this im-portant debate – at least in the context of western penal systems – as to the respective roles of the judge and executive personnel in the determination of formal punishment. This is a debate that is likely to continue and at the same time produce some hybrid institutions that fuse the two functions in question: the British Parole Board or the French *juge de l'application des peines*, for example.[47] Moreover, this point emphasizes the existence of a common tension between penal authority and penal agent.

159

THE PROFESSIONALIZATION OF PUNISHMENT

It may be appropriate at this point to indicate the increasing complexity and sophistication in the practice of punishment in many modern societies, especially in so far as such punishment is supplied by state agencies. It would be no exaggeration to refer, in contemporary terms, to a widespread penal industry, comprising a diverse range of professionals, sometimes with overlapping roles: prison officers and governors, probation officers and correctional agents, medical, psychiatric, and teaching auxiliaries, not to mention those who, one step removed, are now involved in monitoring and assessing various aspects of the state's penal endeavours, the researchers and the penologists. As we have just observed, there is a tendency for such personnel increasingly to distance themselves from the authorities who decide upon punishment and thereby acquire a distinct professional interest based upon their specific roles within the penal system. The outcome of this professional development is a network of differing perspectives, which could be sufficiently demonstrated by a one-hour seminar within a penal institution, involving prison governors, prison officers, and probation personnel. It would be surprising to observe in such a discussion no division of views or purposes, and significant differences in professional self-perception may be revealed in such a situation.

The professionalization of the executory arm of punishment has been stimulated no doubt by the increasingly ambitious role, certainly in western culture, of the state in supplying punishment. It reflects a growth in the quantum of state punishment as well as a developing sophistication of purpose. But contained within this development are the seeds of longer-term problems and tensions. Most importantly, the distance between judicial and technical interests is productive of contradictions in official policy. Thus penal agents, on the one hand, may ponder the difficulty of persuading judicial sentencers to make less use of imprisonment,[48] while judges contemplate the need for and wisdom of their intervention in the internal operation of the prison system to guarantee fair treatment of prisoners.[49]

Such tensions are not novel. Rather, it is the dimension of the problem, most importantly in the context of state penal systems, that is notable. In those situations in which the executory role in the administration of punishment is limited to capital or corporeal action, there is less scope for the emergence of an autonomous professional concern on the part of the penal agent. But even in such cases there remains some possibility of modifying in execution the intentions of the penal authority: the act, for instance, of the merciful executioner who despatches the subject of capital punishment before an act of disembowelling, which has been decreed by the sentencer (or, at an earlier stage and from another source, the deflection of punishment through the process of 'jury equity', to which we have already referred). However, it is more obviously in the case of longer-term penalties, typically those entailing some form of incarceration or supervision, that the more autonomous self-image of the penal agent has evolved. Naturally, for practical reasons, the administration of this kind of punishment needs to be delegated to agents appointed within the penal system. But deviation from or modification of the intention and policy of the sentencer may well trespass against the latter's self-perception as the paramount decision-maker. Judicial sentencers in modern western penal systems have been notoriously suspicious of indeterminate measures, which leave to the penal agencies an important discretion in determining the character and extent of the punishment, and have likewise (especially in a British context) been resistant to legislative attempts to prescribe a more specific structure for their decisions.[50]

None of this should be surprising when the respective roles of penal authority and agent are subject to some little reflection. The former, in deciding upon the punishment, will in many contexts be perceived as acting as the representative of the society or social group in question, being authorized to express and act upon the general disapproval of the offending conduct. In taking this decision, the penal authority or sentencer will naturally be mindful of the wider social interests to be served by the process of punishment: hence the typical concern of the sentencer with issues of proportionality, equivalence, protection of society, and the expression of general sentiment. The task of the penal agent is naturally more specific and individualized, having to carry into effect the measure decided upon and witness the impact of punishment in individual cases. Any tendency to respond to each individual's experience of punishment, in whichever direction, is predictably human, and to a large extent rehabilitative ideas in connection with state punishment have encouraged such a response. Such identification of the distinctive roles performed by those who give effect to penal systems may seem to be stating the

161

obvious. Yet it is an aspect of the subject that deserves emphasis, which then enables us to see more clearly important internal tensions, particularly within state penal systems, and to appreciate the impulse that underlies a number of contemporary attempts to establish greater 'legal' control over the operation of formal punishment.

DIFFUSE PENAL AGENCIES

In some situations, especially outside the framework of formal, legally determined and administered state punishment, the infliction of penal measures may be delegated to or performed by a less specifically identifiable form of agency. The operation of social ostracism and measures of expulsion, of community responses such as *charivaris* and 'rough music' or wider public opinion, of consequential sanctions such as loss of employment and other expected entitlements or of measures of disqualification, and of the punitive reaction of individual states in the context of international relations, may all demonstrate the reliance upon wider social groupings with less immediately apparent structured penal apparatus to give effect to punishment. In such cases the imposition of the penal measure is naturally less predictable. Individual members of a social group may be more or less committed to exercising a penal role and more or less efficient in performing that role. At the same time, such 'popular' sanctions may not be very easy to monitor by those who have authorized them. Banishment depends for its effect on the willingness of individual members of society to maintain the exclusion of the subject of the measure and to limit their intercourse with that person; sanctions ordered by the United Nations depend upon the willingness of individual member states to apply them. In both of these examples, the self-interest or indolence of those to whom the process of punishment has been delegated may obstruct the efficient application of such measures (so further exemplifying the possible tension between authority and agency discussed in the preceding section). In the light of such situations, the relative dependability and efficiency of the 'professional' agents of state penal systems, who have a more rigorous view of the subject of punishment by virtue of their very professionalism, becomes particularly evident. The perception of this fact may be one factor in the tendency to bring a wider range of conduct within the scope of state penal processes, thereby ensuring a more predictable, reliable, and uniform response to rule-breaking. In this way, some instances of what we have referred to as 'popular' punishment have, especially in the context of modern western society, been relegated to a supplementary role, providing an additional expression of disapproval in situations in which the formal response may have been considered inadequate. At the same time, informal responses have more and more come to be regarded with disfavour, since they may appear, in comparison with legal sanctions, as arbitrary and crude in their impact.

However, in the field of international relations diffuse penality remains of much greater practical significance. In a society of sovereign states the implementation of sanctions is inevitably problematical and disapproval of rule-breaking conduct expressed by other states is one of the main factors in securing compliance with rules of international law. In the practice of the United Nations,[51] universally administered sanctions are rarely agreed upon and, even when this does happen, 'sanction-busting' (i.e. non-compliance) in some form must realistically be expected (as for instance in the case of economic sanctions against Rhodesia),[52] or the sanctions themselves may not be the most damaging that could have been employed (as is true of the embargo on the sale of arms to South Africa).[53] On the other hand, we should guard against a glib dismissal of the impact of international penal measures. In the first place, in this context informal disapproval may have greater effect than organized measures. Most governments do not wish to be cast as law-breakers, if only for reasons of long-term self-interest, and would prefer not to be vociferously condemned in a United Nations General Assembly debate. Such penality has a diplomatic rather than a material character. Secondly, unilateral response on the part of individual states may have considerable impact. Targeting of delinquents, especially in the area of human rights violations, may be very effective, particularly if the sanction comprises withdrawal of economic or military aid.[54] Such action is usually justified as a reaction to a perceived breach of international law, the state in question acting as a kind of representative for the wider international community. Again, while self-interest may be an important motivation (for instance, a cynic might argue that Australia and Canada have something to gain in economic terms from the implementation of Commonwealth sanctions, which they urge, against South Africa),[55] such an interest would not affect the penal characterization of such measures, or necessarily their propriety, since they remain a response to international wrongdoing (unless it were in fact the case that the wrongdoing provided only the opportunity, rather than the reason, for the application of the sanction – see the discussion in Chapter 6 on this question). It would seem strange, as a general rule, to oppose the application of punishment on the ground simply that those giving effect to it take an incidental benefit, and this, after all, is one of the rationales of pecuniary penalties. In relation to unilateral measures, the main problem would appear to be related to inconsistency in support and application.

Once again, it may be useful to recall the finding of Willcock and Stokes that the diffuse, informal response of the family and other persons of significance in the personal sphere may be of greater importance to potential offenders than any concern about legal punishment.[56] In seeking to distinguish between formal and informal penal agencies, we should, of course, note the sophistication of the penal apparatus now in the service of the state, but at the same time should not fail to recognize the practical significance of those persons who are not officially designated as penal agents. In reality, the latter may not occupy such a peripheral position as much of the discussion of punishment tends to suggest. The sex offender sentenced to imprisonment will inevitably apprehend the reaction of his fellow prisoners more than that of the prison authorities.[57] The person of reputation and status may fear more for his self-esteem and self-image than the immediate unpleasantness of the penalty imposed by the state. A powerful state may be confident that no formal sanction will ensue from an act of international law-breaking, yet still count the cost of the effect of a general condemnation on its relations with crucial allies.[58] Moreover, we should bear in mind the possibility of incorporating more formally community representation into the penal process: the model of sentencing in some European systems, where the decision is jointly taken by a judge and a jury, clearly demonstrates the potential, beneficial or otherwise, for an osmosis of formal and popular penality.[59] Generally, such points should alert us to the spread of the penal mesh and remind us that penal agents do not have to be uniformed officials but may appear in the guise of the media, friends, or even something as nebulous as posterity.

9

PUNISHMENT: THE SUBJECT

When attempting to supply an answer to the general question 'Who is punished?' it may be helpful to draw distinctions at a number of levels. Firstly, we would say (in contrast to much of the existing discussion of the subject) that the basic subjects of punishment may include, alongside what may appear to be obvious (i.e. human beings), also the less-discussed categories of animals and inanimate objects. Nor, we would argue, is this a fanciful extension of the discussion. The punishment of both the latter categories, although often relegated to the level of primitive social practice, may serve important psychological and social purposes.

Secondly, within the category of human subjects of punishment we may draw some further subdivisions, the most useful of which we would suggest to be: (a) the immediate offender, (b) collective punishment, (c) vicarious punishment, and (d) scapegoats. Situation (a) is said, in some of the philosophical literature,[1] to represent the 'standard' or 'central' case of punishment: that of an offender for committing an offence. Situations (b), (c), and (d) are often considered, at least in terms of western jurisprudence, to give rise to doubts concerning the justice of such measures, since in each of these situations the subject of the penalty is not, or may not be, the perpetrator of the offending conduct that gives rise to punishment. We may also extend the discussion to include the punishment of persons *in absentia*, a situation that suggests an attenuated form of punishment, although, it should be noted, not necessarily for that reason one that lacks impact, as may be seen from the example of the Florentine *pitture infamanti*, to be discussed below. A further departure from the normal range of discussion would be to include, alongside inanimate objects, the question of penal action against the expression of ideas as distinct from measures taken against the physical integrity of the author of such ideas. As elsewhere in our discussion, we would hope that this ramification of the subject will bring into clearer relief some of the debate and practical problems involved generally in the practice of punishment.

Finally, we may note that the character, position or status of the subject may have a bearing on the method of punishment or the likelihood of punishment. Social rank, for example, may have its effects in the practice of punishment, as for instance in the idea that decapitation befits a subject of higher status, whereas hanging is a more appropriate form of execution for somebody of lower rank. Then again, the problem of differential enforcement of criminal law is a well-established topic of contemporary penology. We should not therefore lose sight of the important relation that may exist between the elements of the subject and mode of punishment.

THE PUNISHMENT OF ANIMALS

We should stress at the outset that this is not merely a fanciful area of the discussion of punishment. Firstly, corrective or deterrent functions of punishment (if understood in a purely functional way rather than implying rational calculations) may in some situations be sensibly referred to in relation to animals. It is clear that some animals may respond to adverse human reaction and belief in the practice of 'training' animals to behave in a certain way demonstrates the potential for such an area of penal practice. A dog brought up in a certain household may be expected to act according to the domestic norms for pet animals; if not, we must be forced to ridicule the common sight of a man shouting 'Down Boy!' or growling 'Bad Dog!' at a delinquent animal. Nor is the widespread agricultural practice of hanging up a line of dead birds as a warning to others done without serious intention. The punishment of animals may therefore have a significant practical dimension. But, in addition, the punishment of such subjects may be seen as a response to more elusive psychological needs.

In 1457 in Savigny in Burgundy, a 5-year-old child, Jehan Martin, was savaged and killed by a sow and six piglets. The pigs were taken into custody and brought to trial a month later before the seigneurial justice of Burgundy. The owner of the pigs, Jehan Bailly, was the formal defendant in these proceedings but was on trial only for negligence and ran no risk of personal punishment. He was also given the opportunity to put forward any reason why the sow should be spared (as it were, to present a plea in mitigation) but this right was waived. There was no doubt, from the testimony of the witnesses, concerning the responsibility of the sow for the death of the child and the prosecutor demanded the death sentence. The judge consulted with experts in local law and then pronounced sentence according to the custom of Burgundy: hanging by the hind legs from a suitable tree, the sentence being duly performed at a later date by a hangman from Chalon-sur-Saône. The evidence relating to the piglets was ambiguous, since the most that could be proven was that they were bloodstained. They were therefore remanded to the custody of their owner, who was required to vouch for their future behaviour; when he refused to do so, they were declared forfeit to the local lord's justice, although they were not punished in any way.[2]

Such criminal trial of animals was a common phenomenon in some parts of Western Europe, especially between the fourteenth and seventeenth centuries, and the subject has excited some controversy of interpretation.[3] There appear to have been two main forms of proceeding: secular, as in the case of Jehan Bailly's sow, where the animal was within the reach of the secular authorities; and ecclesiastical, where the animals were not physically in custody and often represented some unwelcome natural invasion (for example, 'plagues' of rats or insects). Both types of proceeding were characterized by a painstaking concern for procedural regularity and due process. Bartholomé Chassenée, when acting as advocate for the rats of Autun, pleaded that their failure to appear in court when summoned was due to their fear of cats, and he therefore demanded a safe conduct for the accused.[4]

It would be presumptuous to dismiss such proceedings and punishment of animals as primitive or superstitious; it is as well to remember that anthropomorphism remains significant as a literary device to the present day. As Esther Cohen argues:

> the trials fulfilled certain necessary functions. While they settled no disputes and kept no peace, they were important in other ways. They defined man's relationship with the animal kingdom by virtue of his judicial rights over it. They re-affirmed society's self-image as universally just. Finally, the ecclesiastical trials

provided the setting for a communal ritual of self and environ-ment purification from inimical forces.[5]

Whilst this argument may represent a rather narrow interpretation of the 'settlement of disputes', its substance would appear to be compelling.

It is in such a context that we can see especially clearly that function of penality that responds to a deep-felt need to provide order in human affairs. Humans have to co-exist with the animal world and to a large extent also control it. When animal behaviour impinges too far upon human arrangements, a punitive response, while it may not be so meaningful in corrective terms, may none the less serve a useful function in reasserting a sense of order and defining the hierarchy normally to be observed amongst various life forms, while admitting that on occasion this natural order may be upset by unruly animal behaviour.[6] Such ideas do not lack literary exploration (witness, for example, the obsessive quest of Captain Ahab in Melville's *Moby Dick*)[7] and this kind of hierarchical instinct is investigated in more abstract terms by D. H. Lawrence:

> Life moves in circles of power and of vividness, and each circle of life only maintains its orbit upon the subjection of some lower circle. If the lower circles of life are not mastered, there can be no higher cycle.[8]

THE HUMAN OFFENDER

Clearly, this is the most commonly perceived subject of punishment. However, there are a number of senses in which a human being may be the subject of a penal measure (as well, obviously, as a number of ways, as we shall discuss in the next chapter). The paradigm subject of punishment in western jurisprudence is the specific perpetrator of the offending conduct: he or she who physically kills, does violence, commits theft, damages property, disobeys orders, commits adultery, or whatever else constitutes prohibited conduct. The idea of imposing punishment upon the physical perpetrator of the offending action presupposes a sense of individual responsibility that is especially strong in western culture. Other cultures may admit a greater degree of collective or group responsibility in interpreting human behaviour and so may extend the net of punishment accordingly (see the discussion below).

In terms of both morality and policy it may not always be regarded as sufficient to punish only the immediate perpetrator of the offence. For instance, a person who physically carries out an act of killing, violence or interference with property may have been encouraged or materially assisted by another or others. In such cases, moral arguments concerning culpability and considerations of penal policy will often bring the accomplice within the reach of the penal measure: certainly, many criminal codes provide for ancillary offences, based on notions such as conspiracy, aiding and incitement.[9] There may also be difficulty in identifying the perpetrator of the offending action if the chain of events leading to the prohibited outcome is attenuated. Is the man who leaves his enemy's senseless body in a perilous situation – in a burning building or across a railway track – with fatal consequences, to be regarded as the killer of such a victim?[10] Such problems of causation and agency may give rise to difficult jurisprudential deliberations, notably within state systems of criminal law, but also under other systems of rules. Such debate concerning the identification of perpetrators of offending conduct provides the meat of systems of substantive criminal law.

Mention above of persons who may be connected in some way with the commission of offending conduct leads naturally to a discussion of the categories of collective and vicarious punishment. But firstly, some explanation of our use of these terms may be helpful. We do not intend to use the term 'collective punishment' to describe the case where a number of individual offenders are proceeded against and punished together for reasons of administrative convenience (for instance, the members of a rioting crowd who are dealt with together in respect of their individual offences committed in the riot). Rather, we use the term to indicate the situation where a group of persons is punished as a group for conduct emanating from that group, irrespective of whether such conduct was perpetrated by all or a limited number of its members. This bears some similarity to the employment of vicarious punishment, whereby a person who stands in some relation to the actual offender is punished in place of that offender. But, for purposes of exposition, we shall treat the two situations separately.

COLLECTIVE PUNISHMENT

The term 'collective punishment', then, is intended here to convey the practice of taking punitive action on the basis of group responsibility for wrongdoing. The notion of collective responsibility for behaviour tends to run counter to the tradition of individual autonomy that is especially pronounced in western culture, but in some other contexts group solidarity has been sufficiently taken for granted as to justify collective penalties. In societies in which the kinship group is of greater social significance than the individual, the kin as a whole may be considered both collectively responsible for an individual member's act and be expected to take action on behalf of a wronged member of the group. Such 'kinship responsibility' is often referred to as giving rise to 'collective punishment' (for instance, some social anthropologists use such terms),[11] but may equally be categorized as a form of vicarious punishment, and so we shall consider it, in the next section of the discussion. Some collective sanctions may also be described as indiscriminate in their impact, since they may affect technically innocent people within the group. But such a view misses an essential point of collective responsibility in one significant formula of its application: that membership of the group in itself gives rise to responsibility for the group's conduct. In this way, the biblical Noah, and his counterparts in numerous other early traditions of a massive deluge,[12] in being exempted from the general destruction rendered that instance of collective punishment somewhat imperfect. On the other hand, pogroms, 'crusades', and other penal persecutions of distinctive or dissident groups may more accurately be described as instances of collective punishment.[13]

In a twentieth-century context, the idea that the people of nations or states may be collectively responsible for conduct not approved in the wider international community has given rise to attempts at internationally organized collective punishment. In the eyes of some national leaders at the end of the First World War, the reparations demanded of Germany took into account the general offence of the German people in conducting the war.[14] Both the British Prime Minister, Lloyd George, and the American President, Woodrow Wilson, spoke forcibly about the need to punish Germany. Lloyd George told his War Cabinet in August 1918 that the terms of peace must amount to 'some penalty for the offence'; and he went on to say in Parliament in July 1919 that since the whole German nation had wholeheartedly backed a war of aggression, the whole nation must be punished.[15] Such moralism in the conduct of international relations also characterized the view of Woodrow Wilson, which was informed by the idea of collaboration between the German people and their government. In a speech in September 1919 he argued: 'The nation

170

permitted itself, through unscrupulous governors, to commit a criminal act against mankind, and it is to undergo the punishment . . . it must pay for the wrongs it has done.'[16] The amount of reparation demanded (132,000,000,000 gold marks) and the consequences for the international community of this demand, represent a great advance on earlier examples of such collective penality. When the German King Henry VII wished to punish the entire city of Florence in 1311 for resisting his attempts to control Italy, it was by means of a publicly posted 'defamatory' proclamation (*in alba*, i.e. in 'black and white').[17]

It is likely that many would now reject the idea of a collective subject of punishment, as revealing an oversimplified interpretation of human behaviour. According to such a view, if it is ever possible to identify wrongdoing on such a large collective scale, it would be unrealistic not to recognize that within such a large collectivity there would be leaders in the offending activity, those who participated through apathy, those who did so through fear or hysteria, and those who did so with reservation or even objection. The psychology of a pogrom, for example, is complex, and the ascription to each participating individual the same degree of moral responsibility a crude calculus.[18] While it is clear that collective responsibility falls foul of the widely accepted concept of individual autonomy, so giving rise to moral objection, the practice may also provoke a critical response on practical grounds: its crudity as a reaction to undesired behaviour reveals a functional weakness, in that its indiscriminate and totalitarian sweep *within* the collectivity fails to address itself to the source of offending or dissent and perceives a spurious and metaphysical unity of action and purpose in the conduct in question. In contrast to the general scope of punishment advocated in 1918, the War Crime Tribunals in 1945 rejected the argument that the individual could submerge his offending role within the greater one of the group.[19] Collective punishment may be seen by some as a convincing strategy only in a context in which the promotion of a greater sense of communal responsibility can be seen as a feasible outcome. In a situation where members of a group are highly interdependent and have a real element of mutual control over each individual's behaviour as a member of the group, collective punishment may have a meaningful role to play. In such a way it may be fruitful to apply a sanction generally to children within a family, a class within a school, or a unit within an army, where the maintenance of standards and

171

discipline may be seen as a matter of communal responsibility, reliant upon mutual scrutiny. But in such situations it is precisely the mutual responsibility for one's fellows that supplies the moral justification for collective punishment. Viewed in this way, the members of the collectivity are then being punished for their own part in the breach of the norm.

VICARIOUS PUNISHMENT

This term is usually applied to the situation where a person is punished, not for physically committing an offence, but on the basis of a particular relationship with the actual perpetrator. The term vicarious derives from the Latin *vicarius*, meaning 'substitute', and so in a literal sense conveys the idea of one who is punished in substitution for another. However, this simple idea of substitution requires some elaboration if the differing possibilities of vicarious punishment are to be fully appreciated.

In the first place, one of the most well-established instances of vicarious penalty arises in the context of kinship groups, who will stand in place of an individual offending member for purposes of receiving punishment (just as in modern state legal systems, parents may be answerable for delinquent acts of their children). This has been (and remains in some areas) a widespread phenomenon.[20] As noted above, such punishment has sometimes been termed 'collective', but we would prefer to categorize it as 'vicarious' since it is not the offence of the group that is being punished but the offence of a particular member or members with punishment being transferred to the members of the group as a whole. This may be more clearly appreciated by noting the practice in some societies of expelling a persistently offending member who has engaged group liability too frequently for the tolerance of the group as a whole. Thus Falk Moore (who, incidentally, uses the expression 'collective responsibility' in this context) argues: 'where every member of a corporate group has the power to commit it in this way to a collective liability, a corollary rule always exists whereby the corporation may discipline, expel or yield up to enemies members who abuse this power'.[21] The Lango, for instance, would drive away one of their number who had imposed upon them too often in this way.[22] Indeed, this would seem to be a general phenomenon: there would appear to be many contexts in which collectivities such as kinship groups or corporations will accept responsibility for their members' wrongs but at the same time may internally discipline such individuals, so evidencing different layers of penality.

There is another, wider and less structured, sense in which we can refer to a practice as vicarious punishment. This involves the situation in which persons related to or associated with the perpetrator of an offence are punished, here literally and intentionally as substitutes for a known or unreachable offender, and not so much through any idea of group responsibility but rather for cruder reasons of deterrence (in the same way that witnessing the torture of a loved one may be equally, if not more, persuasive in extracting information or a confession than torture of the person from whom the latter are sought). The moral, not to say legal, validity of such 'exemplary' vicarious penality is now very much open to doubt and it may be that the objection is rooted in a common popular notion of justice of the kind we have already discussed. Notorious instances of such measures in a state context – for instance, the wholesale flogging of women ordered by the Austrian general Julius Haynau after the suppression of the Hungarian revolt in 1849;[23] or the execution of the entire male population of the Bohemian village of Lidice in 1942 as a reprisal for the assassination of the Gestapo commander Reinhard Heydrich – would now qualify as war crimes under international law.[24] Whatever may be the moral reaction to such punishment of 'innocents', it cannot be doubted that measures of that kind retain for some a seductive deterrent appeal. It is just because actual or potential offenders may be so appalled at such action being taken against their family, friends, or neighbours that they may be induced to conform their behaviour, whereas the prospect of their own punishment may not have achieved that result. One of the major problems faced by those who seek to justify punishment in consequentialist terms is how to avoid conceding propriety to practices that appear manifestly unjust.

In fact, this category of vicarious punishment is a well-established practice, and is clearly evidenced in the custom of hostage-taking. The latter is not simply a device employed by desperate or unscrupulous terrorists; it has often been formalized as a generally accepted means of supplying security for good behaviour. The Romans, for example, were in the practice of taking the sons of tributary princes as a security for the continuing loyalty of the conquered nation and such hostages were liable to punishment or even to be killed in the case of treachery or refusal to fulfil promises.[25] A more recent example of formal hostage-taking may be seen in the French Revolutionary law passed as a means of dealing with the uprising in La Vendée.[26] Under this law, relatives of emigrés were taken from disturbed districts and were imprisoned. Sequestration of their property and deportation from France followed upon the murder of a republican – four to every such murder, with heavy fines imposed on the whole body of hostages. Interestingly, this measure appeared to provoke further insurrection, indicating perhaps the operation of a popular conception of morality. The weight of opinion in modern international law suggests that hostages should be treated as prisoners of war and so should not be subject to such penalties.[27] In addition, both hostage-taking and the use of 'collective' (i.e. vicarious) penalties in relation to civilians are listed as prohibited practices under Articles 33 and 34 of Geneva Convention IV of 1949 and under Protocols I and II of 1977,[28] which contain a presumption of civilian status for all non-combatants. In contemporary terms, therefore, there is an overwhelming moral condemnation of such vicarious penalties.

It is noteworthy that such measures are commonly employed in situations where the validity of the underlying norms is strongly under question, as in the case of the rule of an occupying power, or *a fortiori* in a situation involving a conflict of norms. In this last category, we may include the acts taken by terrorist bodies (the taking hostage or even killing of certain nationals or other representatives of an opposing group) and those favoured by the criminal underworld (which may extend, to use some literary and cinematic examples, to the decapitation of a cherished horse,[29] or the vandalizing of a lawyer's Rolls-Royce car).[30] There may, then, be a double source of objection concerning such instances of vicarious punishment: the suffering of innocent persons (or animals), and the propriety of the normative basis for the imposition of punishment. Moreover, even the deterrent impact of such measures may be open to question, at least in a longer-term view, since moral repugnance may undermine the general respect for a system of rules that employs such methods, and may harden the resolve of those who are actively challenging the punishing authorities within such a system (as appears to have been the case with the French Revolutionary law referred to above). We shall return shortly to the question of punishment of the innocent.

A rather different manifestation of vicarious penalty is provided by contemporary English criminal law, which makes notable use of vicarious liability.[31] This occurs principally in the area of 'regulatory' offences, which are concerned especially with the maintenance of standards in relation to health, safety, public order, and environmental protection. By their nature, such breaches are potentially very numerous and easier to prove in their outcome than in their inception. Put another way, it is often difficult to establish exactly who, among a number of actors, was in fact responsible for the breach of the required standard of behaviour. In order to avoid the cost and drain on resources entailed in extensive investigation and the alternative of not enforcing the prohibition of all in many cases, the expedient of fixing liability on a particular party has evolved: for instance, the legal seller of goods, the owner of the vehicle, the licensee of a public house, or a corporation as distinct from its employees or directors. Not surprisingly, such a version of vicarious liability has provoked charges of injustice, especially as regards the case of the diligent 'offender' who could have done nothing to prevent the commission of the breach by another. An economic justification for such liability is sometimes put forward, to the effect that it is the person who takes the most profit from the activity in question who is thus held responsible; but this justification may not always stand up to closer examination in practice. A more satisfactory response to the problem has been to shift the burden of proof by providing for a 'due diligence' defence,[32] so that it is incumbent on the defendant to establish that he or she took all reasonable action to avoid the breach, although this may leave many breaches untouchable by penal law. Overall, the use of vicarious punishment in this context gives rise to a number of hard questions concerning the purposes and functions of such punishment and both its fairness and deterrent impact may be open to argument. It can be sensibly asked whether penal, as distinct from supervisory, techniques are relevant to these problems and the use of criminal law has been questioned in some such contexts (e.g. by the Committee on Safety and Health at Work, 1972).[33]

SCAPEGOATS

And when he who has made an end of atoning for the holy place and the tent of meeting and the altar, he shall present the live goat; and Aaron shall lay his hands upon the head of the live goat and confess over him all the iniquities of the people of Israel, and all their transgressions and all their sins; and he shall put them upon the head of the goat, and send him away into the wilderness by the hand of a man who is in readiness. The goat shall bear all their iniquities upon him to a solitary land; and he shall let the goat go in the wilderness.

(Leviticus 16: 20–2)

Herein lies the origin of the term 'scapegoat', the innocent goat being exiled with the sins of the people of Israel. This ritual transfer of wrong, which has a parallel in the transfer of demons to the 'innocent' Gadarene swine, which then rush to their destruction (Mark 5: 1–14), has been supplanted by a looser usage of the term to connote a punishment of the innocent. As such it should be regarded as a subclass of categories discussed earlier.

Clearly, as we have seen, the practice is one subject to massive ethical objection, and it is in this context that 'scapegoating' has become a major battlefield in the traditional discourse of punishment. If we consider the purposes to be served by punishment, we may see that some of these are quite capable of being fulfilled by punishment of the innocent in particular instances. So it would appear that scapegoating may serve to reinforce group norms. Early psychological tests on small groups carried out by Lippit established that group co-operation might be increased when the group had the opportunity to blame a scapegoat for its faults.[34] But the question of efficacy in no way determines the justice of the practice. Even in terms of its pragmatic efficacy, however, the impact of two variables may be significant. Firstly, there is the question of how many persons know that the punished entity is innocent (obviously this was not seen as a problem in the original ritual cleansing process of the Leviticus example, but may be when more prosaic penal ends, such as deterrence, are considered). Secondly, the question will arise as to whether a system based upon regular punishment of the innocent will attain any or all of the particular purposes of punishment.

Brief reference may also be made to scapegoating of a more psychological kind: a process of transferred aggression whereby a penal response is diverted from the appropriate target to one that is innocent. This is a phenomenon more easily observed than understood, but may perhaps be viewed as a penal impulse frustrated by an inability, for whatever reason, to act against the desired subject of punishment. Certainly, in an interpersonal context, friends and family may become the unlucky recipients of such diverted penal action, even if only in the form of anger.

176

THE MISSING SUBJECT:
PUNISHMENT *IN ABSENTIA*

A practical problem of punishment may arise in some cases in that, although an offender may be identifiable and the appropriate punishment decided upon, the person of the offender may not be physically available for the penalty to be applied. The subject may have evaded the physical reach of the penal authorities (be 'outside the jurisdiction', to employ legal terminology) or may no longer be alive. In the first case, procedures and machinery may be available, in a legal context, to secure the custody of the fugitive (for instance, extradition) or pursuit of the offender may become an important end in itself (as in the case of some criminal and political organizations who may be very ruthless and determined in their pursuit – a favourite topic of melodrama).[35] In the second case, it may be asked whether there is any further purpose in punishment, to which the answer must be that in some situations there is clearly felt to be some point in punishing something that represents the deceased. Leaving aside the question of the pursuit of penal fugitives, it may be worth reflecting on the practice of punishment *in absentia*.

Such punishment may be regarded by some as notional since it necessarily affects the subject at a distance and may therefore appear to lack impact. But it must be borne in mind that some important interests of the subject, such as esteem and reputation, may be injured by such punishment, and it also serves to underline the expressive function of punishment. Even if at one level the punishment may appear a futile gesture, it may none the less be felt to be an imperative in order to reinforce the authority that the offender has challenged and to emphasize the serious reaction within the normative system in question. These functions can most effectively be served if the punishment *in absentia* at the same time does some injury to the standing of the offender or results in humiliation, even if at a distance. Indeed, the targetting of reputation and an intended humiliation would seem to be an important component in the practice of such punishment and in many cases the physical absence of the subject is significant mainly in that it gives rise to a particular penal method. But discussion of this situation here will serve to emphasize the possibilities of carrying punishment into effect at a physical distance.

While the burning or hanging of an effigy has an obvious symbolic character, other forms of punishment *in absentia* have been more constructive in their attempts to degrade the representation of the offender. Notable examples are provided by the *pitture infamanti* employed in northern Italy during the thirteenth and fourteenth centuries: officially commissioned, displayed in public places, and depicting the offender in ignominious punishment.[36] Thus in 1300 in Bologna, the artist Bartolomeo was commissioned to depict some local culprits sentenced for counterfeiting and murder, the former being shown to be burning at the stake and the latter being seated on a 'throne' being dragged by asses.[37] *Pitture infamanti* could be taken seriously by both the defamed and the public who viewed them. In 1302 the Cavalcanti family, which had joined the dissident White Guelph faction in opposing the prevailing Florentine government, was at great pains to use its political connections to prevent its members being the subject of *pitture infamanti*.[38] The sting of the punishment lay in its impact upon general esteem, causing a 'stain of infamy', which could prejudice political and commercial interests of the wealthy and ambitious. More specifically, for instance, a family's interests could be injured for a considerable time, making impossible the negotiation of advantageous marriages and business arrange-ments. The mocking justice of 'rough music' and *charivari*s may also be viewed as a species of punishment *in absentia*,[39] although in such cases it would often have been possible to act directly against the person of the subject but it was deliberate policy not to do so; again the impact of the punishment was upon standing and esteem. The destruction of statues, images, or other objects representing the rule of a former political leader may also be seen in this light. During the siege of Florence by the troops of Pope Clement VII in 1530 the renegade *condottiere* Baccio Valori was punished by having his house cut in two and the swathe between the halves labelled 'Traitor's Alley'.[40]

In a rather different situation, deceased offenders who have thereby avoided punishment (fortuitously or by suicide) may still be subject to some penalty through the proxy of their reputation or esteem. Images of the deceased may be derided or the corpse may be abused. Consider, for example, the treatment of Richard III of England's corpse, after his death in battle in 1485 at Bosworth Field. Within a few hours of the battle, Henry Tudor's entourage entered Leicester in triumph. At the tail of this procession came Richard's corpse:

> Stark naked, despoiled and derided, with a felon's halter about the neck, the bloody body was flung contemptuously across the back of

a horse, which one of the dead king's heralds was forced to ride. As it was borne across the west bridge of the Soar, the head was carelessly battered against the stone parapet. For two days the body lay exposed to view in the House of the Grey Friars close to the river. It was then rolled into a grave without stone or epitaph.[41]

Although analogous in some respects to the Italian *pitture infamanti*, this treatment of a corpse also suggests another, and perhaps more elusive, penal motivation. In view of the shakiness of the legitimacy of Henry Tudor's claim to the English throne it was all the more necessary to present his predecessor as a wrongful usurper and murderer whose corpse merited this late punishment. Such derisive treatment of the dead king's body therefore served political purposes of a more specific nature than the Italian paintings, and this example should alert us to the fact that it is not easy to generalize too far from these instances of punishment of persons not present or alive to be immediately affected by the measure.

INANIMATE OBJECTS

While there would seem to be no difficulty in describing certain practices in relation to animals as being punishment – indeed, as we have seen, in some of these cases, there may be a highly formal process of punishment – it might be objected that it is nonsensical to speak of punishment as being addressed to corporeal objects and even more so to refer to the punishment of incorporeal things, such as ideas. The problem arises from the proposition that punishment depends upon the infliction of an objective unpleasantness upon a wrongdoer, and also from the fact that the idea of a wrongdoer suggests a capacity to act in some physical manner. How then is it possible to punish that which cannot in itself act independently nor experience a sensation intended to be unpleasant?

We have already noted that systems of compensation may be used as an alternative to the process of punishment, and the role of inanimate objects in relation to compensation presents few problems. Thus English law is familiar with the notion of *deodand*, whereby a personal chattel that has been the immediate cause of the death of a living being is 'given to God'.[42] This may well represent a measure of appeasement of an angry divinity and may also reveal a superstitious fear of that which had killed (although by the time that a railway locomotive was famously declared *deodand* this kind of reasoning might be expected to have declined).[43] But the punishment of inanimate objects may be regarded as altogether less intelligible. None the less, most readers will be familiar with the frustrated reaction of, for instance, kicking a door which will not open, occasionally accompanied by a verbal address of an anthropomorphic kind ('Open, you *****!') and it may be argued that the reasons that underlie such transference of aggression (affirming a proper order in the world by allocating responsibility and guilt) are similar to those that underlie certain applications of punishment.

There are certainly instances that may be fitted within such an explanatory scheme, even though they lack important characteristics of what many would regard as standard forms of punishment. Cases, for example, in which wooden idols have been decapitated for causing the death of a man, or statues banished for falling on men,[44] could be readily recognized as involving the ascription of personality to an object that seems physically appropriate to receive it (as we have noted already in relation to the 'penal' treatment of corpses). This kind of activity bears a relation to, though may be regarded as conceptually distinct from, situations in which the reputation or standing of a living person is attacked by action taken against his image. But other cases are less easily explained in this way. In Russia in 1591 a bell that had sounded the note for insurrection was banished to Siberia.[45] Here it would seem that the familiar rhetoric of punishment is being applied by analogy to make an intelligible point.

The last example leads us to a discussion of the 'punishment' of ideas. It may be argued that, for instance, the burning of 'dangerous' books is no more an act of punishment than the destruction of diseased crops – it is a measure to prevent 'infection'. Similarly, the (to the authors at least) deeply distressing films of ostensibly delighted policemen smashing barrels of beer with axes during the period of Prohibition in the United States might be seen in a number of ways: as the public vindication of police efficiency or the destruction of a dangerous substance, rather than as the 'punishment' of alcohol. Yet this may be to miss some important psychological factors involved in some such cases, which do connect with the psychology associated with 'standard' instances of punishment. In particular it may be important that a clear distinction is drawn between the author of a work and the physical manifestation of that work and, in so far as it is the content of the work that is objected to, it is the book rather than the author that is subjected to penal process. In the same way that the falling statue is regarded as responsible for the injury, not the person who placed it there, so the book is held responsible for its contents, rather than its author. In 1660, the poet John Milton was perhaps fortunate to suffer no direct personal punishment for his role as polemicist for the Republic; however, a royal proclamation ordered the suppression of his books, which were to be surrendered to or seized by public officials and then publicly burned.[46] More recently, following the coup against Salvadore Allende's socialist government in Chile in 1973, Marxist and socialist literature was generally consigned to the pyre in universities and other centres of learning.[47] Clearly, such action may serve a preventive function (further publication, sale, or circulation of Milton's work was prohibited). In so far as the authors are not otherwise punished in relation to their writings it may perhaps be seen as a kind of vicarious penalty. But there may also be a sense in which the targeting of the physical manifestation of ideas in books and other forms represents a desire to punish not authors, artists and the like as such, but rather the wayward intellectual impulse that sought to give expression to those ideas. If we are to talk in terms of the punishment of literature or art, or more precisely, its offending content, we are admittedly referring to an unusual instance of penal process. Yet we would not necessarily want to exclude such activity altogether from the scope of our discussion of punishment.

CLASS AND RANK AND THE
METHOD OF PUNISHMENT

Finally, in the context of the punishment of human beings, it is worth noting how the subject's position within a social group or hierarchy may have consequences, not so much for the choice of that person as a subject for punishment, but as regards whether or what sort of punishment should be applied. Thus, higher status or more 'respectable' offenders may be dealt with by a reprimand or caution, or even not at all if the resources of enforcement are not deployed in their direction, whereas the offender of lower social status may experience the full rigour of formal punishment for substantially the same offence. Thus, Edwin Powers, discussing punishments of humiliation in seventeenth-century Massachusetts, notes that

181

Respected citizens of the upper social strata . . . were not so treated. If they were called to account for some violation of the law – and they not infrequently were – the courts were satisfied with the assessment of a fine, unless, of course, their offenses were particularly heinous.[48]

Historically, many legal systems have employed distinctive methods of capital punishment to reflect the rank or social status of the subject. Commonly, beheading (the literal form of capital punishment) had been reserved for offenders of the highest status:

> beheading, as a form of legal punishment, symbolizes the taking away of rank, that is, the crown. Only members of the upper classes could wear the 'crown' in the first place. When they failed in their duties, their peers performed *poena capitas* upon them, 'punishment of the head' – capital punishment.[49]

Beheading often possessed, therefore, a symbolic and ceremonial significance. Hanging, on the other hand, was frequently seen as appropriate for more vulgar criminality and the spectacle would certainly have been more undignified. Turning to another culture, again of a very hierarchical kind, a similar differentiation was observed in Inca society, whereby different classes would be subject to different forms of punishment.[50] Thus, physical sanctions were used against common people, but psychological measures were taken against the nobility.

Taking a general view of this, class bias in the form of the penalty used is unsurprising in rigidly hierarchical societies, where the punitive distinction then reinforces the existing class difference and discreetly masks the universality of human fallibility and offending.

THE SIGNIFICANCE OF THE SUBJECT OF PUNISHMENT

The foregoing discussion of the range and variety of penal subjects is intended to inform the familiar idea of the 'offender' as the paradigm focus for penal activity. Not only is it important to appreciate that the common idea of 'offending' is rough around the edges, in that notions of responsibility for and participation in offending conduct may be elastic, but also that penal practice may extend to persons or other entities who are not offenders in the conventional sense. To be sure, as we move further away from the 'central' or 'standard' case of penal subject, as some jurists would refer to it, we are likely to encounter both moral and practical doubts and search for a more elusive explanation of the appeal of such penal practice. Many would object (and indeed have objected)[51] that the punishment of animals, objects, intellectual achievement, or representations of absent persons is futile, primitive, and irrational. It is to this kind of objection that we would wish particularly to respond. To see pointlessness in long-standing social practice or acts that serve a strongly felt, if not fully articulated, need is itself to miss the point of the problem. The punitive impulse is neither silly nor primitive; but we may question its practical utility or moral status or wisdom in certain situations. If, as time goes on, we are less likely to use collective punishment or to punish animals or things, it is not so much because we have lost some atavistic instinct to do these things as that we have found other means of coming to terms with the inexplicable or uncontrollable. For instance, as our knowledge of the causes and character of natural phenomena and our insight into the complexities of human behaviour expands, some of the penal directions referred to in this chapter may seem less necessary or more jurisprudentially questionable than they would have appeared in earlier periods. But reflection on what are now less favoured penal practices enables us to appreciate further some of the less frequently articulated functions of punishment, in particular the way in which punishment may be used to confer a sense of getting to grips with a complex or baffling social problem.

Not surprisingly, then, the genuinely serious trial and punishment of animals may strike some twentieth-century observers as bizarre. But, then again, a future generation may view the degree of contemporary resort to vicarious liability under English criminal law as misguided and indeed lawyers from other systems at the present time, which do not deal with the problem of regulatory breaches in this way, may well be baffled by the British predilection for vicarious punishment in this area. The choice of penal subject, therefore, may reveal something about the underlying view and understanding of the origin and significance of certain social problems.

10

METHODS OF PUNISHMENT

It is interesting to note that this aspect of punishment, the question of how it is put into effect, has been productive of the most debate and controversy. This may not be surprising in one sense, since the method of punishing comprises its most visible and sensitive element, and the means employed is often used as an interpretative aid in tracing developments and shifts in the practice of punishment. It has typically provided a major focus of attention for those who have been interested to observe punishment as a type of state activity and have therefore been less concerned with questions of authority and subject. In such a context, it has been largely taken for granted that punishment is a process whereby the state takes action against a criminal offender; the method used is then naturally perceived as the principal variable and a major indicator of tendencies within the practice. So, for instance, the Foucauldian analysis,[1] which traces a shift from corporeal to juridical to carceral types of punishment, derives its impetus from a concern with methods employed within the practice of state penality. In that analysis the transition from corporal punishment to incarceration then assumes a major explanatory role in the attempt to penetrate the social functioning of punishment. But as a result, other important tendencies, such as the shift from community to state punishment, or the growing moral doubts concerning the use of collective or vicarious punishment, receive little treatment: the mode is seen as the most important expression of the practice. Similarly, penological debate concerning the effectiveness of punishment tends to centre upon the different forms and their comparative impact and does not concern itself overmuch with such subjects as the investigation of non-state penality, self-punishment, and taboo, or the rationale of vicarious measures. And popular discussion also evinces a faith in methodology for purposes of supplying more effective and appropriate penal measures, as demonstrated for example by a popular yearning for discarded measures of capital and corporal punishment.

This is not to suggest that the penal method is unimportant, but rather to question the centrality of the topic in much of the discussion. We have already stressed our concern to open out the boundaries of the debate to encompass instances of penal practice beyond the limits of state penality. But, having done that, we may return finally to the question of – whoever may be punishing whomever – how this punishment is carried out. And in coming to this question our main purpose will be to assess the significance of method for penal practice generally. In turn, an attempt to do this will require an effort of categorization, since the question of method cannot be usefully tackled without some form of typology. This kind of exercise may inevitably prove controversial. When Michel Foucault, in *Surveiller et Punir* (translated into English as *Discipline and Punish*), referred to the transition from corporeal through juridical to carceral modes of punishment, he was basing his analysis upon the external features and perceived purposes of particular types of penal measure.[2] Such analysis is based not upon a totality of penal practice but upon a selection of what are considered to be key developments in what are perceived to be key forms of state punishment. Crudely interpreted, Foucault's argument suggests a shift from deterrent and expressive concerns (as evidenced by the spectacle of corporeal punishment) to corrective preoccupations (as manifested by the discreet disciplinary apparatus of the closed institution). But such an account leaves aside much that was happening both within and without the arena of state penality. Moreover, investigation of different societies at different times reveals a complex mix of deterrent, corrective, expressive, preventive, and reparative functions within penal practice. True, the mix may change from time to time and from place to place, but the sweep of penal development indicated by Foucault's kind of analysis may be too categorical and unilinear in its argument.

THE OBJECTS OF PUNISHMENT

If we are to work out a categorization of penal methods that will accommodate the range and variety of penal activity we have been concerned to emphasize in our discussion, it may be helpful to talk initially about the *object* of punishment. While punishment is

185

addressed to a subject in the sense of a person (or more exceptionally an animal or even an inanimate entity) the punishment achieves its impact by action taken against an object that relates to the penal subject. Such objects (and the term is being used in a wide sense) will necessarily be of significance and value to the subject (cf. Finnis's term: 'likeable goods'),[3] or else the essential unpleasantness of the penal experience will not come about. The essence of the penal method, therefore, is to focus effectively and appropriately on such objects in order to achieve the purposes discussed in Chapter 6. When those objects that are typically under attack in the practice of punishment are scrutinized throughout the range of penal activity in different societies at different times, certain main types emerge. Again, we need to bear in mind that this kind of categorization, although possessing some explanatory value, cannot be hard-and-fast. Having said that, we can proceed to identify the following main objects of punishment: (a) the body of the subject; (b) material possessions and comforts of the subject; (c) the freedom of action and movement of the subject; (d) the reputation or status of the subject; (e) the social relations of the subject; and (f) the spiritual well-being of the subject. Again acknowledging the possibility of overlap, measures taken against such valued objects would typically be represented by (a) a physical beating; (b) a monetary fine; (c) incarceration; (d) the humiliation of standing in the pillory; (e) banishment; and (f) excommunication. We shall in due course consider in more detail the first five of these 'objects' of punishment; the targeting of spiritual well-being has already been discussed at some length in Chapter 8 in the context of supernatural penality.

Now, it is important to appreciate that measures taken against any of these typical objects of punishment may have one or a number of penal purposes – expressive, retaliatory, compensatory, preventive, or whatever else. Thus, as a society moves from a preference for attacking one of these objects to that for another (for instance from corporal punishment to incarceration), that does not necessarily mean that the penal purposes or the rationale of punishment has thereby changed. Rather, it suggests that the perception of the value of the object has shifted and it is no longer seen as appropriate or effective for achieving the underlying penal purpose. Some objects of punishment may well be more suitable than others for achieving the relevant penal purpose and the preference may depend on psychological or symbolic factors, which are themselves culturally determined. In a society in which life is harsh, corporal or capital punishment may have less impact than in more affluent and comfortable environments; conversely, spiritual well-being or belief in otherworldly experience may be much more vulnerable objects in the former kind of situation. Individual freedom is highly prized in modern western society but would, it has been argued, be a less-sensible object for punitive action in more regimented, immobile, and hierarchical societies, such as the earlier feudal society of Western Europe. Physical exclusion or banishment is more meaningful in the hostile environment of Eskimo tribes; it is largely unworkable in a highly populated industrialized society. Penal method, therefore, takes its cue from societal and environmental possibilities and needs to be assessed in that light.

We return once again to our earlier assertion that punishment should be viewed not as an institution but as a technique. Therefore, punishment *qua* technique may be seen in a sense as a constant, though its underlying purposes may vary and its methods are adapted to achieve these purposes as best as possible. The shift from corporal to carceral methods tells us as much about the societies in which that shift is located as about the rationale of employing punishment. Moreover, we must take care, in comparing penal methods, not to fall into the trap of perceiving evolutionary developments, from 'primitive' to more 'sophisticated' techniques, from 'cruel' to 'humane' treatment. The self-congratulatory modern text that confidently distinguishes between the 'civilized' and the 'uncivilized' and shudders at the thought of 'gruesome punishments of bygone days' misses some important comparative points. The psychological torment of prolonged incarceration or loss of esteem amongst one's peers may be subjectively as unbearable as a severe whipping or a spell in the pillory. In particular, we should guard against the idea of any necessary progressive softening of the impact of punishments; what has occurred in the modern period is perhaps viewed more usefully in many contexts as a shift from the visible corporeal methods to the less manifest attacks at a psychological level.[4] Not for little reason do the authors of a 1970s work on imprisonment entitle their book *Psychological Survival*.[5]

CORPORAL PUNISHMENT

Perhaps we should develop this last point by considering part of Foucault's famous argument: the modern period has witnessed not so much a shift from corporal methods of punishment to incarceration (see in particular the arguments put forward by Cohen and Bottoms in this respect)[6-7] as a general decline in the use of corporal measures in favour of a number of other methods. As Foucault puts it:

> The body . . . is caught up in a system of restraints and privations, obligations and prohibitions. Physical pain, the pain of the body itself, is no longer the constituent element of the penalty. From being an art of unbearable sensations punishment has become an economy of suspended rights.[8]

At one time a major weapon in the armoury of state legal systems, corporal measures have now become widely unlawful in the hands of state authorities, capital punishment has been abolished in a number of systems and is used in limited circumstances in others, and there is an increasing legal control of punishment in the private sphere of family and educational sanctions.

This movement in penal practice can be illustrated with little effort. It is well documented in the area of state penality and we need do little more here than point out the contrast between, for example, the spectacle of corporal and capital punishment of the regicide Damiens as portrayed in the opening part of Foucault's *Surveiller et Punir*,[9] and the condemnation of 'cruel, inhuman and degrading treatment' in Article 3 of the European Convention on Human Rights and the body of case-law that has accumulated on the basis of that provision.[10] In the domestic sphere, parallel developments could perhaps be usefully illustrated a little further.

We may begin with the example supplied by David Hunt, in his discussion of family life in early modern France, of the upbringing of the future King Louis XIII.[11] Louis' father, Henri IV, wrote to the dauphin's governess Madame de Montglat at one point:

> 'I have a complaint to make: you do not send word that you have whipped my son. I wish and command you to whip him every time that he is obstinate or misbehaves, knowing well for myself that there is nothing in the world which will be better for him than that. I know it from experience, having myself profited, for when I was his age I was often whipped. That is why I want you to whip him and to make him understand why.[12]

And Hunt comments: 'Surely other fathers were capable of such logic. If the dauphin was regularly beaten, I would assume that most children were no less severely treated.' From there, let us move forward just over two hundred years.

In 1859, a 13-year-old boy, Reginald Cancellor, was entrusted by his parents to the care of a schoolmaster at Eastbourne.[13] He was described as 'dull' and by the schoolmaster, Hopley, as 'obstinate'; and for such truculence he was 'chastized' before the Christmas of 1859. On 18 April 1860, Hopley wrote to Cancellor's father complaining that his son was 'obstinate' and that, if he were his own child he should, after due warning, subdue this obstinacy by chastizing him severely and would, if necessary, repeat the punihsment and 'continue it at intervals, even if he held out for hours'. The father wrote promptly in reply that he did not wish to interfere with this plan. On the night of the 21st of April, Hopley took Cancellor into a downstairs room in the school and beat him for about two hours with a thick stick and a skipping rope. The stick was at one end about an inch thick and at the other edged with brass 'about the circumference of a sixpence'. Afterwards Hopley was heard either dragging or pushing Cancellor upstairs to his bedroom, where he beat him again for about half an hour until the beating and noise of crying suddenly stopped. Cancellor died before the morning.

At Hopley's trial, Lord Chief Justice Cockburn directed the jury:

> By the law of England a parent or a schoolmaster (who for this purpose represents a parent and has the parental authority delegated to him) may for the purposes of correcting what is evil in the child inflict moderate and reasonable corporal punishment, always, however, with this condition, that it is moderate and reasonable. If it be administered for the gratification of passion or of rage, or if it be immoderate or excessive in its nature or degree, or if it be protracted beyond the child's powers of endurance, or with an instrument unfitted for the purpose and calculated to produce danger to life and limb; in all such cases the punishment is excessive, the violence is unlawful, and if evil consequences to life or limb ensue, then the person inflicting it is answerable to the law.[14]

Not surprisingly, the jury decided that this was a case of excessive punishment; Hopley was convicted of manslaughter and sentenced to four years' penal servitude.

Just over one hundred years later, on 25 April 1978, the European Court of Human Rights had to consider in the Tyrer case whether the penalty of being birched under judicial sentence in the Isle of Man was contrary to Article 3 of the Convention.[15] In paragraph 33 of its judgment, the Court stated:

> The very nature of judicial corporal punishment is that it involves one human being inflicting physical violence on another human being. Furthermore, it is institutionalised violence ... Thus, although the applicant did not suffer any severe or long-lasting physical effects, his punishment – whereby he was treated as an object in the power of the authorities – constituted an assault on precisely that which it is one of the main purposes of Article 3 to protect, namely a person's dignity and physical integrity. Neither can it be excluded that the punishment may have had adverse psychological effects.
>
> The institutionalised character of this violence is further compounded by the whole aura of official procedure attending the punishment and by the fact that those inflicting it were total strangers to the offender.[16]

The Court concluded by saying:

> the applicant was subjected to a punishment in which the element of humiliation attained the level inherent in the notion of 'degrading punishment' ... The indignity of having the punishment administered over the bare posterior aggravated to some extent the degrading character of the applicant's punishment but it was not the only or determining factor.[17]

This significant questioning of the propriety of corporal punishment in the context of state action can be seen as having an even more forceful application as regards domestic situations. Although the point is not wholly within the scope of the European Convention, the subsequent case of *Campbell and Cosans* v. *UK* touched upon these issues.[18] The European Court of Human Rights had to consider whether the threat of corporal punishment in a school in Scotland amounted to a breach of Article 3 of the Convention. Since corporal punishment had not been applied to the applicants themselves, the Court found no actual violation of Article 3, but did refer back to the interpretation of 'degrading treatment' that it had given in its judgment in the Tyrer case and went on to say, significantly:

> corporal chastisement is traditional in Scottish schools and, indeed, appears to be favoured by a large majority of parents ... of itself, this is not conclusive of the issue before the court for the threat of a

190

particular measure is not excluded from the category of 'degrading', within the meaning of Article 3, simply because the measure has been in use for a long time or even meets with general approval.[19]

There would appear to be a potent principle implicit in that statement. For without doubt the official abandonment of corporal punishment in the modern period has had to contend with a fair amount of popular support for such measures (this is particularly evident in the case of capital punishment). The European Court is here in effect overriding arguments based upon longstanding popular approval and asserting the primacy of official over domestic or popular ideas of punishment. Whatever the precise legal position in relation to corporal punishment in these various contexts, it is clear that the overall drift in terms of legal development is towards condemnation or at least stricter control of the use of corporal measures. Whether there has been any significant change in the day-to-day severity of the practice of child punishment is a more difficult issue to which we shall return below.

This shift in 'official' or 'formal' penal practice is manifest, at least in western society. But it may be more difficult to capture its significance. It does not help, in this respect, simply to assert that twentieth-century man is more 'humane' or 'civilized' than his forebears: we need only to refer to the recent, world-wide annals of torture, genocide, and massive waste of human life through indifference or carelessness to refute such a complacent observation. Admittedly, there is now a more marked distaste for bodily suffering, which may have been a less sensitive issue for people of earlier societies. In so far as this is true, it may well be a result of the more healthy physical conditions and greater longevity enjoyed by members of many (though not all) contemporary societies. Advances in health care, sanitation, and the general increase in standards of material comfort, not to mention a fuller understanding of the physical world and its pathologies and abnormalities, have encouraged us to respect more our own and others' bodies and so be less ready to accept the deliberate infliction of physical suffering. In short, it is possible to detect in many modern societies a fuller sensitivity towards the integrity of the body. However, more needs to be done to explain convincingly this aspect of the demise of corporal penality. For it is not simply a question of discovering more effective or appropriate objects for punishment (such as individual freedom or reputation): there is, *in tandem* with the search for more effective methods, a definite moral repugnance towards the use of violence, the deliberate infliction of physical pain, and the violation of bodily integrity. Human sensibilities have altered significantly and the body is commonly not regarded now as an appropriate (though it may still be an effective) object for punishment.

At the same time, care must be taken not to overstate this shift in penal method. As we have remarked, there remains a huge residual capacity for violence and for destructive responses in human relations, most obviously in the realms of organized crime, terrorism, military conflict, and political strife. To be sure, much of this is officially deplored and condemned. But the late twentieth century has witnessed the irony of a formal reduction in the use of violent measures while experiencing a flourishing underworld of extreme physical force and terror. Colombia and Venezuela, for instance, may have abolished the death penalty for all crimes, but in both states during the early 1980s there occurred assassinations and 'disappearances' for which the state was allegedly responsible and reports of torture in custody.[20]

Moreover, in some social groupings, there remains a strong and openly practised habit of violent reaction and corporeal penalty. Leaving aside the possibility of an attempted external control (as regards, for instance, family, educational, or military punishments), it may be difficult to change such attitudes and practices from within. Kaplan and Dubro, in their study of Japanese organized crime, *Yakuza*,[21] report on a frustrated attempt to reform the widespread practice of *yubitsume*, the punitive ritual of finger-cutting for breaches of gang rules, on the part of the modern Tokyo gang-leader, Kakuji Inagawa:

> A lowly soldier in the Inagawa army had committed some grievous error, so his immediate boss demanded he slice off a fingertip as punishment. When Inagawa learnt of this, he was enraged and berated the boss for ordering such an act. The boss, humiliated and ashamed, responded in the only way he knew how: he cut off his finger and presented it to Inagawa.[22]

The tension between a continued resort to corporal punishment in practice and 'official' (i.e. state) condemnation is clearly indicated in those areas where there is a co-existence of tribal and state norms. For instance, Hoebel, in discussing Pueblo tribal sanctions, comments: 'The actual use of the whip as a legal penalty is now done most circumspectly, for fear of punishment of the officers by nonpueblo agencies. In the early phases of our fieldwork it was flatly denied that there is any whipping. Subsequently, it was readily acknowledged.'[23] Köbben points to a similar collision of normative systems, in relation to the Djuka of Surinam. A man and a woman among the Djuka had been beaten by the woman's kin for committing adultery. When two of the beaters were subsequently arrested by the Surinam police, the local community is indignant: 'The police are stupid, they should ask what was the reason for the fight.'[24]

It must be concluded, therefore, that the impulse behind corporeal penality remains strong in some contexts. And we need not search very far to appreciate some of its 'appeal'. It is, in the first place, a form of punishment characterized by an ease of application and ready availability: it can often be carried into effect quickly and with no special skill, usually requiring a minimum of penal apparatus. It has the advantage of a general availability, attaching to the basic condition of the subject. When the latter has no wealth or freedom, the body is still available to receive punishment. Moreover, bodily punishment has a simple appeal in talionic terms, particularly as a response to bodily harm, so enabling a sense of balance to be achieved in the penal process. And finally, we should note the flexibility of corporeal punishment. The range of punishments that may be inflicted upon the body is vast and infinitely variable, from the slapped wrist to capital punishment. In addition, the body can serve as a permanent noticeboard for guilt: thus mutilation, and, more especially, branding, may serve not only as an infliction of pain, but also affixes a permanent badge of stigma. It is at this point that we encounter the borderland of corporeal and stigmatic measures, between which there may, of course, be some overlap, and we shall return to the subject of physical stigmatization below.

MATERIAL ASSETS

Here the target of punishment is not the body but those things the body enjoys: material possessions, wealth, objects of comfort; put another way, things of a quantifiable value of which the subject of punishment may be deprived. The main forms of this penal method will be familiar enough – monetary fines, confiscation of property, refusing to supply or cutting off access to desired commodities, as exemplified more specifically by the fine and compensation order under criminal law, forfeiture of property and property rights under an act of attainder, refusal to supply essential goods as a commercial or economic sanction, or the withdrawal of 'pocket-money' in a domestic context.

Penalties involving loss of goods are interesting in a number of ways. Firstly, there is the question of the destination of that which is taken. If such property is handed over to the wronged person, then the process is likely to be described as compensation and not as punishment (see the discussion above, in Chapter 7, on the relation between the two systems). It may, incidentally, be of great importance in understanding the difference between punishment and compensation to know whether it is the deprivation of the wrongdoer's goods or their allocation to the injured person that is significant within the psychology of the group in question. (This assumes that such a difference may be meaningfully drawn in the context of particular belief structures.) The property in question may, however, be handed over to other bodies or individuals. In such cases, it may be that a propitiatory urge is predominant, the underlying idea being that the goods may 'buy off' the wrath of an angry lord within whose territory or 'place' the offence has occurred, or that of an angry god or spirit. Or, then again, what is taken may be used for reward or to provide for the upkeep of the system that imposed the punishment or initiated the penal process. It should not be thought that the latter is a reference only to modern state systems: among the Cheyenne, for example, such goods might be given to the soldier bands who occasionally assumed a peace-keeping role.[25]

In quantitative terms, pecuniary penalties are of great significance, especially at the level of state action. The great majority of criminal cases dealt with in the English legal system result in the imposition of a fine.[26] At the same time, its widespread use and convenience for dealing with a vast number of less-serious infringements of the criminal law results in a loss of stigma within such measures, and subjectively the imposition of a fine may be more likely to be felt as a nuisance than a painful experience in any real sense. The use of tariffs and fixed penalties for administrative convenience supplies a mechanical and neutral character, which also affects the penal impact of these measures. In this respect, the pecuniary penalty exemplifies

Foucault's idea of juridical penality: it is representational, short-term, and neutral, and leaves no permanent or long-term mark on the subject of the measure, as is likely to be the case with corporal punishment, incarceration, or measures of degradation. It is cleanly applied and relatively easily forgotten. In the same way, a measure of attainder could be reversed and property rights restored and none of this affect much the general perception of the subject of punishment as distinct from his or her material position. Of all the main methods or ideal types of punishment within the contemporary western legal world, this is the most detached from the subject, that which is least likely to strike at the roots of personal sensibility. Not surprisingly, therefore, this method is seen as especially appropriate in the area of regulatory offending, where the imposition of stigma is a matter of less concern, and is, practically speaking, a necessity as regards corporate offenders.

The other significant feature of this form of punishment is the ease with which a range of material goods or a system of currency may accommodate the requirement of proportionality. Reference has already been made to the detailed compensation codes of the Anglo-Saxon and Nuer societies. We may add here one further example of how easily the notion of monetary equivalence may be achieved. In a Zambian customary court in 1950 the wrongdoer appealed on the ground that the award of compensation against him was excessive: 'I have appealed because the money was too much. In my opinion for the two teeth that he had lost I should have been made to pay only £2. If three teeth had come out I should have paid £3.'[27] A similar idea of equivalence may be seen in cases where the goods or money are not paid over as 'compensation' but as a 'fine'.

INCARCERATION

Let us consider the assertion made by Melossi and Pavarini that there is a crucial relation between the origins of the modern prison (or incarceration as a method of punishment; for practical purposes those authors might not draw the distinction) and the rise of the capitalist mode of production.[28] The basis of this thesis is that only in such an economic context could human labour measured as time be a meaningful object of punishment, and hence the emergence of penal incarceration in the post-feudal period. It also rests upon the assumption that imprisonment did not exist as a form of punishment in pre-capitalist societies and also that in post-industrial societies of the late twentieth century there is a tendency towards methods of penal control 'in conditions of liberty' (in the form, for example, of probation, suspension of imprisonment, and community service). Penal incarceration is thus inextricably linked, in this view, with the nature of capitalist society.

This argument, taking its inspiration from Rusche and Kirchheimer's *Punishment and Social Structure*, is thus firmly located within the Marxist critique of imprisonment and is further nourished by a perception of 'crisis' within the prison system.[29] Like so many bold explanations, it combines an insight with a tendency towards monolithic theory, and the latter may obfuscate the former. It is difficult to deny the significance of incarceration in the modern period, and its potential as a punitive method is clearly enhanced by the degree of individual mobility and freedom of action to be found in western society during this time; but its continuing appeal as a penal method may extend beyond a coincidence with capitalist modes of production. Like much of the western literature on the subject, Melossi and Pavarini's study is based on the use of imprisonment by the state, for the most part in Western Europe and North America. It does not consider the use of imprisonment in non-capitalist or largely unindustrialized Third World countries, nor does it extend to other types of deprivation of liberty. Imprisonment in pre-capitalist Europe is defined as not being punitive, but rather as 'preventive' or 'custodial' and 'without going into the historiographic debate on the nature of certain atypical punishments (pro-correction prisons, prisons for prostitutes and "sodomites", etc.)'.[30] This may be an over-simplified assessment. Indeed, those authors state at the beginning of their work that there is 'a rather precise temporal (and spatial) definition' to their theme, which coincides with the dimensions 'of the formation of a determinate social structure' (i.e. capitalism).[31] Well, if one seeks to study the phenomenon of imprisonment within the temporal and spatial confines of capitalist social structures, it is not surprising to discover a system that reflects the conditions of such a society. Moreover, it is important not to be misled by the use of the specific term 'imprisonment'. There are a number of institutions of incarceration and, as we have asserted in our discussion of the purposes of punishment, a number of different purposes that may underlay a resort to penal measures, including incarceration. House arrest or banishment to an inhospitable location are as much a part of the network of deprivation of liberty and free movement as the conventional prison of western design. 'Prison' is a widely used and emotive term: on the one hand, it may be used in the context of academic argument in a precise and narrowly located sense; on the other, it may have a looser, metaphorical application, and it is not stretching the use of language too far to talk of the 'Man in the Iron Mask' (according to Voltaire and Dumas – actually, it was a velvet mask)[32] being 'imprisoned' within his headgear or, as many poets and songsters would have it, being a 'prisoner of love'. We need to guard against a domination by the study of specifics and, as we have argued earlier stipulative definitions. Imprisonment or incarceration is a general technique and can be used as a punishment in a number of different contexts.

Certainly, it would be useful to stress a wider perspective on the use of incarceration than that which has engaged the attention of many writers. Consider, for example, the use of imprisonment in African countries. In the early 1970s the United States imprisoned roughly 200 per 100,000 of its inhabitants; in the same period African countries generally imprisoned around 400 per 100,000 of their populations.[33] Imprisonment, therefore, appears as a relatively popular method of state punishment in an African context, but, as W. Clifford indicates:

> Recourse to imprisonment in Africa is not, however, so much a desire to punish an offender by segregation, as it is a reflection of the failure so far to devise suitable alternatives. . . . While there is undoubted scope for experimentation in adapting the penal systems of Africa to something more locally appropriate and less dependent upon prisons, the poverty of most countries south of the Sahara makes it difficult to envisage alternatives on a genuinely country-wide basis . . . the fact that extra-mural labour schemes have not always extended into rural areas has not been due to the unwillingness to use this in preference to prison but to the absence of an administrative structure to supervise and guide it.[34]

In the case of Africa it seems clear that imprisonment as a major means of punishment was first introduced by the colonial powers and is now to some extent at least retained through lack of resources to develop alternative methods. On the surface, imprisonment in Africa would not appear to be a fundamentally different phenomenon from that in Europe or America; yet the reasons for its original development there and its continuing use may be very different. It may be

197

then that, while the use of incarceration by the state as a major penal form might have its origins in the capitalist modes of production, its development and continuing use may depend upon other factors.

Indeed, it would be helpful, we suggest, to view imprisonment in its conventional form as just one on a scale of measures generally concerned with the restriction of freedom of action. The familiar and imposing physical form of the prison marks it out as an obvious and impressive example of such a measure, and this physical manifestation provides state imprisonment with a pronounced symbolic significance. But there are variations on this general theme of action and it is important to recognize them as such: political exile, reduction to slavery, house arrest, labour camps, reformatories for juveniles, a range of hospitals and treatment centres, and curfew and attendance requirements as part of community supervision; and, beyond the direct sphere of state action, various forms of detention and confinement for penal purposes: children being sent to bed early, detention outside school hours, soldiers being put in the 'glasshouse', and prisoners forfeiting remission of sentence. The carceral method can therefore be seen to be of wide application and its preventive uses should also be borne in mind when seeking to explain its appeal: it is naturally suited to cases where it is sought to punish and at the same time provide protection for others. To regard imprisonment by the state as the 'standard case' of deprivation of liberty (so that some community-based measures, for example, may be referred to as 'part-time' imprisonment) and to emphasize the problems or 'state of crisis' within contemporary prison systems may lead to an underestimate of the effectiveness and utility, in terms of the purposes usually associated with punishment of incarceration generally and of its potential applications.

REPUTATION, HUMILIATION, AND STIGMA

The targeting of reputation, self-esteem, and community standing is a pervasive penal practice and the effect of stigma should not be underestimated: indeed, stigmatization may be viewed as a central component within the penal process, as our discussion in Chapter 6 should already have made clear.[35-6] We have also stressed already that in many modern societies the formal penalty imposed by the state legal system may subjectively be less a matter of concern than the accompanying stigmatization, either in society generally or with particular individuals or groups. Naturally, the impact of such stigma may vary from one social context to another and will depend upon both individual and cultural variables. In modern western society, it may lead to ashamed reclusion or even suicide; in some other societies it may have minimal impact. Köbben, discussing the Djuka of Surinam, indicates that being put to shame in a public palaver may not always prove to be an efficacious sanction ('it seems that their ego-image can very well stand it';[37] although contrast in this respect Pospisil's study of another simple society, the Kapauku of Papua, mentioned earlier, where the opposite was observed).[38] Clearly, in each case the target has to be areas of vulnerability in the subject's ego and it is a question not only of identifying such weakness but successfully exploiting it as well.

Some punishments may be specifically concerned with producing humiliation or leaving marks of stigma. Penalties of degradation have been widely employed at different times in western legal systems, to deal in particular with moral and political offences: devices such as the pillory,[39] the stool of repentance,[40] being chained in a public place (e.g. the use of jougs in Scotland),[41] and the enforced wearing of large symbolic letters or inscriptions,[42] rely largely for their impact upon the humiliation of the penal subject. Similarly, there is a resort to such methods in popular penality, again very often in relation to breaches of moral or political norms. Thus, much 'rough music' had a shaming character and no doubt proved very effective in this respect in the context of a local community; the use of tar and feathers and the head shaving of female collaborators in the aftermath of German occupation in the Second World War are further well-attested examples of this method of punishment.[43] To a large extent, formal punishment has now abandoned such blatant resort to techniques of humiliation, in the same way that corporal punishment has been used increasingly less in that sphere. What may be detectable here is a tendency towards less personalized (as distinct from individualized) action in state systems of punishment, which now focus upon more 'neutral' objects, such as freedom and material assets.

None the less, it remains true that a significant experience of humiliation or degradation may accompany the imposition of other kinds of penalty and in this respect it may be the publicity or spectacle of punishment that is important. Indeed, the measures referred to above have a pronounced element of public spectacle, such as the degrading posture of the pillory or being publicly paraded in a ridiculous fashion or with degraded appearance. In a more modern context it is rather the process of public condemnation and potentially widespread subsequent knowledge of this through media dissemination that are likely to injure the sensitive parts of the ego. Wide notoriety is now more easily established and the relative anonymity that may have been possible in earlier periods in larger societies is no longer there as consolation for the punished. (The use of mass-media publicity referred to earlier should be borne in mind, and the interesting question of 'who punishes?' in such a case should be considered.)

There is a further aspect to this kind of penal method, in that sometimes a physical stigma of criminality may be used for deterrent purposes, or to warn others in their dealings with convicted offenders, or to facilitate the custody of prisoners. Typical penal markings of earlier periods were branded marks or cropped ears[44] (even the ears of a man's horse, as in the case of the Cheyenne Indians),[45] the dunce's cap and ass's ears in educational settings.[46] The prison uniform developed in a number of systems at the end of the eighteenth century served a number of practical purposes, including sanitation and making escapes more difficult, but also, in the words of the Penitentiary Act of 1779, prison clothing was to be of 'coarse and uniform Apparel, with certain Obvious Marks or Badges affixed to the same, as well as to Humiliate the wearer as to facilitate Discovery in Case of Escapes'.[47] The cutting of prisoners' hair has also been a widespread practice and may reflect a complex psychology. Although there may have been pragmatic grounds in some cases (e.g. to deal with lice), there are undoubtedly other potent reasons for this practice. I. M. Lewis has suggested that there may exist in many societies a linked idea between short hair and the acceptance of discipline and authority (as in the case of monks and soldiers) and between long hair and defiance of an established order.[48] But, whatever the explanation, there can be little doubt that the process of admission to prison, often involving a change of appearance and certainly emphasizing a change of status, may be subjectively experienced by many convicted offenders as an extra element of punishment, a humiliation overlaying the loss of liberty.

EXPULSION AND OSTRACISM

There is a clear relation between incarceration and measures of expulsion, since both involve a restriction on freedom of movement and in some instances, such as the use of overseas penal colonies or internal exile within large states, the two terms could be used interchangeably (as Sally Falk Moore puts the matter: 'Imprisonment may be a form of internal expulsion').[49] But the distinguishing feature of many forms of expulsion is the element of rejection and that of severing of pre-existing relations. The essence of banishment is the exclusion of its subject, without necessarily taking any further steps to restrict freedom of movement once banished.[50] Indeed, in contrast to the model of the remote penal colony, where a regime of confinement is prescribed, there is a large measure of indifference to the fate of the excluded person. In this way, the impact of such measures lies only partly in the act of physical exclusion; a significant element lies at the psychological level, experienced through the knowledge that one is no longer a matter of interest or concern to one's former friends and acquaintances. We shall, therefore, use the general term 'expulsion' in the distinctive sense of ostracism as well as physical removal. And it is the process of ostracism in itself that remains highly significant in interpersonal relations, while banishment in the more traditional territorial sense of being ordered away has declined in importance as a formal measure of punishment.

We have made the point earlier that, while expulsion may be a meaningful measure in the context of tightly knit pre-industrial societies and of a hostile natural environment, it is less feasible in a contemporary industrialized society.[51] Not surprisingly, therefore, it is easier to find historical examples of territorial banishment, but it may still be encountered more recently in some tribal societies (see, for example, the discussions by Llewelyn and Hoebel of Cheyenne practice;[52] J. H. Driberg and T. T. Hayley of the Lango;[53] and Hoebel of the Pueblo).[54] A significant relation is posited in some of this discussion (for instance by Sally Falk Moore) between collective responsibility in tribal societies and expulsion of an individual whose behaviour has given rise so often to such responsibility that the group will no longer answer for him, and so he is rejected from the society[55] (and compare in this respect, at a different level, the decision in 1976 of the United Kingdom to no longer be a defendant in any proceedings under the European Convention on Human Rights in relation to acts occurring within the Isle of Man).[56] In some societies, expulsion could also serve to protect other members of society from further violent or antisocial behaviour on the part of the banished member, a function that in many cases is now more commonly served by imprisonment.[57] For as communications have improved and the wilder environment has been progressively tamed, the punitive and protective potential of expulsion has been reduced and the measure has evolved through transportation, internal exile, and the like to merge to a large extent with incarceration.

But while physical expulsion has become less of a practicable option, psychological banishment, or social ostracism as it may be sometimes called, remains a penal process with real impact in interpersonal relations. The individual whose own fulfilment is dependent upon membership of a particular social group is especially vulnerable in this way (for a literary exploration of this idea, see George Eliot's novel, *Silas Marner*).[58] Also, in this respect the international community is closer to a group of individuals than a state legal system, and states may experience an analogous form of ostracism, through such processes as non-recognition, severance of diplomatic relations, or refusal to have dealings in particular matters, such as trade or cultural or sporting exchanges. South Africa comes to mind as a kind of contemporary international pariah, but other states too have experienced a degree of ostracism at times, such as Soviet Russia in its early days, while the Jewish nation experienced territorial expulsion and forcible diaspora.[59]

Finally, it may be added that the effects of penal expulsion may be very difficult to assess and this is an issue highly dependent upon context. The point is summed up by Sally Falk Moore: 'The seriousness of the penalty of expulsion depends on how easy it is to attach oneself to another community and to what extent one is a second-class citizen in that community. Does one become an "outlaw", a refugee or a welcome immigrant?'[60] This statement has a general validity, whether in the context of simple societies or of interpersonal relations. In the context of the international community, the issue appears rather differently, in terms of the degree of ostracism experienced and how that affects different aspects of inter-state relations.

CONTINUITY AND CHANGE: THE BOUNDARIES OF PUNISHMENT AND THE IDEA OF PROPORTION

The factors that may change the form of punishment employed over a period of time may be many and complex and it will be impossible to provide anything approaching an exhaustive account. Foucault, who has made a significant contribution in charting the transition in the nature and social meaning of European judicial punishment, identifies this transition with a number of broad historical processes, which include demographic, economic, and scientific developments. Beyond generalizations and hypotheses, within such broad outlines, it is difficult to go.[61] We shall content ourselves with a few observations.

Firstly, we have already argued that certain penal methods may be associated particularly, though not, we would maintain, exclusively, with particular forms of social organization. So, for example, ostracism may be more feasible among nomadic hunter-gatherers than among settled village cultivators, for whom mutual support may be vital for survival. Physical violence administered vicariously within the feud system will depend on the existence of a settled kinship structure. Evidently, then, changes that affect major factors of social organization – an expanding population, a destruction of settled kinship ties, e.g. by resettlement or a technological change related to cultivation – may well have an influence on the phenomenology of punitive technique. Changing conceptions of pain – which may be brought about by any number of factors, from the discovery of analgesics, to an improved diet, to the formulation of tools that are less likely to break, causing injury – may similarly be influential. It is more than probable, we feel, that a person who is a member of a society in which individuals are born in pain, will live with pain and die early and in pain will have a different perception of corporal punishment (as regards their criminals, children, and domestic animals) from that of the twentieth-century Western European.

Similarly, we have seen that reputation as an object of punishment may be more obviously suited to such a role in a small-scale hierarchical community. The punishment of reputation may also be affected by the availability of mass communication, by literacy or technology, as may other penal forms. Where once the site of the gallows or the pillory was the locus of 'live theatre', the television, the film, and the newspaper may now have allowed it to retreat indoors or even disappear altogether. Certainly there is now no need for the electric chair to be taken to the scene of the crime as it was in the United States only thirty years ago,[62] when a description of its operation can now be provided to accompany the breakfast cereal or to speak from the corner of the lounge. Such factors may affect not only the physical location of the punishment, but also the theatricality of its gestures.

Proportionality in punishment is another point that deserves our attention. The idea, we have argued, is very widely dispersed in the administration of punishments. We know of no society, wherever it draws its boundaries of acceptable penal activity, in which there is no understanding of the doctrine of 'excessive' punishment, no notion of 'going too far'. Proportionality, we have suggested, is an integral element in many conceptions of justice and it has, no doubt because of this feature, an important sociological role in preventing the escalation of disputes. Yet this assertion, of course, begs many questions about how graduations of both offence seriousness and seriousness of punishment are arrived at.

Piaget maintained that very young children attribute blame objectively, apportioning it in accordance with the amount of damage produced.[63] Later in their development, he argued, subjective factors, intention and motive, were added to this simple objective criterion but apparently without depriving it of its force. Yet however it is judged, there does seem to be a considerable measure of consensus in the relative weighting of seriousness of 'criminal' wrong, a consensus that seems to be consistent even across divisions (albeit not enormous) of time and culture, and within social groups within a country.[64] Seriousness of the perceived offence does seem, at least in some instances, to be a factor of great importance in the decision as to the gravity of punishment deemed to be suitable, although it is conceded that the relationship may not be a simple one.[65]

The idea of proportionality retains an importance, we would maintain, even within a system employing penal techniques that would be regarded by many as excessive, though the idea of lack of proportion may be voiced only as a moral criticism of the punishing system. In Foucault's famous example, Damiens, a regicide and hence the most dangerous type of criminal for a penal authority centred on the monarchical state, is awarded the most hideous of punishments. Yet, as we have pointed out, this is not to assume that the same penalty for all offences would have been acceptable to a popular notion of penality, which, as we have indicated, may act as a mediating agent in state punitive systems.[66] This is not to say, of course, that it is impossible to impose a regime that runs entirely contrary to popular notions of desert, but it may not be easy to maintain such a regime without difficulty.

Foucault's analysis of the public execution in the age of corporeal state punishment urges that the spectacle of terror was not intended to represent proportionate response to the wrong done – it was indeed deliberately disproportionate.[67] Yet Foucault also stresses, without explaining in any detail the differential response, that in many instances popular reaction at the scaffold was not evidenced by the crowd's acceptance of the spectacle but could result in disorder and riot. In these cases spectators themselves 'enter by force the punitive mechanism'.[68] Evidently, this reaction may have been sparked off by many things external to the spectacle of the punishment and to which it may have acted as a point of focus. But it may also have been (and Foucault's own examples at times support this) that popular penality (here the penality of the attendant masses, not that of the jurors, whose role we have considered elsewhere) and a sense of proportion assert themselves. For a crowd might react when it sees that a man has been unjustly convicted but might also do so when it sees, even within a code, the penalties of which are widely regarded as disproportionate, an extra disproportionate element added. Hence, Foucault instances a riot after a murderer's execution was bungled and immense pain was caused in the attempt to hang him.[69]

Peter Linebaugh's survey of the popular reaction to the practice of dissection undertaken by the surgeons upon the corpses of hanged men in eighteenth-century England suggests a similar sentiment.[70] Even though an extreme penal code may be, if not accepted, then at least tolerated, an extra disproportion – either too much pain being caused or the attempt to meddle with death in addition to the taking of life – may be enough to provoke the oppositional reaction. Whether, of course, the reaction is directed against the 'extra' disproportion or the 'wider' disproportion would be a matter difficult to determine. It is interesting, in view of Linebaugh's evidence, to note that the idea of additional mutilation to a corpse is still regarded with abhorrence in at least some penal systems that still employ capital punishment. An assistant warden at Louisiana State Penitentiary commented with regard to the contemporary operation of the electric chair: 'The idea is not to have any overkill – excessive scarring for example.'[71]

Let us recapitulate the point we are making here. Proportion in punishment, we have argued earlier, is a widely found and deeply rooted principle in many penal contexts. It is, we have suggested, integral to many conceptions of justice and as such the principle of proportion in punishment seen generally acts to annul, rather than to exacerbate, social dysfunction. Even within penal regimes in which the scales of penality are set high, even 'disproportionately' high, ideas of proportion may still be significant within those regimes and indeed may well be clearly evidenced – as, for example, when popular penality interposes itself in an attempt to moderate the disproportion, or where, even within a system enforced against popular conceptions of justice, an additional injustice or additional disproportion is introduced. The reaction may be direct, as in the case of jury equity or the riot at the scaffold, or may be restricted to criticism, 'growling' at the wrong involved in the breach of proportion.

So too in the case of the punishment of children. Although the boundaries of punishment regarded as legitimate may differ across time and space, within those boundaries a sense of proportion will still generally, it would appear, be considered proper – severity being graduated within the canon of permitted punitive action. This may even be spelled out in terms of an almost formal graduated table of different kinds and extents of penalty. So, in the diary of C. Mather (1663–1728) we learn:

> The *first Chastisement*, which I inflict for an ordinary Fault, is, to lett the Child see and hear me in an Astonishment, and hardly able to beleeve that the Child could do so *base* a Thing, but beleeving that they will never do it again. I would never come to give a child a *Blow* except in Case of Obstinacy or some gross Enormity. To be chaste for a while out of my Presence, I would make to be looked upon the sorest Punishment in the Family.[72]

The question as to how far the boundaries of permissible child discipline have shifted historically is a vexed one. Many authors consider that child discipline has declined generally in severity over the years,[73] but Linda Pollock, in a recent text, has doubted this thesis.[74] Certainly the intervention acknowledged as proper by state agencies in such matters has increased, and it may be that the boundaries acknowledged as proper by those agencies in this respect have become more restrictive, as they have in respect of the treatment of convicts or of animals.[75] This, of course, raises a number of questions, in particular whether this is simply a case of more active state setting guidelines in areas that have traditionally been left to self-regulation, and whether state regulation follows changed public perceptions or leads them.

NOTES

1 THEMES AND ANALYSES

1 *De Universo*, Hrabanus Maurus, ninth century. Cf. the work of Isidore in the seventh century.

2 See the discussion in ch. 4.

3 For a useful overview of the development and present state of this discipline, see I. M. Lewis, *Social Anthropology in Perspective: the Relevance of Social Anthropology*, 2nd edn (Cambridge University Press, 1985).

4 This problem will be explored more fully in ch. 6. On the problem of cultural relativism, see Piers Beirne, 'Cultural relativism and comparative criminology', *Contemporary Crises* 7 (1983), 371.

5 Immanuel Kant, *The Philosophy of Law: An Exposition of the Fundamental Principles of Jurisprudence as the Science of Right*, 1797, trans. W. Hastie (T. & T. Clark, Edinburgh, 1887), p. 198.

6 Images conjured by the work of Jeremy Bentham [see *An Introduction to the Principles of Morals and Legislation*, ed. J. H. Burns and H. L. A. Hart (Athlone Press, London, 1970)] and Baroness Wootton [see *Crime and the Criminal Law*, 2nd edn (Stevens, London, 1975)].

7 For use of the term with the qualifying adjective, see e.g. H. L. A. Hart, *Punishment and Responsibility: Essays in the Philosophy of Law* (Oxford University Press, London, 1968), p. 1; Torstein Eckhoff, 'Justifications of punishment', in A. Duff and N. Simmonds (eds), *Philosophy and the Criminal Law* (Steiner, Stuttgart, 1984).

8 Cf. Hart's discussion of retribution in distribution (Hart, *Punishment and Responsibility*, pp. 11–13) and see ch. 4.

9 Eckhoff, 'Justifications of punishment', p. 9.

10 Ibid., p. 9.

11 See in particular Hart, *Punishment and Responsibility*, ch. 1.

12 Ibid., p. 5.

13 Ibid., pp. 3–4.

14 This statement is, of course, empirically verifiable only with considerable difficulty. At the same time, it is one that would be difficult to dispute convincingly.

15 R. J. Gerber and P. D. McAnany, *Contemporary Punishment* ('Views,

207

explanations and justifications', in the introduction to the paper by Antony Flew) (Notre Dame Press, Indiana, 1972).

16 Ibid., p. 9.

17 David Garland and Peter Young (eds), *The Power to Punish: Contemporary Penality and Social Analysis* (Heinemann, London, 1983), pp. 9, 36. See also the review of Garland and Young by Arie Freiberg, *Contemporary Crises* 9 (1985), 387.

18 E.g., Michael Ignatieff, 'State, civil society and total institutions: a critique of recent social histories of punishment', in M. Tonry and N. Morris (eds), *Crime and Justice: An Annual Review of Research*, vol. 3 (University of Chicago Press, 1981), p. 153; Stanley Cohen, 'The punitive city: notes on the dispersal of social control', *Contemporary Crises* 3 (1979), 340.

19 See in particular the discussion by Michel Foucault, *Discipline and Punish: the Birth of the Prison* (Allen Lane, London, 1977); Steven Spitzer, 'Punishment and social organisation: a study of Durkheim's theory of penal evolution', *Law and Society Review* 9 (1975), 613; Stanley Cohen, *Visions of Social Control: Crime, Punishment and Classification* (Polity Press, Cambridge, 1985) on this question.

2 PUNISHMENT, STATE, AND SOCIETY

1 Michael Ignatieff, 'State, civil society and total institutions: a critique of recent social histories of punishment', in M. Tonry and N. Morris (eds), *Crime and Justice: An Annual Review of Research*, vol. 3 (University of Chicago Press, 1981), pp. 99–100. Stanley Cohen makes a similar point: agencies of social control 'need locating within the physical space of the city, but more important in the overall social space'; see 'The punitive city: notes on the dispersal of social control', *Contemporary Crises* 3 (1979), 340.

2 See generally, Martin L. Friedland, *Double Jeopardy* (Clarendon Press, Oxford, 1969).

3 H. D. Willcocks and J. Stokes, *Deterrents and Incentives to Crime Among Boys and Young Men Aged 15–21 Years* (Office of Population Censuses and Surveys, Social Survey Division, London, 1968).

4 Peter Young, 'Sociology, the state and penal relations', in David Garland and Peter Young (eds), *The Power to Punish: Contemporary Penality and Social Analysis* (Heinemann, London, 1983), p. 90.

5 J. D. Mabbott, 'Punishment', in H. B. Acton (ed.), *The Philosophy of Punishment* (Macmillan, London, 1969), p. 42; originally published in *Mind* XLVIII: 190 (1939).

6 Ibid., p. 42.

7 J. D. Mabbott, 'Professor Flew on punishment', in Acton (ed.), *Philosophy of Punishment*, p. 119; originally published in *Philosophy* 30 (1955).

8 H. J. McCloskey, 'The complexity of the concept of punishment', *Philosophy* 37 (1962), 307.

9 Ibid., p. 315.

10 David Garland and Peter Young, 'Towards a social analysis of penality', in Garland and Young (eds), *The Power to Punish*, p. 14.
11 Ibid., p. 36.
12 Young, 'Sociology, the state and penal relations'.
13 Michael Mann, *The Sources of Social Power* (Cambridge University Press, 1986), pp. 2, 14.
14 Michel Foucault, *The History of Sexuality*, vol. 1 (Allen Lane, London, 1979), p. 92 (translated from *La histoire de la sexualité*, Gallimard, Paris, 1976).
15 Leopold Pospisil, *Anthropology of Law: a Comparative Theory* (Harper & Row, New York, 1971), p. 99.
16 See Pospisil, *Anthropology of Law*, generally on these other writers, pp. 102 *et seq.* and his comment at p. 102: 'it is interesting to learn that credit for the nontraditionalist school of thought which did not limit its inquiry to the level of state or society must be given to jurisprudence rather than the social sciences'.
17 Eugen Ehrlich, *Fundamental Principles of the Sociology of Law* (Harvard University Press, 1936). For Otto Von Gierke, see *Das deutsche Genossen Schaftrecht* (Wiedmann, Berlin, 1868).
18 Max Weber, *Law in Economy and Society*, ed. Max Rheinstein (Simon & Schuster, New York, 1967).
19 A. L. Epstein, *s.v.* 'Sanctions', *International Encyclopaedia of the Social Sciences*, ed. D. L. Sills, vol. 14 (Macmillan/The Free Press, New York, 1968), p. 1.
20 E. Adamson Hoebel, *The Law of Primitive Man* (Harvard University Press, 1954), p. 50.
21 J. Middleton, *Lugbara Religion* (Oxford University Press for the International African Institute, London, 1960).
22 *Observer*, 13 June 1987.
23 See: A. C. Bickley, 'Some notes on a custom at Woking, Surrey', *Home Counties Magazine* IV (1902), 25; Violet Alford, 'Rough music or charivari', *Folklore* 70 (1959), 505; Natalie Zemon Davis, 'The reasons of misrule: youth groups and charivaris in sixteenth century France', *Past and Present* 50 (1971), 41; E. P. Thompson, 'Rough music! Le charivari anglais', *Annales: économies, sociétés et civilisations* 27 (1972), 285.
24 See Thompson, 'Rough music'.
25 Davis, 'Reasons of misrule', p. 75.
26 See Herbert R. Lottman, *The People's Anger: Justice and Revenge in Post-Liberation France* (Hutchinson, London, 1986), for a discussion of this phenomenon in post-Second World War France.
27 See Lottman, *The People's Anger*; and Thompson, 'Rough music', where reference is made to 'tribunals'.
28 Philip Priestley, *Community of Scapegoats: The Segregation of Sex Offenders and Informers in Prisons* (Pergamon Press, Oxford, 1980).
29 P. Marsh, E. Rosser, and R. Harré, *Rules of Disorder* (Routledge & Kegan Paul, London, 1978).
30 Ibid., p. 45.

3 CONFLICTS AND TENSIONS WITHIN THE PENAL NETWORK

1 See generally, Martin L. Friedland, *Double Jeopardy* (Clarendon Press, Oxford, 1969), Part I.
2 Justinian's Digest, D.48.2.7.2. and C.9.2.9. See also 'Jurisdiction with respect to crime', *Harvard Research in International Law*, supplement to *American Journal of International Law* 29 (1935), 602.
3 See Friedland, *Double Jeopardy, passim.*
4 See, e.g., Article 13 of the Harvard Research Draft Convention on Jurisdiction with Respect to Crime, supplement to *American Journal of International Law* 29 (1935), 602.
5 See Friedland, *Double Jeopardy*, pp. 326 *et seq.*
6 See, e.g., in connection with the regulation of anti-competitive practices within the EEC: Case 14/68, *Wilhelm* v. *Bundeskartellamt* (1969) E.C.R. 1; Case 7/72, *Boehringer Mannheim* v. *Commission* (1972) E.C.R. 1281.
7 See the judgment of the Court of Criminal Appeal in *R* v. *Dawson, R* v. *Wenlock* (1960) 1 All E.R. 558.
8 D. A. Thomas, *Principles of Sentencing*, 2nd edn (Heinemann, London, 1979), pp. 211 *et seq.*: Andrew Ashworth, *Sentencing and Penal Policy* (Weidenfeld & Nicolson, London, 1983), pp. 425–7; and see the remarks of Scarman LJ in *R* v. *Daryl Parker* (1977) 2 All E.R. 37.
9 For examples of recent studies of prosecutorial practice in the UK, see S. R. Moody and J. Tombs, *Prosecution in the Public Interest* (Scottish Academic Press, Edinburgh, 1982); Graham Mansfield and Jill Peay, *The Director of Public Prosecutions* (Tavistock, London, 1987).
10 See the results of the study by H. D. Willcock and J. Stokes, *Deterrents and Incentives to Crime Among Boys and Young Men Aged 15–21 Years* (Office of Population Censuses and Surveys, Social Survey Division, 1968).
11 See, e.g. V. A. C. Gatrell, 'The decline of theft and violence in Victorian and Edwardian England', in V. A. C. Gatrell, Bruce Lenman, and Geoffrey Parker (eds), *Crime and the Law: the Social History of Crime in Western Europe since 1500* (Europa Publications, London, 1980), p. 251.
12 Especially 'moral' offences and the breach of local and community sensibility. This has often been the subject of family and local community sanctions: adultery, for example, not an offence under English criminal law, but behaviour that may still be subject to localized, unofficial responses, such as 'rough music'.
13 On the legal powers of the Roman *Paterfamilias*, see: Barry Nicholas, *Introduction to Roman Law* (Clarendon Press, Oxford, 1962; 1975), pp. 65 *et seq.*: J. A. C. Thomas, *Textbook of Roman Law* (North Holland, Amsterdam, 1976), ch. 37.
14 On the parental power of chastisement of children, see *Bromley's Family Law*, 7th edn (Butterworth, London, 1987), p. 274; Stephen M. Cretney, *Principles of Family Law*, 4th edn (Sweet & Maxwell, London, 1984), p. 304; *R* v. *Hopley* (1860) 2 F & F 202; and see the discussion of punishment of children in ch. 10.

15 As under s. 1 of the UK Children and Young Persons Act 1969.

16 See, e.g., the judgment of Lord Denning, MR in *Fraser* v. *Mudge* (1975) 3 All E.R. 78.

17 For a useful account of the development of prisoners' rights, especially within the UK, see Mike Maguire, John Vagg, and Rod Morgan (eds), *Accountability and Prisons* (Tavistock, London, 1985).

18 See Edward Fitzgerald, 'Prison discipline and the courts' and Genevra Richardson, 'Judicial intervention in prison life', chs 2 and 3 in Maguire *et al.* (eds), *Accountability and Prisons*.

19 See further discussion of this question in ch. 8.

20 Such shifts, resulting in 'supervised' and 'delegated' penality may be identified in certain less obvious contexts, for instance in the case of financial institutions in the City of London undertaking to 'keep their own house in order'; or, very different again, increasing intervention in relation to 'socialization' processes, such as initiation ceremonies in educational and military contexts.

21 Especially in relation to war crimes, crimes against humanity, terrorist activities, international or cross-frontier economic crime, drug trafficking, and the uniformity of punishments.

22 See e.g. Benjamin Ferencz, *An International Criminal Court: a Step Towards World Peace* (Oceana Publications, New York, 1980).

23 Consider, for instance, the denouement of Fritz Lang's film *M* (1931), with its implication that the trial and punishment of a child-molester and child-murderer by criminal organizations rather than the state would be unacceptable.

24 Moreover, it may not be easy to identify such objectives, or distinguish them from rationalizations of penal practice. See the discussion in ch. 6.

25 This is reflected, in a contemporary context of 'official' state action in the UK, in the important choice in many cases between cautioning and prosecuting offenders.

26 *Oxford English Dictionary* definition. The role of penology will be more fully considered in ch. 4.

27 The term used in the legal system of the Federal Republic of Germany; see J. H. Langbein, 'Controlling prosecutorial discretion in Germany', *University of Chicago Law Review* 41 (1973), 439.

28 Willcock and Stokes, *Deterrents and Incentives*.

29 Nigel Walker, *Sentencing in a Rational Society* (Penguin, Harmondsworth, 1969), p. 89.

30 Vigilantism, or self-help in imposing law and order, is an interesting phenomenon. It is especially associated with American frontier activity in the days of fledgling municipal organization (see the entry by Glenn S. Dumke in the *Encyclopaedia Americana*, vol. 28 (Americana Corporation, New York, 1968), pp. 113–14), but the term 'vigilante activity' has been given a variety of applications, more recently in relation to citizen 'self-help' against street crime in cities such as New York.

31 It may be argued, for instance, that it is the higher visibility of legal proceedings, and the greater opportunity for public scrutiny, that may

lend them a higher content of 'due process' as compared to family and other procedures.

32 See ch. 8.

33 See: *United Nations Action in the Field of Human Rights* (United Nations, New York, 1983), para. 143 *et seq*. For information, see Charles Humana, *World Human Rights Guide* (Pan Books, London, 1987).

34 Edward Peters, *Torture* (Basil Blackwell, Oxford, 1985).

35 Declaration of the Protection of All Persons from Being Subjected to Torture and Other Cruel, Inhuman or Degrading Treatment or Punishment, G. A. Res. 3452 (XXX) of 9 December 1975.

36 See generally on this area: Karel Vasak (gen. ed.), *The International Dimensions of Human Rights* (Greenwood Press, Westport, Conn. and UNESCO, Paris, 1982), revised and edited for the English edition by Philip Alston.

37 An accommodation of this fact – in effect, a kind of agreement to disagree – is reflected, for example, in recent arrangements for the transfer of alien prisoners to complete their sentences in their own countries. See e.g. the Treaty between the US and Turkey on Extradition and Mutual Assistance in Criminal Matters, 7 June 1979 and the discussion by E. A. Nadelmann, 'Negotiations in criminal law assistance treaties' *American Journal of Comparative Law* 33 (1985), 467.

38 In particular, the introduction of such measures in 'renascent' Islamic systems, such as Pakistan and Sudan (under Numeiri) provoked special criticism from western observers. See also the discussion by M. A. Abdelrahman, 'Medicine, psychiatry and human rights' (unpublished Ph.D thesis, University of Wales, 1987), pp. 31 *et seq*.

39 Does or should a convicted person have the right to choose death rather than life imprisonment? Cf. the case of Gary Gilmore, executed in Utah in January 1977: Gilmore had expressed strongly his wish to die and had made two attempts at suicide in protest against two stays of execution. And cf. the splendid blues song performed by Bessie Smith, 'Send me to the 'lectric chair'.

40 *Ireland* v. *UK*, judgment of 18 January 1978, *Publications of the European Court of Human Rights*, series A, vol. 25.

41 Ibid., pp. 66–7.

42 *Amnesty International Report*, 8 September 1987; *Observer*, 13 September 1987. The term 'stubborn disease' was used in *Chinese Legal News*, in 1985.

4 LORE AND DOCTRINE: FROM A REFLEXIVE TO A REFLECTIVE EXPERIENCE OF PUNISHMENT

1 David Garland and Peter Young, 'Towards a social analysis of penality', in David Garland and Peter Young (eds), *The Power to Punish: Contemporary Penality and Social Analysis* (Heinemann, London, 1983).

2 See in particular Michel Foucault's *Les mots et les choses* (Gallimard, Paris, 1966), transl. *The Order of Things* (Tavistock, London, 1970) and

L'archéologie du savoir (Gallimard, Paris, 1969), transl. *Archaeology of Knowledge* (Tavistock, London, 1972).

3   H. L. A. Hart, *Punishment and Responsibility* (Oxford University Press, 1968), p. 3.

4   Jeremy Bentham, *An Introduction to the Principles of Morals and Legislation*, ed. J. H. Burns and H. L. A. Hart (Athlone Press, London, 1970), p. 158: 'But all punishment is mischief: all punishment in itself is evil.'

5   Ted Honderich, *Punishment: the Supposed Justifications* (Penguin, Harmondsworth, 1971; 1976), p. 9.

6   Garland and Young (eds), *The Power to Punish*, p. 11. See also Garland's critique of the 'Grand Debate' in 'Philosophical argument and ideological effect', *Contemporary Crises* 7 (1983), 79.

7   Antony Flew, 'The justification of punishment', *Philosophy* 29 (1954), 291; S. I. Benn, 'An approach to the problems of punishment', *Philosophy* (1958) 325–6; Hart, *Punishment and Responsibility*, pp. 4–5.

8   Hart, *Punishment and Responsibility*, pp. 5–6.

9   Immanuel Kant, *The Philosophy of Law: an Exposition of the Fundamental Principles of Jurisprudence as the Science of Right*, 1797 transl. W. Hastie, (T. & T. Clark, Edinburgh, 1887).

10 Bentham, *Principles of Morals and Legislation*, ch. XIII.

11 Hart, *Punishment and Responsibility*, ch. 1. Cf. Dean H. Clarke, 'Justifications for punishment', *Contemporary Crises* 6 (1982), 25.

12 Hart, *Punishment and Responsibility*, p. 1.

13 Stanley E. Grupp (ed.), *Theories of Punishment* (Indiana University Press, 1971), p. 4.

14 Honderich, *Punishment*, p. 9.

15 See e.g., Baroness Wootton, *Social Science and Social Pathology* (Allen & Unwin, London, 1959), ch. VIII.

16 Hart, *Punishment and Responsibility*, p. 9.

17 See, e.g., Harry Elmer Barnes, ch. 1 in Harry Elmer Barnes (ed.), *An Introduction to the History of Sociology*, 7th edn (University of Chicago Press, Chicago and London, 1965); Robert Bierstedt, 'Sociological thought in the eighteenth century', in Tom Bottomore and Robert Nisbet (eds), *A History of Sociological Analysis* (Heinemann, London, 1978).

18 See Emile Durkheim, *The Rules of Sociological Method*, 8th edn, transl. Sarah Solovay and John Mueller (Collier Macmillan, London, 1938).

19 Much of this writing is conveniently summarized in the Bibliography in Leon Radzinowicz and Roger Hood, *A History of English Criminal Law*, vol. 5 (Stevens, London, 1985), section IV(1), pp. 890–925.

20 Garland and Young (eds), *The Power to Punish*, p. 13.

21 G. Rusche and O. Kirchheimer, *Punishment and Social Structure* (Columbia University Press, New York, 1939; reissued 1968).

22 Rusche and Kirchheimer, *Punishment and Social Structure*; Michel Foucault, *Discipline and Punish: the Birth of the Prison* (Allen Lane, London, 1977); Michael Ignatieff, *A Just Measure of Pain: the Penitentiary in the Industrial Revolution 1750–1850* (Macmillan, London, 1978); Andrew Scull, *Decarceration: Community Treatment and the Deviant*, 2nd edn

(Polity Press, Cambridge, 1984); Dario Melossi and Massimo Pavarini, *The Prison and the Factory: Origins of the Penitentiary System* (Macmillan, London, 1981); Stanley Cohen, *Visions of Social Control* (Polity Press, Cambridge, 1985); David Garland, *Punishment and Welfare: a History of Penal Strategies* (Gower, Aldershot, 1985).

23 Garland, *Punishment and Welfare*, pp. 3–4.
24 C. Z. Weiner, 'Sex roles and crime in late Elizabethan Hertfordshire', *Journal of Social History* 8 (1975), 38.
25 J. A. Beattie, 'Crime and the courts in Surrey, 1736–1753', in J. S. Cockburn (ed.), *Crime in England 1550–1800* (Methuen, London, 1977).
26 Eric Stockdale, *A Study of Bedford Prison, 1660–1877* (Phillimore, London, 1977).
27 J. A. Sharpe, *Crime in Seventeenth Century England* (Cambridge University Press, 1983).
28 W. J. Forsythe, *A System of Discipline: Exeter Borough Prison 1819–1863* (University of Exeter, 1983).
29 John L. McMullan, 'Crime, law and order in early modern England', *British Journal of Criminology* 29 (1987), 252.
30 John Howard, *The State of the Prisons*, Bicentennial edn (Professional Books, Abingdon, 1977).
31 H. Mayhew and J. Binny, *The Criminal Prisons of London and Scenes of Prison Life* (Griffin, Bohn & Co., London, 1862).
32 Ibid.
33 Charles Dickens, 'Philadelphia and its solitary prison', in *American Notes* (Collins, London, 1842).
34 John Galsworthy, *The Spirit of Punishment* (Humanitarian League, 1910).
35 See Jo Manton, *Mary Carpenter and the Children of the Streets* (Heinemann, London, 1976); for her publications, see Radzinowicz and Hood, *History of English Criminal Law*, vol. 5, Bibliography, pp. 896–7.
36 See, e.g., William Tallack, *Humanity and Humanitarianism* (Howard Association, London, 1871); *Penological and Preventive Principles* (Wertheimer, Lea & Co., London, 1889; 1896).
37 See Radzinowicz and Hood, *History of English Criminal Law*, vol. 5, Bibliography, under: Frederic Hill, Rev. J. T. Burt, W. L. Clay, W. D. Morrison, G. L. Chesterton, and Sir Edmund Du Cane. For Joshua Jebb, see his *Report and Observations on the Discipline and Management of Convict Prisons* (London, 1863).
38 W. D. Morrison, 'The increase of crime', *Nineteenth Century* (1892), 950; Sir Edmund Du Cane, 'The decrease of crime', *Nineteenth Century* 33 (1893), 480.
39 The centrality of the criminal law and the state penal system in penological discussion is reinforced by the titles of some of the British literature, e.g., 'The war against crime' (UK Government White Paper, 1964, Cmnd 2296); *Society Against Crime*, ed. Howard Jones (Penguin, Harmondsworth, 1981).
40 Garland and Young (eds), *The Power to Punish*, p. 4.
41 There is a large literature here; for a useful overview and bibliography,

see Michael Ignatieff, 'State, civil society and total institutions: a critique of recent social histories of punishment', in M. Tonry and N. Morris (eds), *Crime and Justice: an Annual Review of Research*, vol. 3 (University of Chicago Press, 1981).

42 Foucault, *Discipline and Punish*, p. 113.

43 Ibid., p. 301.

44 For an overview of the literature in this area, see I. M. Lewis, *Social Anthropology in Perspective*, 2nd edn (Cambridge University Press, 1985).

45 See David Stafford-Clark, *What Freud Really Said* (Penguin, Harmondsworth, 1967); Sigmund Freud, *Introductory Lectures on Psychoanalysis* (Pelican Freud Library, no. 1, Harmondsworth, 1973); for the Rat Man, see no. 9 in the same series.

46 B. F. Skinner, *Beyond Freedom and Dignity* (Jonathan Cape, London, 1972).

47 Ibid., p. 62. See also H. Wheeler, 'A non-punitive world?', in H. Wheeler (ed.), *Beyond the Punitive Society* (Wildwood House, London, 1973).

48 For a useful and generally informative account of the 'intellectual jump' in European culture, see J. M. Roberts, *The Triumph of the West* (BBC Publications, London, 1985), ch. VIII. A particular theoretical view of this phenomenon is presented by Foucault in *The Order of Things*, although some would undoubtedly regard his analysis as contestable.

49 See J. T. McNeill and H. M. Gamer, *Medieval Handbooks of Penance* (Octagon Books, New York, 1965).

50 To take just one example: the rise of Islam. Parts of the *Qur'an* (Koran) constitute a movement towards social reform inspired by a radical sense of justice.

51 See the discussion of these transitions in ch. 10.

52 This point may be related to our earlier discussion of cross-cultural tensions in the use of punishment, see ch. 3.

5 PUNISHMENT, RULE, AND SOCIAL ORGANIZATION

1 Further criticisms of H. L. A. Hart's position are developed later. For views on the empirical/analytical ambiguity in Hart's work, see R. N. Moles, *Definition and Rule in Legal Theory* (Basil Backwell, Oxford, 1987), pp. 88 *et seq.* on the question of social rules generally, and see also J. W. Harris, *Law and Legal Science* (Clarendon Press, Oxford, 1979), p. 58, and P. M. S. Hacker, 'Hart's philosophy of law', in P. M. S. Hacker and J. Raz (eds), *Law, Morality and Society: Essays in Honour of H. L. A. Hart* (Clarendon Press, Oxford, 1977), esp. at p. 12.

2 A. M. Honoré, 'Groups, laws and obedience', in A. W. B. Simpson (ed.), *Oxford Essays in Jurisprudence*, 2nd series (Clarendon Press, Oxford, 1973), p. 3.

3 Ibid., p. 3.

4 S. Roberts, *Order and Dispute* (Penguin, Harmondsworth, 1979), p. 25.

5 S. E. Asch, *Social Psychology* (Oxford University Press, 1952; repr. 1987), p. 5.
6 Roberts, *Order and Dispute*, p. 32.
7 Honoré, 'Groups, laws and obedience', p. 14. The idea of efficiency as underlying the generality of rules goes back at least as far as von Jhering.
8 Ibid., p. 6.
9 I. M. Lewis, *Social Anthropology in Perspective*, 2nd edn (Cambridge University Press, 1985), p. 340.
10 E. Adamson Hoebel, *The Law of Primitive Man* (Harvard University Press, 1954), pp. 74–9.
11 Ibid., p. 139.
12 H. L. A. Hart, *The Concept of Law* (Clarendon Press, Oxford, 1961), pp. 189–95. For criticisms, see, e.g., N. McCormick, *H. L. A. Hart* (Edward Arnold, London, 1981), pp. 92–102.
13 C. M. Turnbull, *The Mountain People* (Jonathan Cape, London, 1973).
14 D. Hume, *Treatise of Human Nature*, 1739, ed. L. A. Selby Bigge, 2nd edn with revisions by P. H. Nidditch (Oxford University Press, 1978), p. 469.
15 Hart, *The Concept of Law*, pp. 54, 56.
16 Hence Hart's test of legal validity is dependent on conformity to the 'rule of recognition' rather than popular sentiment. See on this point Moles, *Definition and Rule in Legal Theory*, pp. 90 *et seq.*
17 See Hart, *The Concept of Law*, pp. 27, 41. Other jurists have recognized that legal material encompasses more than simply one type of rule: cf. the notion of 'performatory imperatives' discussed by Karl Olivecrona, *Law as Fact*, 2nd edn (Stevens, London, 1971), ch. 8; or the 'norms of competence' discussed by Alf Ross, *On Law and Justice* (Stevens, London, 1974).
18 At the time of writing there are discussions concerning possible change in the law. The relevant legislation at present is contained in the Shops Act 1950.
19 It is interesting to note that the phrase 'send to Coventry' may have related originally to Coventry gaol: see *The Penguin Dictionary of Historical Slang*, compiled by E. Partridge, abridged by J. Simpson (Harmondsworth, 1972), p. 216.
20 Moles, *Definition and Rule in Legal Theory*, p. 85.
21 Ibid., p. 87.
22 For the use of the term 'growling' see R. R. Marett, *The Threshold of Religion*, 1914, as quoted in F. Steiner, *Taboo* (Penguin, Harmondsworth, 1967).
23 R. Nozick, *Philosophical Explanations* (Harvard University Press, 1981), p. 369.
24 Ibid., p. 370, where a notion of Karma is discussed.
25 Hoebel, *Law of Primitive Man*, p. 70.
26 The issues of homosexuality and of AIDS were both discussed at the Church of England General Synod of 1987. See e.g. *The Times*, 11 and

12 November 1987. A great deal of popular and journalistic discussion was provoked at that time.

27 Antony Flew, 'The justification of punishment', *Philosophy* 29 (1954), 291, at p. 294.

28 See, e.g. *The Times*, 11 November 1987.

29 See, e.g., J. Bryce, *Studies in History and Jurisprudence*, cited in T. O. Elias, *The Nature of African Customary Law* (Manchester University Press, 1956), p. 58 and the discussion therein.

30 I. M. Lewis, *Social Anthropology*, p. 17.

31 Elias, *African Customary Law*, p. 61.

32 For the central role of sanctions in key classical legal theories see, for example, John Austin's *Province of Jurisprudence Determined* of 1832 (repr. Weidenfeld & Nicolson, London, 1954), Hans Kelsen's *General Theory of Law and State*, 1945, transl. A. Wedberg (reissued by Russell & Russell, New York, 1961). For the anthropological views see, for example, G. St J. Orde-Browne, cited in Elias, *African Customary Law*, p. 61, on the sanction and custom, and cf. Radcliffe-Browne's views also discussed there. For the classic synopsis of the early anthropological position, see B. Malinowski, *Crime and Custom in Savage Society*, 1926 (the text used here is of a 1932 issue, Kegan Paul, Trench, Trubner & Co., London).

33 Malinowski, *Crime and Custom*, p. 13.

34 See pp. 122 *et seq.*

35 R. A. LeVine, 'The internalization of political values in stateless societies', *Human Organization* 19: 2 (1960), pp. 51–8.

36 Ibid., p. 57.

37 J. and E. Newsom, *Four Years Old in an Urban Community* (Penguin, Harmondsworth, 1970), p. 450.

38 See our discussion on p. 206.

6 THE PURPOSES OF PUNISHMENT

1 R. Tannahill, *Sex in History* (Abacus, London, 1981), p. 365. See also Lloyd De Mause (ed.), *The History of Childhood* (Souvenir Press, London, 1976), p. 44.

2 C. Fitzmaurice and K. Pease, *The Psychology of Judicial Sentencing* (Manchester University Press, 1986), ch. 3.

3 Ibid., pp. 49–51. The argument is suggestive rather than conclusive, but the points raised demand serious consideration.

4 Ibid., pp. 52–9, reviewing the work of Wilkins, Gottfredson, Kress, *et al.*, in the US, and available British material.

5 We are aware of the danger of overstating this point but there is, we feel, considerable substance to it. A general overview of penal theory and practice, such as that provided by C. Harding, B. Hines, R. Ireland, and P. Rawlings, *Imprisonment in England and Wales: a Concise History* (Croom Helm, Beckenham, 1985) would, hardly surprisingly, support this contention.

6 Torstein Eckhoff, 'Justifications of punishment', in A. Duff and N.

Simmonds (eds), *Philosophy and the Criminal Law* (Steiner, Stuttgart, 1984).

7　See pp. 103 and 117.

8　Lord Denning's statement to the Royal Commission on Capital Punishment is quoted in H. L. A. Hart, *Punishment and Responsibility* (Oxford University Press, 1968), p. 170.

9　C. L. Ten, *Crime, Guilt and Punishment* (Clarendon Press, Oxford, 1987), p. 42. See also, Nigel Walker, *Sentencing in a Rational Society* (Penguin, Harmondsworth, 1972), pp. 36–8.

10　Ten, *Crime, Guilt and Punishment*, p. 41.

11　J. and E. Newsom, *Four Years Old in an Urban Community* (Penguin, Harmondsworth, 1970), p. 450; on verbalization in socialization, see ibid., ch. 14.

12　Leopold Pospisil, *Anthropology of Law: a Comparative Theory* (Harper & Row, New York, 1971), p. 90.

13　Ibid., p. 95. This is the case among the Nunamiut.

14　See *The Times*, 12 November 1987.

15　*Independent*, 22 December 1987.

16　Pospisil, *Anthropology of Law*, pp. 89–111.

17　See Lynda Nead's article 'The long and the short and the normal', which appeared in the *Guardian* in 1987, discussing the 'Guinness World of Records'. Unfortunately, we do not have a note of the date of the article.

18　A. R. Radcliffe-Brown, *s.v.* 'Sanction', *Encyclopaedia of Social Sciences* (Macmillan, New York, 1934), vol. 13, p. 533.

19　J. Toby, 'Is punishment necessary?' *Journal of Criminal Law, Criminology and Police Science* 55 (1964), 332, at p. 333.

20　Sigmund Freud, *Totem and Taboo* (Routledge, London, 1923), p. 57.

21　On ostracism generally, see S. Roberts, *Order and Dispute* (Penguin, Harmondsworth, 1979), pp. 65–7; on abjuration of the realm in medieval England, see R. F. Hunnisett, *The Medieval Coroner* (Cambridge University Press, 1961), ch. 3; on outlawry and excommunication in medieval England, see F. Pollock and F. W. Maitland, *History of English Law*, 2nd edn, 1898 (reissued 1968, Cambridge University Press), vol. 2, p. 449, vol. 1, pp. 478–80, respectively.

22　See generally, Geoffrey Pearson, *Hooligan: a History of Respectable Fears* (Macmillan, London, 1983). For the derivation of 'mugger', see Stuart Hall, Chas Critcher, Tony Jefferson, John Clarke and Brian Roberts, *Policing the Crisis* (Macmillan, London, 1978), p. 3.

23　See pp. 128 *et seq.*

24　These are the factors that, as we indicated earlier, appear to be of great importance in the area of criminal law sentencing. See n. 4, above.

25　Newsom and Newsom, *Four Years Old in an Urban Community*, p. 447.

26　See p. 204.

27　R. Nozick, *Philosophical Explanations* (Harvard University Press, 1981), p. 367.

28　Ibid., p. 366.

29 See p. 148.
30 R. C. Sherman and M. D. Dowdle, 'The perception of crime and punishment: a multidimensional scaling analysis', *Social Science Research* 3 (1974), 109, at p. 125.
31 For a discussion of the nature of feud see Pospisil, *Anthropology of Law*, pp. 2–9.
32 E. Adamson Hoebel, *The Law of Primitive Man* (Harvard University Press, 1954), p. 89.
33 See p. 154.
34 A. A. Ehrenzweig, *Psychoanalytic Jurisprudence* (Sijthoff, Leiden, 1971), p. 208.
35 Ted Honderich, *Punishment: the Supposed Justifications* (Hutchinson, London, 1969), p. 233.
36 R. M. Hare, *Moral Thinking: its Levels, Method and Point* (Oxford University Press, 1981), as discussed in Ten, *Crime, Guilt and Punishment*, pp. 27–32.
37 Nicola Lacey, 'Punishment, justice and consequentialism: a reply to Professor Eckhoff', in A. Duff and N. Simmonds (eds), *Philosophy and the Criminal Law* (Steiner, Stuttgart, 1984), pp. 24–5.
38 H. Morris, 'Persons and punishment', in J. G. Murphy (ed.), *Punishment and Rehabilitation* (Wadsworth, Belmont, 1973); J. M. Finnis, 'The restoration of retribution', *Analysis* 32 (1971–2), 131 and in *Natural Law and Natural Rights* (Clarendon Press, Oxford, 1980), pp. 262–6; J. G. Murphy, 'Marxism and retribution' in J. G. Murphy (ed.), *Retribution, Justice and Therapy* (D. Reidel, Dordrecht, 1979). For discussion, see Ten, *Crime, Guilt and Punishment*, pp. 52–65.
39 B. Malinowski, *Crime and Custom in Savage Society* (Kegan, Paul, Trench, Trubner & Co., London, 1932), *passim*, but chs 4, 8, and 9 in particular.
40 T. O. Elias, *The Nature of African Customary Law* (Manchester University Press, 1956), p. 70.
41 A. W. Gouldner, 'The norm of reciprocity: a preliminary statement *American Sociological Review* 25 (1960), 161.
42 Ibid., p. 72.
43 Malinowski, 'Argonauts of the Western Pacific (Routledge & Kegan Paul, London, 1922), cited in I. M. Lewis, *Social Anthropology in Perspective*, 2nd edn (Cambridge University Press, 1985), p. 200.
44 J. Piaget, *The Moral Judgement of the Child* (Routledge & Kegan Paul, London, 1932), p. 321.
45 Ibid., p. 323, and see generally ch. 3 of this classic work.
46 See p. 82.
47 H. Morris, as quoted in Ten, *Crime, Guilt and Punishment*, p. 53.
48 J. G. Murphy, 'Marxism and retribution', *passim*.
49 Finnis, *Natural Law and Natural Rights*, *passim*.
50 P. Ziegler, *The Black Death* (Penguin, Harmondsworth, 1970), pp. 98–111.
51 Ibid., pp. 87–98.
52 Cited in De Mause (ed.), *History of Childhood*, p. 33.
53 M. J. Lerner, 'The desire for justice and reactions to victims', in

J. McCaulay and L. Berkowitz (eds), *Altruism and Helping Behavior* (Academic Press, New York, 1970), p. 227.

54 See p. 111, and Lacey, 'Punishment, justice and consequentialism'.

55 For a discussion and critique, see, e.g., S. E. Asch, *Social Psychology* (Oxford University Press, 1952; repr. 1981), ch. XII.

56 See B. F. Skinner, *Beyond Freedom and Dignity* (Jonathan Cape, London, 1971).

57 See e.g. S. S. Diamond and C. J. Herhold, 'Understanding criminal sentencing: views from law and social psychology', in G. M. Stephenson and J. M. Davis (eds), *Progress in Social Psychology*, vol. 1 (John Wiley, Chichester, 1981), p. 71.

58 Discussions of deterrent theories of punishment may be found in many of the traditional theoretical works on punishment. See, e.g., Honderich, *Punishment*, ch. 3; on the efficacy of deterrence, see D. Beyleveld, *The Effectiveness of General Deterrence Against Crime: an annotated Bibliography of Evaluative Research* (Cambridge University Press, 1978); and see Diamond and Herhold, 'Understanding criminal sentencing'.

59 See, e.g., Statute of Westminster 1 (1275). For medieval penal theory, Harding *et al.*, *Imprisonment in England and Wales*, pp. 14–17 and R. W. Ireland, 'Theory and practice in the medieval English Prison', *American Journal of Legal History* 31 (1987), 56.

60 See p. 154.

61 So, for example, see Nils Christie, as quoted in Eckhoff, 'Justifications of punishment'; Ten, *Crime, Guilt and Punishment*, pp. 141 *et seq.*

62 Jeremy Bentham, *An Introduction to the Principles of Morals and Legislation*, ed. J. H. Burns and H. L. A. Hart (Athlone Press, London, 1970), p. 168.

63 Ten, *Crime, Guilt and Punishment*, p. 146.

64 Ehrenzweig, *Psychoanalytic Jurisprudence*, p. 211.

65 Ibid., p. 212.

66 Ibid., p. 214.

67 Interestingly, 'habilitation' is not a frequently used term.

68 The insights of P. J. Rawlings in this area are gratefully acknowledged. On children being taken to the gallows, see De Mause, *History of Childhood*, p. 14.

7 SIMILARITIES, COMPARISONS, AND CONTRASTS

1 For further consideration of this term, see our discussion on p. 9.

2 In philosophical discourse, see the discussion of the relative roles of reward and punishment: Jeremy Bentham, *Of Laws in General*, ed. H. L. A. Hart (Athlone Press, London, 1970), ch. XI; cf. J. Austin, *Province of Jurisprudence Determined*, ed. H. L. A. Hart (Weidenfeld & Nicolson, London, 1954), pp. 16–17. For anthropological use of the term 'positive sanction' see, e.g., the views of the anthropologist Radcliffe-Brown, *Encyclopaedia of Social Sciences* (Macmillan, New York,

1934), vol. 13, p. 531.

3   B. Malinowski, *Crime and Custom in Savage Society* (Kegan Paul, Trench, Trubner & Co., London, 1932), p. 26.

4   See p. 136.

5   A. M. Honoré, 'Groups, law and obedience', in A. W. B. Simpson (ed.), *Oxford Essays in Jurisprudence*, 2nd series (Clarendon Press, Oxford, 1973), p. 10.

6   For the Nuer, see P. P. Howell, *A Manual of Nuer Law* (Oxford University Press, 1954); for the Ifugao, see E. Adamson Hoebel, *The Law of Primitive Man* (Harvard University Press, 1954); for the Yurok, see ibid., pp. 51 *et seq*. On Anglo-Saxon Law, see T. F. T. Plucknett, *Edward I and the Criminal Law* (Cambridge University Press, 1966); J. Goebel, *Felony and Misdemeanour* (Commonwealth Fund, New York, 1937), vol. 1.

7   On state responsibility under international law, see Ian Brownlie, *Principles of Public International Law*, 3rd edn (Oxford University Press, 1979), ch. 20.

8   I. M. Lewis, *Social Anthropology in Perspective*, 2nd edn (Cambridge University Press, 1985), p. 341.

9   Howell, *Nuer Law*, p. 236.

10 Laws of Ethelbert of Kent, 51. See F. L. Attenborough, *The Laws of the Earliest English Kings* (Cambridge University Press, 1922), p. 10.

11 Note the distinction made under English law in the thirteenth century between 'mayhem' and 'wounding' as offences: *De Legibus et Consuetudinibus Angliae*, transl. and rev. by S. E. Thorne (Harvard University Press, 1968), vol. 2, p. 410.

12 For the Somali evidence, see Lewis, *Social Anthropology*, p. 329, on the distinction between internal and external group homicide.

13 Howell, *Nuer Law* pp. 27, 41–2.

14 Hoebel, *Law of Primitive Man*, pp. 100 *et seq*., especially p. 119.

15 See p. 151.

16 P. Einzig, *Primitive Money in its Ethnological, Historical and Economic Aspects* (Pergamon Press, London, 1966), cited in Lewis, *Social Anthropology*, p. 213.

17 Howell, *Nuer Law*, pp. 206–10.

18 Lewis, *Social Anthropology*, p. 342.

19 Ibid., p. 342.

20 Howell, *Nuer Law*, p. 207. Howell's evidence for the Nuer attitude is based on a wider understanding of the culture than we possess and we would not dispute it, but the general risk remains. Cf. the habit of describing compensation-based systems as pertaining to 'civil wrongs' rather than 'crimes', which may conceal a similar confusion of social attitude with enforcement agency. For the use of the term (though admittedly in a neutral sense) 'civil wrong' to encompass the taking of life, see, e.g., Sir Norman Anderson, 'Criminal sanctions', in J. Stott and N. Miller (eds), *Crime and the Responsible Community* (Hodder & Stoughton, London, 1980), pp. 66–7.

21 Lewis, *Social Anthropology*, p. 345.

22 A. W. B. Simpson, 'The laws of Ethelbert', in *Legal Theory and Legal History* (Hambledon, London, 1987), p. 1.
23 W. W. Lehman, 'The first English law', *Journal of Legal History* 6 (1985), 1.
24 See the reference concerning Anglo-Saxon law, n. 6 above.
25 N. D. Hurnard, *The King's Pardon for Homicide Before A.D. 1307* (Clarendon Press, Oxford, 1969), ch. 8.
26 Offences Against the Person Act 1861, ss. 42–5.
27 Powers of Criminal Courts Act 1973, ss. 35–8, as amended by the Criminal Justice Act 1982, s. 67. See Christopher Harding and Laurence Koffman, *Sentencing and the Penal System* (Sweet & Maxwell, London, 1988), pp. 228–31.
28 E. Berscheid, D. Boye, and E. Walster, 'Retaliation as a means of restoring equity', *Journal of Personality and Social Psychology* 10 (1968), 370–6. See also E. Walster, E. Berscheid, and G. W. Walster, 'The exploited: justice or justification?', in J. McCaulay and L. Berkowitz (eds), *Altruism and Helping Behavior* (Academic Press, New York, 1970), pp. 179–204.
29 M. B. Voyce, 'The communal discipline of the Buddhist order of monks: the "sanction" of the Vinaya Pitaka', *American Journal of Jurisprudence* 29 (1984), 123.
30 Hoebel, *Law of Primitive Man*, p. 73.
31 J. and E. Newsom, *Four Years Old in an Urban Community* (Penguin, Harmondsworth, 1970), p. 450.
32 R. F. Hunnisett, *The Medieval Coroner* (Cambridge University Press, 1961), ch. 3.
33 On police cautions see, e.g., J. E. Hall Williams, *Criminology and Criminal Justice* (Butterworth, London, 1982), pp. 207–8.
34 D. A. Thomas, *Principles of Sentencing*, 2nd edn (Heinemann, London, 1979), pp. 50–2. See also J. R. Baldwin and M. McConville, *Negotiated Justice* (Martin Robertson, London, 1977).
35 See p. 128 and Malinowski, *Crime and Custom*.
36 R. Nozick, *Philosophical Explanations* (Harvard University Press, 1981), pp. 366–70.
37 Ibid., p. 366.
38 Ibid., p. 388.
39 See p. 89.
40 See Barbara Wootton, *Crime and the Criminal Law*, 2nd edn (Stevens, London, 1981).
41 R. B. Clay, *The Medieval Hospitals of England* (Frank Cass, London, 1966 reprint), p. 54; C. Harding, B. Hines, R. Ireland, and P. Rawlings, *Imprisonment in England and Wales: a Concise History* (Croom Helm, Beckenham, 1985), p. 37.
42 See Suicide Act 1961; Glanville Williams, *Textbook of Criminal Law*, 2nd edn (Sweet & Maxwell, London, 1983), p. 578.
43 Mental Health Act 1983, s. 37(2) (a)(i).
44 Glanville Williams, *Textbook of Criminal Law*, p. 694.
45 Lewis, *Social Anthropology* pp. 101–2.

46   Ibid., p. 69 *et seq.*, 95.
47   A. R. Radcliffe-Brown, *Encyclopaedia of Social Sciences*, vol. 13, p. 532.
48   Wootton, *Crime and the Criminal Law*.
49   See, e.g., Thomas S. Szacz, *The Myth of Mental Illness* (Paladin, London, 1972); Raymond Cochrane, *The Social Creation of Mental Illness* (Longman, London, 1983).
50   *The Mirror of Justices*, Bk 11, ch. IX, ed. W. J. Whittaker (Selden Society Publications, 1893), p. 52; Harding *et al.*, *Imprisonment in England and Wales*, pp. 16–17.
51   Hoebel, *Law of Primitive Man*, p. 70.
52   A. A. Ehrenzweig, *Psychoanalytic Jurisprudence* (Sijthoff, Leiden, 1971), p. 215.
53   R. A. Duff, *Trials and Punishments* (Cambridge University Press, 1986). See also, Nozick, *Philosophical Explanations*, p. 370.

8 PUNISHMENT: AUTHORITIES AND AGENTS

1   H. L. A. Hart, *Punishment and Responsibility* (Oxford University Press, 1968), p. 5. Such 'decentralized sanctions' are relegated by Hart to the secondary level of punishment.
2   For an example of the possibility of professional disciplinary action following from conviction for an (unrelated) criminal offence, see the remarks of Scarman LJ in the case of *R* v. *Daryl Parker* (1977) 2 All E.R. 37, 40.
3   Exodus 10:4.
4   See p. 116 and note 52 to ch. 6.
5   For an account of societies in which interpersonal violence is employed as a form of dispute-settlement, and the restrictions placed on its use, see S. Roberts, *Order and Dispute* (Penguin, Harmondsworth, 1979), pp. 57–9.
6   Lloyd de Mause, *The History of Childhood* (Souvenir Press, London, 1976).
7   On public executions in Britain, see Leon Radzinowicz, *A History of English Criminal Law*, vol. 1, *The Movement for Reform* (Stevens, London, 1948), ch. 6.
8   Capital Punishment Amendment Act 1868, s. 2 (31 Vict. 24).
9   *Independent*, 23 July 1987.
10   This is, it is conceded, an impression based on no detailed investigation of press reporting. But for a discussion of some press reports, see Siân Hughes, 'The reporting of crime in the press: a study of newspaper reports in 1985', *Cambrian Law Review* 18 (1987), 36.
11   There was some flexibility within the system. See R. W. Ireland, 'First catch your toad: medieval attitudes to ordeal and battle', *Cambrian Law Review* 11 (1979), 50. On ordeal generally, see R. Bartlett, *Trial by Fire and Water* (Oxford University Press, 1986).
12   See H. R. T. Summerson, 'The early development of the peine forte et dure', in E. W. Ives and A. H. Manchester (eds), *Law, Litigants and the Legal Profession* (Royal Historical Society, London, 1983), p. 116.
13   See B. Malinowski, *Crime and Custom in Savage Society* (Kegan Paul,

Trench, Trubner & Co., London, 1932), pp. 77 *et seq.*, for discussion of
the reaction to breach of rules relating to exogamy. Note as well that
the punishment is carried out by the culprit himself.

14   Ibid., p. 104.

15   Radzinowicz, *History of English Criminal Law*, vol. 1, parts 1–3.

16   Ibid., pp. 94–7. See also T. A. Green, *Verdict According to Conscience:*
Perspectives on the English Criminal Trial Jury 1200–1800 (University of
Chicago Press, 1985).

17   R. W. Ireland, 'Theory and practice within the medieval English
prison', *American Journal of Legal History* 31 (1987), 64–7.

18   The work of W. Robertson Smith is discussed in F. Steiner, *Taboo*
(Penguin, Harmondsworth, 1967), pp. 50 *et seq.*

19   Steiner, *Taboo*, quoted at p. 66.

20   E. Adamson Hoebel, *The Law of Primitive Man* (Harvard University
Press, 1954), p. 70.

21   J. Middleton, *Lugbara Religion* (Oxford University Press for the
International African Institute, London, 1960).

22   Emile Durkheim's work and views on religion are discussed in I. M.
Lewis, *Social Anthropology in Perspective*, 2nd edn (Cambridge University
Press, 1985), pp. 46 *et seq.*, esp. p. 51.

23   See the discussion of this work in Steiner, *Taboo*.

24   See, e.g., J. T. McNeill and H. M. Gamer, *Medieval Handbooks of Penance*
(Octagon Books, New York, 1965).

25   Samuel Y. Edgerton Jr, *Pictures of Punishment: Art and Criminal Prosecution
during the Florentine Renaissance* (Cornell University Press, 1985).

26   Ibid., pp. 66–8.

27   See S. Asch, *Social Psychology* (repr. Oxford University Press, 1987),
p. 415.

28   De Mause, *History of Childhood*, p. 12.

29   Ibid., pp. 11–12.

30   Ibid., pp. 11–12.

31   On the origin of the legend of Bluebeard, see Iona and Peter Opie,
The Classic Fairy Tales (Oxford University Press, London, 1974), pp.
103–9.

32   De Mause, *History of Childhood* reports the use of 'bearded man',
'chimney sweep', and 'werewolf' in Europe at the present day.

33   Heinrich Hoffmann, *The English Struwwelpeter* (George Routledge &
Sons, London, 1909).

34   M. Bateson, *Borough Customs*, vol. 1 (Selden Society Publications,
London, 1904), p. 75.

35   See *Encyclopaedia Britannica*, 11th edn, vol. XII (Cambridge University
Press, London, 1910), *s.v.* 'Guillotine', p. 695.

36   See Sophocles, *Oedipus Tyrannus*.

37   See Plato, *Phaedo*.

38   David E. Kaplan and Alec Dubro, *Yakuza* (Macdonald, London, 1987),
p. 25.

39   *The Oxford Book of Local Verses*, ed. J. Holloway, (Oxford University
Press, 1987), p. 180. Cf. the thirteenth-century Portsmouth penalty for

petty theft: 'his ere to be nayled to the pelery, he to chese whether he woll kytt or tere it of' (Bateson, *Borough Customs*, p. 55).

40 Quoted in 'The routine of the chair', *Independent*, 28 August 1987.

41 Bateson, *Borough Customs*. p. 74.

42 *Njal's Saga*, transl. M. Magnusson and H. Pálsson (Penguin, Harmondsworth, 1960).

43 See the discussion of this issue generally in C. Harding and L. Koffman, *Sentencing and the Penal System* (Sweet & Maxwell, London, 1988), pp. 81–92.

44 See, e.g. Louis Blom-Cooper, 'Sentencing structure: a paradigm for the future', in L. Blom-Cooper (ed.), *Progress in Penal Reform* (Oxford University Press, 1974).

45 Both as regards the use of custody (the 'prison service') and in the non-custodial sphere (probation officers and social workers).

46 See, e.g., D. A. Thomas (ed.), *The Future of Sentencing* (University of Cambridge, Institute of Criminology, Occasional Paper no. 8, 1982); Harding and Koffman, *Sentencing and the Penal System*, pp. 102–14.

47 See the European Committee on Crime Problems, *Sentencing* (Strasbourg, Council of Europe, 1974), pp. 61–5 (report by B. Dutheillet-Lamonthézie).

48 This may be achieved, e.g., via recommendations in social enquiry reports submitted to courts by the probation service prior to sentence in England and Wales. But, as Andrew Ashworth argues in *Sentencing and Penal Policy* (Weidenfeld & Nicolson, London, 1983), pp. 63 *et seq.*, the sentencing autonomy of the judiciary operates as a kind of taboo.

49 See, e.g., M. Maguire, J. Vagg, and R. Morgan (eds), *Accountability and Prisons* (Tavistock, London, 1985).

50 See Ashworth, *Sentencing and Penal Policy*, ch. 2.

51 See the papers by K. R. Nossal and D. G. Anglin, chs 2 and 3 in David Leyton-Brown (ed.), *The Utility of International Economic Sanctions* (Croom Helm, Beckenham, 1987).

52 D. G. Anglin, 'United Nations economic sanctions against South Africa and Rhodesia', in Leyton-Brown (ed.), *Utility of International Economic Sanctions*.

53 Ibid., p. 48.

54 On the impact of economic sanctions generally, see the papers by Lawrence J. Brady and David Leyton-Brown, chs 15 and 16 in Leyton-Brown (ed.), *Utility of International Economic Sanctions*. On making conditional the grant of military aid, see Stephen B. Cohen, 'Conditioning US security assistance on human rights practices', 76 (1982) *American Journal of International Law* 246. And see generally the discussion of the problems involved in 'targeting' states for such sanctions in Richard Falk, *Human Rights and State Sovereignty* (Holmes & Meier, New York, 1981).

55 On the adoption of such sanctions by Commonwealth states, see 1986 *Keesing's Contemporary Archives*, vol. XXXII, 34647.

56 H. D. Willcock and J. Stokes, *Deterrents and Incentives to Crime Among Boys*

and Young Men Aged 15–21 Years (Office of Population Censuses and Surveys, Social Survey Division, London, 1968).

57 See generally, Philip Priestley, *Community of Scapegoats: the Segregation of Sex Offenders and Informers in Prisons* (Pergamon Press, Oxford, 1980).

58 Note, for instance, the consequences for the United States of its intervention in Grenada in 1983 as regards its relations with other states: Scott Davidson, *Grenada* (Gower, Aldershot, 1987), ch. 5.

59 See W. R. Cornish, *The Jury* (Allen Lane, London, 1968), pp. 269–71; Lars Molin, 'The role of lay assessors in Swedish courts', in Nigel Walker (ed.), *The British Jury System* (University of Cambridge, 1975).

9 PUNISHMENT: THE SUBJECT

1 E.g. H. L. A. Hart, *Punishment and Responsibility* (Oxford University Press, 1968), ch. 1.

2 E. P. Evans, *The Capital Punishment and Criminal Prosecution of Animals* (first published by Heinemann, London, 1906; repr. Faber & Faber, London, 1987), pp. 153–4.

3 Evans, *Punishment of Animals*; J. J. Finkelstein, *The Ox That Gored, Transcriptions of the American Philosophical Society* 71, Part 11 (1981); G. MacCormack, 'On thing liability in early law', *Irish Jurist* (1984) 19, 322; Esther Cohen, 'Law, folklore and animal law', *Past and Present* 50 (1986), 6.

4 Evans, *Punishment of Animals*, pp. 18–19.

5 Cohen, 'Law, folklore and animal law', p. 37.

6 See Nicholas Humphreys, Foreword to Evans, *Punishment of Animals*, p. xvi.

7 Herman Melville, *Moby Dick; or, The Whale* (Harper & Brothers, New York, 1851).

8 D. H. Lawrence, 'Reflections on the death of a porcupine', *Selected Essays* (Penguin, Harmondsworth, 1950), p. 63.

9 See, e.g., on English criminal law, Glanville Williams, *Textbook of Criminal Law*, 2nd edn (Sweet & Maxwell, London, 1983), chs 15, 18, and 19.

10 Williams, *Textbook of Criminal Law*, ch. 16.

11 E.g. Sally Falk Moore, *Law as Process* (Routledge & Kegan Paul, London, 1978), pp. 111 *et seq.*

12 Alexander Heidel, *The Gilgamesh Epic and Old Testament Parallels* (University of Chicago Press, Chicago, 1946).

13 Indeed, genocidal acts, in so far as they may be fitted within a penal framework, constitute collective punishment in a 'pure' form, since it is the group identity that is the principal target of genocidal action.

14 See generally, Marc Trachtenberg, *Reparation in World Politics* (Columbia University Press, 1980).

15 *Parliamentary Debates*, Commons, 3 July 1919, cols 1221–2.

16 Woodrow Wilson, *Messages* (Doran, New York, 1924), p. 807.

17 Samuel Y. Edgerton Jr, *Pictures and Punishment: Art and Criminal Prosecution during the Florentine Renaissance* (Cornell University Press, Ithaca, NY, 1985), p. 74.

18 Leo Kuper, *Genocide* (Penguin, Harmondsworth, 1981), ch. 3.

19 *Judgment of the International Military Tribunal, for the Trial of German Major War Criminals*, Nuremberg, 30 September and 1 October 1946 (HMSO, London, Cmd. 6964), pp. 41–2.

20 Falk Moore, *Law as Process*, pp. 111 *et seq.*

21 Ibid., p. 121.

22 J. H. Driberg, *The Lango* (Unwin, London, 1923).

23 Though note that Haynau's reputation for brutality was such that he was mobbed by hostile crowds on subsequent visits to London and Brussels.

24 On the massacre at Lidice see Kuper, *Genocide*, p. 21. The incident provoked a declaration by US President Roosevelt concerning the punishment of those responsible.

25 *Encyclopaedia Britannica*, 11th edn, vol. XIII (Cambridge University Press, London, 1910), pp. 801–2.

26 Ibid., p. 802.

27 Jean Pictet, *Development and Principles of International Humanitarian Law* (Martinus Nijhoff, Dordrecht, 1985).

28 Geneva (Red Cross) Convention IV (Protection of Civilian Persons in Time of War), 12 August 1949, 75 U.N.T.S. 31; Additional Protocols to the Geneva Conventions, 8 June 1977, 16 I.L.M. 1391.

29 *The Godfather* (1972, dir. Francis Ford Coppola, and based on the novel by Mario Puzo).

30 *Performance*, (1970, dir. Nicholas Roeg and Donald Cammel).

31 Williams, *Textbook of Criminal Law*, ch. 43.

32 Ibid., pp. 978–80.

33 Robens Committee Report (HMSO, London, 1972, Cmnd 5034).

34 Quoted in S. Asch, *Social Psychology* (repr. Oxford University Press, 1987), p. 509.

35 See generally on extradition: M. Cherif Bassiouni, *International Extradition and World Public Order* (Sijthoff, Leyden, 1974); I. A. Shearer, *Extradition in International Law* (Manchester University Press, 1971).

36 Edgerton, *Pictures and Punishment*, ch. 2.

37 Ibid., p. 77.

38 Ibid., p. 76.

39 See ch. 2.

40 Edgerton, *Pictures and Punishment*, p. 40; cf. the discussion on p. 179 concerning the punishment of inanimate objects.

41 Paul Murray Kendal, *Richard III* (Allen & Unwin, London, 1955), p. 369.

42 See further on *deodand*, Finkelstein, *The Ox That Gored*, pp. 73–81.

43 See *R* v. *The Eastern Counties Railway Co.* (1842) 10 M&W 59, 152 E.R. 380. The monetary value of the locomotive was being claimed.

44 Evans, *Punishment of Animals*, pp. 171–5.

45 Ibid., p. 175. Another example concerns a bell from the Belfry in

Ghent, temporarily removed on account of its 'participation' in a rebellion against the Emperor Charles V.
46 J. Milton French, *The Life Records of John Milton*, vol. IV (Rutgers University Press, 1949–58), pp. 328–33.
47 Ian Roxborough, Philip O'Brien, and Jackie Roddick, *Chile: the State and Revolution* (Macmillan, London, 1977), p. 244.
48 Edwin Powers, *Crime and Punishment in Early Massachusetts, 1620–1692* (Beacon Press, Boston, 1966), p. 195.
49 Edgerton, *Pictures and Punishment*, pp. 128–9.
50 See P. A. Means, *Ancient Civilisations of the Andes* (Scribner's, New York, 1931), p. 348; Leopold Pospisil, *Anthropology of Law* (Harper & Row, New York, 1971), p. 115.
51 H. Ascough, 'Review of Evans, *The Punishment of Animals*, 84 (1987) *Law Society's Gazette* 3348.

10 METHODS OF PUNISHMENT

1 Michel Foucault, *Discipline and Punish: the Birth of the Prison* (Allen Lane, London, 1977).
2 Ibid.
3 We are unsure whether Finnis has committed this term to paper; it was used in a lecture course. Cf. his account in J. M. Finnis, *Natural Law and Natural Rights* (Oxford University Press, 1980), pp. 263–4.
4 This argument is, of course, discussed extensively by Foucault in *Discipline and Punish*: see, e.g., pp. 16–17.
5 Stanley Cohen and Laurie Taylor, *Psychological Survival: the Experience of Long-Term Imprisonment*, 2nd edn (Penguin, Harmondsworth, 1981).
6 Stanley Cohen, *Visions of Social Control* (Polity Press, Cambridge, 1985), ch. 1.
7 A. E. Bottoms, 'Neglected features of contemporary penal systems', in David Garland and Peter Young (eds), *The Power to Punish: Contemporary Penality and Social Analysis* (Heinemann, London, 1983).
8 Foucault, *Discipline and Punish*, p. 11.
9 Ibid., pp. 3–6.
10 On Article 3 of the European Convention on Human Rights, see J. E. S. Fawcett, *The Application of the European Convention on Human Rights*, 2nd edn (Oxford University Press, 1987), pp. 41 *et seq.*
11 David Hunt, *Parents and Children in History: the Psychology of Family Life in Early Modern France* (Basic Books, New York, 1970).
12 Ibid., p. 135.
13 *R v. Hopley* (1860) 2 F & F 202.
14 Ibid., p. 206.
15 *Tyrer v. UK*, judgment of 25 April 1978, 2 *European Human Rights Reports* p. 1; *European Court of Human Rights Publications*, series A, no. 26.
16 2 *European Human Rights Reports*, p. 11.
17 Ibid., pp. 11–12 (para. 36 of the judgment).
18 *Campbell and Cosans v. UK*, judgment of 25 February 1982, 4 *European Human Rights Reports* 293; *European Court of Human Rights Publications*,

228

series A, no. 48.
19 4 *European Human Rights Reports* 301 (para. 29 of the judgment).
20 See Michael Kidron and Ronald Segal, *The New State of the World Atlas* (Pan Books, London, 1984), map 25.
21 David E. Kaplan and Alec Dubro, *Yakuza* (Macdonald, London, 1987).
22 Ibid., p. 152.
23 E. Adamson Hoebel, 'Keresan Pueblo law', in Laura Nader (ed.), *Law in Culture and Society* (Aldine, Chicago, 1969), p. 102.
24 Andre J. F. Köbben, 'Law at the village level: the Cottica Djuka of Surinam', in Nader (ed.), *Law in Culture and Society*, p. 127.
25 E. Adamson Hoebel, *The Law of Primitive Man* (Harvard University Press, 1954), p. 156. Cf. the role of attainder in earlier English law: see, e.g., J. R. Lander, 'Attainder and forfeiture, 1453–1509', *Historical Journal* 4 (1961), 119.
26 In 1986, for instance, fines were imposed on 39% of offenders sentenced for indictable offences in England and Wales; on 90% of those sentenced for summary non-motoring offences; and 98% of those sentenced for summary motoring offences. *Criminal Statistics for England and Wales, 1986* (HMSO, London, Cmd 233), p. 120.
27 A. L. Epstein, 'Injury and liability in African customary law in Zambia', in M. Gluckman (ed.), *Ideas and Procedures in African Customary Law* (Oxford University Press, 1969), p. 298.
28 Dario Melossi and Massimo Pavarini, *The Prison and the Factory: Origins of the Penitentiary System* (Macmillan, London, 1981). Cf. the review of this work by Ivan Jancovic, *Contemporary Crises* 7 (1983), 393.
29 G. Rusche and O. Kirchheimer, *Punishment and Social Structure* (Columbia University Press, New York, 1939; reissued 1968).
30 Melossi and Pavarini, *The Prison and the Factory*, p. 2.
31 Ibid., p. 1.
32 The tradition of a 'masked' political prisoner held in the Bastille and other French prisons in the late seventeenth and early eighteenth centuries has attracted a large scholarship. It was Voltaire and subsequently Dumas, in his novel *The Man in the Iron Mask*, who promoted the idea of a mask of iron – imprisonment of the head indeed – but the historical records refer to a velvet mask.
33 William Clifford. *An Introduction to African Criminology* (Oxford University Press, Nairobi, 1974), p. 212.
34 Ibid., at pp. 190–1.
35 See p. 104
36 Ibid.
37 Köbben, 'Law at the village level', p. 138.
38 Leopold Pospisil, *Kapauka Papuans and their Law* (Yale University Press, 1958), p. 255.
39 See, e.g., Edwin Powers, *Crime and Punishment in Early Massachusetts* (Beacon Press, Boston, 1966), pp. 195–8; Derek Jarrett, *England in the Age of Hogarth* (Granada Publishing, London, 1974), pp. 56–8.
40 Joy Cameron, *Prisons and Punishment in Scotland* (Canongate, Edinburgh, 1983), pp. 20 *et seq.*

41 Ibid., p. 10.

42 Powers, *Crime and Punishment in Early Massachusetts*, pp. 198–201.

43 Herbert R. Lottman, *The People's Anger: Justice and Revenge in Post-Liberation France* (Hutchinson, London, 1986), pp. 66–8; cf. E. P. Thompson, 'Rough music! Le charivari anglais', *Annales: économies, sociétés, civilisations* 27 (1972), 307 (for the account of the 'Rebecca' tribunal in Radnorshire in 1898).

44 Powers, *Crime and Punishment in Early Massachusetts*, p. 170.

45 Hoebel, *Law of Primitive Man*, p. 152.

46 See L. A. Pollock, *Forgotten Children: Parent–Child Relations from 1500 to 1900* (Cambridge University Press, 1983), p. 197 for the asses' ears in the early nineteenth century. Cf. the use of 'markes of approbation and of disgrace . . . pinned on our frocks', in the late eighteenth century, ibid., p. 193. The dunce's cap humiliates both the wearer and, etymologically, the philosopher Duns Scotus (ob. 1308).

47 Michael Ignatieff, *A Just Measure of Pain: the Penitentiary in the Industrial Revolution, 1750–1850* (Macmillan, London, 1978), pp. 93–4.

48 I. M. Lewis, *Social Anthropology in Perspective*, 2nd edn (Cambridge University Press, 1985), pp. 117 *et seq.*

49 Sally Falk Moore, *Law as Process* (Routledge & Kegan Paul, London, 1978), p. 123.

50 Ibid., p. 124, where it is argued: 'Expulsion is surely the ultimate withdrawal of reciprocity'.

51 Cf. Rusche and Kirchheimer, *Punishment and Social Structure*, p. 66 where economic and public policy arguments against the use of banishment are referred to.

52 K. N. Llewelyn and E. Adamson Hoebel, *The Cheyenne Way: Conflict and Case Law in Primitive Jurisprudence* (University of Oklahoma Press, 1941), *passim*.

53 J. H. Driberg, *The Lango* (T. Fisher Unwin, London, 1923); T. T. Hayley, *The Anatomy of Lango Religions and Groups* (Cambridge University Press, 1947).

54 Hoebel, 'Keresan Pueblo Law'.

55 Falk Moore, *Law as Process*, pp. 121 *et seq.*

56 Declaration of the UK under Article 46 of the Convention, 30 July 1976, *Council of Europe Yearbook of the European Convention on Human Rights 1976*, p. 16.

57 See, e.g., Llewelyn and Hoebel, *The Cheyenne Way*, and note the indeterminate character of some of the Cheyenne expulsions: cf. the function of life imprisonment in many contemporary western societies.

58 George Eliot, *Silas Marner, the Weaver of Raveloe* (William Blackwood & Sons, London, 1861). In the novel, the eponymous hero is expelled for an alleged theft from a close-knit Nonconformist community in a northern English industrial town, and resettles in a distant rural location.

59 On the Jewish diaspora, see Hugh Seton-Watson, *Nations and States* (Methuen, London, 1977), pp. 387–91.

60 Falk Moore, *Law as Process*, pp. 124–5.

61 See B. Smart, 'On discipline and social regulation', in Garland and Young (eds), *The Power to Punish*, p. 62.
62 'The routine of the chair', *Independent*, 28 August 1987.
63 J. Piaget, *The Moral Judgement of the Child* (Routledge & Kegan Paul, London, 1932), ch. 2. The relation between the forms of moral judgement is not a simple one.
64 See the review of evidence in C. Fitzmaurice and K. Pease (eds), *The Psychology of Judicial Sentencing* (Manchester University Press, 1986), ch. 5.
65 See R. C. Sherman and M. D. Dowdle, 'The perception of crime and punishment: a multi-dimensional scaling analysis', 3 (1974) *Social Science Research* 3 (1974), 109.
66 See pp. 151–2.
67 Foucault, *Discipline and Punish*, p. 49.
68 Ibid., p. 61
69 Ibid., p. 64.
70 See P. Linebaugh, 'The Tyburn riot against the surgeons', in D. Hay, P. Linebaugh, J. G. Rule, E. P. Thompson, and C. Winslow, *Albion's Fatal Tree* (Penguin, Harmondsworth, 1977).
71 Richard Peabody, quoted in 'The routine of the chair'.
72 As quoted in Pollock, *Forgotten Children*, p. 152.
73 E.g. Lloyd de Mause, *The History of Childhood* (Souvenir Press, London, 1976).
74 Pollock, *Forgotten Children*.
75 For state intervention in the lives of prisoners, see C. Harding, B. Hines, R. Ireland and P. Rawlings, *Imprisonment in England and Wales: a Concise History* (Croom Helm, Beckenham, 1985). For the protection of animals by law, see G. Sandys-Winsch, *Animal Law*, 2nd edn (Shaw & Sons, London, 1984), ch. 8.

SELECT BIBLIOGRAPHY

Note: the works listed below are those frequently referred to in the course of this book or which would be useful in developing discussion of any of the points we have made.

Acton, H. B. (ed.) (1969) *The Philosophy of Punishment*, London: Macmillan.

Alford, Violet (1959) 'Rough music or charivari', *Folklore* 70: 505.

Ariès, Philippe (1960) *L'Enfant et la Vie Familiale sous l'Ancient Régime*, Paris: Librairie Plon, English trans: *Centuries of Children*, Harmondsworth: Penguin.

Asch, S. E. (1952; repr. 1987) *Social Psychology*, Oxford University Press.

Ashworth, Andrew (1983) *Sentencing and Penal Policy*, London: Weidenfeld & Nicolson.

Bean, Philip (1976) *Rehabilitation and Deviance*, London: Routledge & Kegan Paul.

—— (1981) *Punishment: a Philosophical and Criminological Enquiry*, Oxford: Martin Robertson.

Beattie, John (1964) *Other Cultures*, London: Cohen & West.

Beirne, Piers (1983) 'Cultural relativism and comparative criminology', *Contemporary Crises* 7: 371.

Bentham, Jeremy (1970) *Principles of Morals and Legislation* (1789), ed. H. L. A. Hart and J. H. Burns, London: Athlone Press.

Berscheid, E., Boye, D., and Walster, E. (1968) 'Retaliation as a means of restoring equity', *Journal of Personality and Social Psychology* 10: 370.

Bickley, A. C. (1902) 'Some notes on a custom at Woking, Surrey', *Home Counties Magazine* IV: 25.

Blom-Cooper, Louis (ed.) (1974) *Progress in Penal Reform*, Oxford University Press.

Bottoms, Anthony E. (1983) 'Neglected features of contemporary penal systems', in David Garland and Peter Young (eds), *The Power to Punish: Contemporary Penality and Social Analysis*, London: Heinemann.

Cameron, Joy (1983) *Prisons and Punishment in Scotland, from the Middle Ages to the Present*, Edinburgh: Canongate Publishing.

Charvet, John (1966) 'Criticism and punishment', *Mind* 75: 573.

Clarke, Dean H. (1982) 'Justifications for punishment', *Contemporary Crises* 6: 25.

Clifford, William (1974) *An Introduction to African Criminology*, Nairobi: Oxford University Press.

Cohen, Esther (1986) 'Law, folklore and animal lore', *Past and Present* 50: 6.

Cohen, Stanley (1974) 'Criminology and the sociology of deviance in Britain: a recent history and current report', in P. Rock and M. McIntosh (eds), *Deviance and Social Control*, London: Tavistock.

—— (1979) 'The punitive city: notes on the dispersal of social control', *Contemporary Crises* 3: 339.

—— (1985) *Visions of Social Control: Crime, Punishment and Classification*, Cambridge: Polity Press.

—— and Scull, Andrew (eds) (1983) *Social Control and the State: Comparative and Historical Essays*, London: Martin Robertson.

Council of Europe, Directorate of Legal Affairs (1984) *Historical Research on Crime and Criminal Justice*, Strasbourg: Sixth Criminological Colloquium, November 1983.

Davis, Natalie Zemon (1971) 'The reasons of misrule: youth groups and charivaris in sixteenth century France', *Past and Present* 41.

—— (1975) *Society and Culture in Early Modern France*, London: Duckworth.

De Mause, Lloyd (ed.) (1976) *The History of Childhood*, London: Souvenir Press.

Diamond, S. S. and Herhold, C. J. (1981) 'Understanding criminal sentencing: views from law and social psychology', in G. M. Stephenson and J. M. Davis (eds), *Progress in Social Psychology*, vol. 1, Chichester: John Wiley.

Duff, A. and Simmonds, N. (eds) (1984) *Philosophy and the Criminal Law*, Conference Report, Association for Legal and Social Philosophy, Stuttgart: Franz Steiner.

Duff, R. A. (1976) *Trials and Punishments*, Cambridge University Press.

Durkheim, Emile (1938) *The Rules of Sociological Method*, 8th edn, transl. Sarah Solovay and John Mueller, London: Collier Macmillan.

—— (1973) 'Two laws of penal evolution', transl. T. A. Jones and Andrew Scull, *Economy and Society* 2: 285.

Earle, Alice Morse (1896) *Curious Punishments of Bygone Days*, Chicago: Herbert S. Stone.

Eckhoff, Torstein (1984) 'Justifications of punishment', in A. Duff and N. Simmonds (eds), *Philosophy and the Criminal Law*, Conference Report, Association for Legal and Social Philosophy, Stuttgart: Franz Steiner.

Edgerton, Samuel Y. Jr (1985) *Pictures and Punishment: Art and Criminal Prosecution during the Florentine Renaissance*, Ithaca, NY: Cornell University Press.

Ehrenzweig, A. A. (1971) *Psychoanalytic Jurisprudence*, Leiden: Sijthoff.

Ehrlich, Eugen (1936) *Fundamental Principles of the Sociology of Law*, transl. W. E. Mell, Harvard University Press.

Elias, T. O. (1956) *The Nature of African Customary Law*, Manchester University Press.

234

Epstein, A. L. (1968) *s.v.* 'Sanctions', *International Encyclopaedia of the Social Sciences*, ed. D. L. Sills, vol. 14, p. 1, New York: Macmillan/The Free Press.

Erikson, Kari (1966) *Wayward Puritans: a Study of the Sociology of Deviance*, New York: John Wiley.

Evans, E. P. (1906) *The Criminal Prosecution and Capital Punishment of Animals*, London: William Heinemann (reissued in 1987 by Faber & Faber, London).

Fine, Bob, Kinsey, Richard, Lea, John, Picciotto, Sol, and Young, Jock (eds) (1979) *Capitalism and the Rule of Law: from Deviancy Theory to Marxism*, Harmondsworth: Penguin.

Finkelstein, J. J. (1981) *The Ox That Gored, Transcriptions of the American Philosophical Society*, 71, Part II.

Finnis, J. M. (1981) *Natural Law and Natural Rights*, Oxford University Press.

Fitzmaurice, C. and Pease, K. (1986) *The Psychology of Judicial Sentencing*, Manchester University Press.

Flew, Antony (1954) 'The justification of punishment', *Philosophy* 29:291.

Foucault, Michel (1970) *The Order of Things*, London: Tavistock (originally published as *Les mots et les choses*, Paris: Editions Gallimard, 1966).

—— (1977) *Discipline and Punish: the Birth of the Prison*, London: Allen Lane (originally published as *Surveiller et Punir*, Paris: Editions Gallimard, 1975).

—— (1979) *History of Sexuality*, vol. I, London: Allen Lane (originally published as *Histoire de la sexualité*, Paris: Editions Gallimard, 1979).

Freiberg, Arie (1985) 'Review of D. Garland and P. Young (eds), *The Power to Punish*', *Contemporary Crises* 9: 387.

Freud, Sigmund (1973) *Introductory Lectures on Psychoanalysis*, Pelican Freud Library, vol. I, Harmondsworth: Penguin.

—— (1923) *Totem and Taboo*, London: George Routledge.

Friedland, Martin L. (1969) *Double Jeopardy*, Oxford: Clarendon Press.

Garland, David (1983) 'Philosophical argument and ideological effect', review of Philip Bean, *Punishment*, *Contemporary Crises* 7: 79.

—— (1983) 'Durkheim's theory of punishment', in David Garland and Peter Young (eds), *The Power to Punish: Contemporary Penality and Social Analysis*, London: Heinemann.

—— (1985) *Punishment and Welfare: a History of Penal Strategies*, Aldershot: Gower.

—— and Young, Peter (eds) (1983) *The Power to Punish: Contemporary Penality and Social Analysis*, London: Heinemann.

—— and —— (1983) 'Towards a social analysis of penality', in David Garland and Peter Young (eds) *The Power to Punish: Contemporary Penality and Social Analysis*, London: Heinemann.

Gatrell, V., Lenman, B., and Parker, G. (eds) (1980) *Crime and the Law*, London: Europa.

Grupp, Stanley, E. (ed.) (1971) *Theories of Punishment*, Indiana University Press.

Harding, C., Hines, B., Ireland, R. W., and Rawlings, P. (1985) *Imprisonment in England and Wales: a Concise History*, Beckenham: Croom Helm.

Harding, Christopher and Koffman, Laurence (1988) *Sentencing and the Penal System: Text and Materials*, London: Sweet & Maxwell.

Hart, H. L. A. (1961) *The Concept of Law*, Oxford University Press.

—— (1968) *Punishment and Responsibility: Essays in the Philosophy of Law*, Oxford University Press.

Hoebel, E. Adamson (1954) *The Law of Primitive Man*, Harvard University Press.

Honderich, Ted (1969) *Punishment: the Supposed Justifications*, London: Hutchinson.

Honoré, A. M. (1973) 'Groups, laws and obedience', in A. W. B. Simpson (ed.), *Oxford Essays in Jurisprudence*, 2nd series, Oxford University Press.

Hunt, David (1970) *Parents and Children in History: the Psychology of Family Life in Early Modern France*, New York: Basic Books.

Ignatieff, Michael (1978) *A Just Measure of Pain: the Penitentiary in the Industrial Revolution, 1750–1850*, London: Macmillan.

—— (1981) 'State, civil society and total institutions: a critique of recent histories of punishment', in M. Tonry and N. Morris (eds), *Crime and Justice: an Annual Review of Research*, vol. 3, University of Chicago Press.

—— (1983) 'Total institutions and working classes: a review essay', *History Workshop Journal* 15:167.

Jankovic, Ivan (1983) 'Review of D. Melossi and M. Pavarini, *The Prison and the Factory*', *Contemporary Crises* 7:393.

Kant, Immanuel (1887) *The Philosophy of Law: an Exposition of the Fundamental Principles of Jurisprudence as the Science of Right* (1797) transl. W. Hastie, Edinburgh: T. & T. Clark.

Kaplan, David E. and Dubro, Alec (1987) *Yakuza*, London: Macdonald

Khadduri, Majid (1984) *The Islamic Conception of Justice*, Baltimore: Johns Hopkins University Press.

Kuper, Leo (1981) *Genocide: its Political Use in the Twentieth Century*, Harmondsworth: Penguin.

Lander, J. R. (1961) 'Attainder and forfeiture, 1453–1509', *Historical Journal* 4:119.

Lang, Olga (1946) *Chinese Family and Society*, Yale University Press.

Lerner, M. J. (1970) 'The desire for justice and reactions to victims', in J. McCaulay and L. Berkowitz (eds), *Altruism and Helping Behavior*, New York: Academic Press.

LeVine, R. A. (1960) 'The internalization of political values in stateless societies', *Human Organization* 19: 2, 51.

Levy, Marion J. (1949) *The Family Revolution in Modern China*, Harvard University Press.

Lewis, I. M. (1985) *Social Anthropology in Perspective: the Relevance of Social Anthropology*, 2nd edn, Cambridge University Press.

Leyton-Brown, David (ed.) (1987) *The Utility of International Economic Sanctions*, Beckenham: Croom Helm.

Llewelyn, K. N. and Hoebel, E. A. (1941) *The Cheyenne Way: Conflict and Case Law in Primitive Jurisprudence*, University of Oklahoma Press.

Lottman, Herbert R. (1986) *The People's Anger: Justice and Revenge in Post-Liberation France*, London: Hutchinson.

Mabbott, J. D. (1939) 'Punishment', *Mind* 48:152.
—— (1955) 'Professor Flew on punishment', *Philosophy* 30:256.
Malinowski, B. (1932) *Crime and Custom in Savage Society*, London: Kegan
 Paul, Trench, Trubner & Co.
Mann, Michael (1986) *The Sources of Social Power*, Cambridge University
 Press.
Manser, A. R. (1962) 'It serves you right', *Philosophy* 37:293.
McCall, Andrew (1979) *The Medieval Underworld*, London: Hamish
 Hamilton.
McCloskey, H. J. (1962) 'The complexity of the concept of punishment',
 Philosophy 37:307.
McMullan, John L. (1987) 'Crime, law and order in early modern
 England', *British Journal of Criminology* 27:252.
Maguire, M., Vagg, J., and Morgan R. (eds) (1985) *Accountability and
 Prisons*, London: Tavistock.
Marsh, P., Rosser, E., and Harré, R. (1978) *Rules of Disorder*, London:
 Routledge & Kegan Paul.
Melossi, Dario and Pavarini, Massimo (1981) *The Prison and the Factory:
 Origins of the Penitentiary System*, London: Macmillan.
Middleton, J. (1960) *Lugbara Religion*, London: Oxford University Press for
 the International African Institute.
Minson, Jeffrey (1980) 'Review of Michael Ignatieff, *A Just Measure of Pain*
 and Andrew Scull, *Museums of Madness'*, *Sociological Review* 28:195.
Moles, R. N. (1987) *Definition and Rule in Legal Theory*, Oxford: Basil
 Blackwell.
Moore, Sally Falk (1978) *Law as Process: an Anthropological Approach*, London:
 Routledge & Kegan Paul.
—— (1986) *Social Facts and Fabrications: Customary Law on Kilimanjaro
 1880–1980*, Cambridge University Press.
Morse, H. B. (1909) *The Gilds of China*, London: Longmans, Green & Co.
Murphy, J. G. (1979) *Retribution, Justice and Therapy*, Dordrecht: D. Reidel.
Nader, Laura (ed.) (1969) *Law in Culture and Society*, Chicago: Aldine.
Newsom, J. and Newsom, E. (1970) *Four Years Old in an Urban Community*,
 Harmondsworth: Penguin.
Nozick, R. (1981) *Philosophical Explanations*, Harvard University Press.
Parry, L. A. (1975) *The History of Torture in England*, Montclair, NJ:
 Patterson Smith.
Perrot, Michelle (ed.) (1980) *L'impossible prison: recherches sur le système
 pénitentiaire au XIXe siècle*, Paris: Seuil.
Peters, Edward (1985) *Torture*, Oxford: Basil Blackwell.
Piaget, J. (1932) *The Moral Judgement of the Child*, London: Routledge &
 Kegan Paul.
Pollock, L. A. (1983) *Forgotten Children: Parent–Child Relations from 1500 to
 1900*, Cambridge University Press.
—— (1987) *A Loving Relationship: Parents and Children over Three Centuries*,
 London: Fourth Estate.
Pospisil, Leopold (1971) *Anthropology of Law: a Comparative Theory*, New
 York: Harper & Row.

Powers, Edwin (1966) *Crime and Punishment in Early Massachusetts 1620–1692*, Boston: Beacon Press.

Priestley, Philip (1980) *Community of Scapegoats: the Segregation of Sex Offenders and Informers in Prisons*, Oxford: Pergamon Press.

Radcliffe-Brown A. R. (1934) *s.v.* 'Sanction', in *Encyclopaedia of the Social Sciences*, vol. 13, p. 531. New York: Macmillan.

Radzinowicz, Leon and Hood, Roger (1986) *A History of English Criminal Law*, vol. 5, *The Emergence of Penal Policy*, London: Stevens.

Roberts, Simon (1979) *Order and Dispute*, Harmondsworth: Penguin.

Rodman, Barbee-Sue (1968) 'Bentham and the paradox of penal reform', *Journal of the History of Ideas* 29:197.

Rusche, G. and Kirchheimer, O. (1939) *Punishment and Social Structure*, New York: Columbia University Press (reissued 1968).

Scull, Andrew T. (1977) *Decarceration – Community Treatment and the Deviant*, Englewood Cliffs, NJ: Prentice-Hall, 2nd edn, 1984, Cambridge: Polity Press.

—— (1979) *Museums of Madness: the Social Organisation of Insanity in Nineteenth-Century England*, London: Allen Lane.

Senkevicz, Robert S. J. (1985) *Vigilantes in Gold Rush San Francisco*, Stanford University Press.

Skinner, B. F. (1972) *Beyond Freedom and Dignity*, London: Jonathan Cape.

Spitzer, Steven (1975) 'Punishment and social organisation: a study of Durkheim's theory of penal evolution', *Law and Society Review* 9:613.

—— (1979) 'The rationalisation of crime control in capitalist society', *Contemporary Crises* 3:187.

—— and Scull, Andrew T. (1977) 'Social control in historical perspective: from private to public responses to crime', in D. F. Greenberg (ed.), *Corrections and Punishment*, Beverley Hills: Sage.

Ten, C. L. (1987) *Crime, Guilt and Punishment*, Oxford University Press.

Thomas, D. A. (1979) *Principles of Sentencing*, 2nd edn, London: Heinemann.

Thomas, K. (1971) *Religion and the Decline of Magic*, London: Weidenfeld & Nicolson.

Thompson, E. P. (1972) 'Rough music! Le charivari anglais', *Annales: économies, sociétés, civilisations* 27:285.

Turnbull, C. M. (1973) *The Mountain People*, London: Jonathan Cape.

Weber, Max (1967) *Law in Economy and Society*, ed. Max Rheinstein, New York: Simon & Schuster.

Weisser, Michael R. (1979) *Crime and Punishment in Early Modern Europe*, Hassocks: Harvester Press.

Whitely, C. H. (1956) 'On retribution', *Philosophy* 31:154.

Willcock, H. D. and Stokes, J. (1968) *Deterrents and Incentives in Crime Among Boys and Young Men Aged 15–21 Years*, London: Office of Population Censuses and Surveys, Social Survey Division.

Young, Peter (1983) 'Sociology, the state and penal relations', in David Garland and Peter Young (eds), *The Power to Punish: Contemporary Penality and Social Analysis*, London: Heinemann.

NAME INDEX

Asch, S. E. 79

Benn, S. I. 61
Bentham, J. 20, 60, 62, 119, 121
Berscheid, E. 134
Binny, J. 69, 70
Boye, D. 134
Bottoms, A. E. 188
Burt, J. T. 70

Carpenter, M. 70
Chesterton, G. L. 70
Clay, W. L. 70
Clifford, W. 197
Cohen, E. 167–8
Cohen, S. 2, 67, 188

De Mause, L. 149
Denning, Lord A. 100
Dickens, C. 70
Dowdle, M. D. 109
Driberg, J. H. 201
Dubro, A. 192
Du Cane, E. 70
Duff, R. A. 145
Durkheim, E. 65, 67, 133, 153

Eckhoff, T. 20, 98
Ehrenzweig, A. A. 111, 121–2, 144
Ehrlich, E. 36, 37
Einzig, P. 131
Eliot, G. 202
Epstein, A. L. 37

Finnis, J. M. 186
Fitzmaurice, C. 97, 98
Flew, A. 23, 33, 61, 88–9
Foucault, M. 35, 59, 65, 67, 184, 185,
   187–8, 195, 202, 204–5

Freud, S. 73, 104, 106, 121

Galsworthy, J. 70
Garland, D. 9, 23, 34, 59, 61, 67, 71
Gouldner, A. W. 113
Grupp, S. E. 62

Hare, R. M. 111
Harré, R. 42
Hart, H. L. A. 20, 21, 22, 60–4, 81 *et
   seq.*, 146
Hayley, T. T. 201
Hill, F. 70
Hoebel, E. A. 37, 193, 201
Hoffmann, H. 155
Hogarth, W. 124
Honderich, T. 61–2
Honoré, A. M. 78, 80, 128
Howard, J. 169
Howell, P. P. 132–3
Hume, D. 82
Hunt, D. 188

Ignatieff, M. 26, 67

Jebb, J. 70

Kaplan, D. E. 192
Kirchheimer, O. 67, 196
Köbben, A. J. F. 193, 199

Lacey, N. 111, 117
Lawrence, D. H. 168
Lehman, W. W. 133
Lerner, M. J. 116
LeVine, R. A. 92
Lewis, I. M. 81, 90, 129, 132, 133, 200
Linebaugh, P. 205
Llewelyn, K. N. 200

239

SUBJECT INDEX

For Product Safety Concerns and Information please contact our EU
representative GPSR@taylorandfrancis.com
Taylor & Francis Verlag GmbH, Kaufingerstraße 24, 80331 München, Germany

www.ingramcontent.com/pod-product-compliance
Lightning Source LLC
Chambersburg PA
CBHW050420280326
41932CB00013BA/1934